Under the Color of Law

Under the Color of Law

The Bush Administration's Subversion of U.S. Constitutional and International Law in the War on Terror

Martin Henn

LEXINGTON BOOKS
A division of
ROWMAN & LITTLEFIELD PUBLISHERS, INC.
Lanham • Boulder • New York • Toronto • Plymouth, UK

Published by Lexington Books
A division of Rowman & Littlefield Publishers, Inc.
A wholly owned subsidiary of The Rowman & Littlefield Publishing Group, Inc.
4501 Forbes Boulevard, Suite 200, Lanham, Maryland 20706
http://www.lexingtonbooks.com

Estover Road, Plymouth PL6 7PY, United Kingdom

British Library Cataloguing in Publication Information Available

Library of Congress Cataloging-in-Publication Data

Henn, Martin J., 1968-
Under the color of law : the Bush administration's subversion of U.S. constitutional and international law in the War on Terror / Martin Henn.
p. cm.
Includes bibliographical references and index.
ISBN 978-0-7391-4329-2 (cloth : alk. paper)
1. War on Terrorism, 2001-2009. 2. Terrorism--Prevention--Law and legislation--United States. 3. War and emergency powers--United States. 4. Executive power--United States. 5. Constitutional law--United States. 6. War (International law) 7. International and municipal law--United States. I. Title.
KF7225.H46 2010
343.73'01--dc22 2010001244

™ The paper used in this publication meets the minimum requirements of American National Standard for Information Sciences—Permanence of Paper for Printed Library Materials, ANSI/NISO Z39.48-1992.

Printed in the United States of America

This book is dedicated to
Kelly Gerling, who held fast to the truth,
when the rest of us were outfoxed.

CONTENTS

INTRODUCTION

Under the Color of Law

My present purpose is to provide to the general reading public an informed and critical commentary on five key Bush administration legal memoranda formative of U.S. counterterrorism policy from 2001 to 2009. This volume is dedicated to the idea that these documents are worthy of being read and critically examined in themselves as primary text, precisely because the act of critical assessment may yield meaningful policy reform in the ongoing debate facing the nation over balancing security interests with the preservation of civil liberties. The issues surrounding this balancing are not at all easy to resolve; and this author makes no pretensions to that effect, but rather frames each document around one central dialectical question—the Bush administration Office of Legal Counsel documents supplying arguments that weigh in favor of an *affirmative* response to the question, this present commentary supplying a series of arguments posited in favor of the *negative* opposing side of the question.

This volume is, therefore, intended merely to provide counterpoint for and antithesis to positions vigorously defended by President Bush's attorneys working at the OLC inside the Department of Justice, and is designed to be used primarily *in conjunction with* and examined *as response to* the Bush-era documents themselves. This volume supplies alternative perspectives to what are a series of largely one-sided legal opinions weighed, to all appearances, deliberately in favor of the policy predispositions of high Bush II administration officials after 9/11. The novelty of this book is that it provides the reader with a close commentary to primary text documents, while at the same time combing through the original texts of the jurists, statesmen, and philosophers of classical antiquity in order to definitively establish customary international law norms immediately relevant to the documents formative of U.S. counterterrorism policy, norms jettisoned by Bush administration OLC attorneys post-9/11 as overly cumbersome to the exercise of presidential war-making power and irrelevant to operational decision making in a new age of global terrorism.

Thankfully, much has changed since the first raw draft of this book was completed in October of 2008. Barack Hussein Obama, a man born of a Muslim father from Kenya and a mother from Kansas, has been elected President of the United States. His new administration has made several changes to the policies of his predecessor. To begin with, the Obama administration no longer defines torture by raising the threshhold of acceptable pain and suffering to the point of organ failure and cardiac arrest the way former Assistant Attorney General Jay Bybee defined it in 2002, but in a manner more consistent with the text and humanitarian spirit of the United Nations Convention Against Torture and the Geneva Conventions.

In addition, President Obama's Attorney General Eric Holder is currently leaning toward finding a special prosecutor to review whether federal laws were broken during Bush-era interrogations.[1] This bold move has caused new tensions to emerge between the Justice Department and the CIA[2] but marks a new era of Justice Department operational independence from the will of the Executive.

Obama has also committed himself to closing once and for all the detention facility established at Guantánamo Bay, Cuba by his predecessor for the original purpose of housing suspected terrorists rounded up after 9/11. President Obama also appears far more committed to a policy of public disclosure of official government documents, along with open debate within his own administration than his predecessor. Four previously classified Bush-era memos were made public in April of 2009[3] amid charges that Obama and Holder were giving away state secrets by revealing counter-resistance techniques to potential enemies. Yet these techniques are the very ones that have presumably been abandoned by U.S. officials on the grounds of being inconsistent with ratified humanitarian treaties.

While the Obama administration is currently debating openly as never before the extent of America's committment to rebuilding Afghanistan,[4] it nevertheless continues utilizing many of the same policy definitions laid down by its predecessors, including so-called "failed-state" doctrine in application to the war ongoing in Afghanistan—a doctrine whose authenticity is seriously challenged in *Question Three* of this book. In addition, little has been done by Obama in the way of challenging or rejecting limits to the excercise of certain civil liberties brought on by the Patriot Act.

President Obama has also recently signed into law a Homeland Security appropriations bill (October 28, 2009) that grants the Department of Defense the authority to continue suppressing photos of prisoner abuse.[5] The current administration has brushed aside grave concerns expressed by Jameel Jaffer, Director of the American Civil Liberties Union National Security Project, who has recently called for release of interrogational abuse photos on the grounds that "no democracy has ever been made stronger by concealing evidence of its wrongdoing"and that "the failure of the country's current leadership to fully confront the abuses of the prior administration—a failure embodied by the suppression legislation at issue now—will only compound these harms."[6]

In addition, despite promises of a January 2010 closed date by President Obama, the detention facility established by the previous administration at Guantánamo Bay Naval Base remains open and functioning, notwithstanding the fact that under the Geneva Conventions Relative to the Protection of Civilian Persons in Time of War, Article 49, ¶1, individual or mass forcible transfers of protected persons from occupied territory (such as Afghanistan) to the territory of the Occupying Power or to that of *any other country, occupied or not,* are prohibited.

But while a number of Bush-era policies are being challenged under the current administration—for instance, Eric Holder's recent decision to try those complicit in the 9/11 attacks as criminals in civilian court in New York City—a move that accords with the customary standard of treating as crime rogue acts of brigandage, piracy, and terrorism—little if any attempt has been made by other organs of governemnt to atone for the mistakes of the previous administration. On November 2, 2009, the Second Circuit Court of Appeals, by a vote of 7-4 in *Arar v. Ashcroft,* exempted federal officials from prosecution for violations of Maher Arar's constitutional rights when he was rendered to Syria for invasive interrogation and torture after landing at JFK Airport on his way home to Canada in 2002. Arar possessed dual Canadian and Syrian citizenship at the time he was held incommunicado by U.S. authorities for twelve days. Arar was then transported to Syria for brutal interrogation and torture against his wishes. Yet, because the Executive has practiced a *de facto* policy of extraordinary rendition since at least 1995, the Court held that

> a suit seeking a damages remedy against senior officials who implement such a policy is in crucial respects a suit against the government as to which the government has not waived sovereign immunity. Such a suit unavoidably influences government policy, probes government secrets, invades government interests, enmeshes government lawyers, and thereby elicits government funds for settlement. . . . A suit seeking a damges remedy against senior officials who implement an extraordinary rendition policy would enmesh the courts ineluctably in an assessment of the validity and rationale of that policy and its implementation in this particluar case, matters that directly affect significant diplomatic and national security concerns. (*Arar v. Ashcroft et al.* 06-4216-cv (2009), §X(A), at 38-40)

Although Canada has already admitted its complicity in this case by awarding Arar roughly $10 million victimization compensation for its role in falsely tipping U.S. officials that he was a member of al-Qaeda, United States courts continue to use the imperatives of national security in a wartime state of emergency to exempt U.S. officals from prosecution for violations of U.S. federal laws. A recurring theme in the Bush-era OLC memoranda on counterterrorism policy formation is that government officials acting under executive aegis are free to do virtually anything they want in a national security context, including torture or causing others to be tortured through rendition.[7]

It is the hope of this author, therefore, that in fleshing out the deficiencies of the Bush-era opinions examined herein new light may be shed on finding viable solutions in the contemporary policy debate over balancing United States security interests with the preservation of civil liberties and the maintenance of good faith in our international agreements.

I seek, then, to demonstrate how high officials within the Bush administration, eager to suspend the application of longstanding humanitarian treaties and War Powers Resolution limits to the exercise of presidential power, have established, by means of policy directives grounded in highly questionable legal analysis, a series of repressive and patently unconstitutional measures decreed into law in the days, weeks, and months following the al-Qaeda attacks of September 11, 2001, measures which, because of their perceived necessity in a wartime emergency of indefinite duration brought on by global terrorist activity, continue to seriously imperil the fabric of liberties that safeguard the delicate viability of our democracy. In this work I shall describe in precise detail how good faith in the formation of United States foreign policy along with adherence to the rule of law itself came to be America's first casualty in her new global war on terror, and how she came to jettison too many liberties in the wake of too few dangers, liberties guaranteed by the Fourteenth Amendment to citizens and noncitizens alike.

A close examination of administration documents makes clear that high Bush II officials working in the Office of Legal Counsel inside the Department of Justice, openly declared the American president to operate within a realm of authority existing beyond the rule of law. OLC officials have baldly asserted blanket immunity from criminal prosecution for violations of extant federal laws by *any* executive branch official who acts on Presidential orders pursuant to the president's constitutional authority to wage a military campaign.

Armoring President Bush with so-called "unenumerated" executive powers not defined anywhere in the text of the Constitution, then-Assistant Attorney General Jay S. Bybee claimed (in a memorandum for Alberto Gonzales, then-Counsel to the president) that although it could be argued Congress enacted the law criminalizing torture, 18 U.S.C. §2340A[8], with the intention of restricting the president's discretion in the interrogation of enemy combatants, nevertheless "the Department of Justice could not enforce Section 2340A against federal officials acting pursuant to the president's constitutional authority to wage a military campaign."[9] Bybee even speculates that "both courts and prosecutors should reject prosecutions that apply federal criminal laws to activity that is authorized pursuant to one of the president's constitutional powers." In other words, if a piece of federal law or some provision of a ratified treaty (such as the Geneva Conventions, or the United Nations Convention Against Torture, or the International Covenant on Civil and Political Rights) should impede or constrain the president's free exercise of plenary executive power in prosecuting the global war on terror, then that law represents an unconstitutional infringement of executive power, and does not restrict the president, his principals, or any of his subordinates acting pursuant to executive orders from engaging in behavior that openly violates existing federal anti-torture statutes.

Bybee reminds Gonzales that "although Congress may define federal crimes that the President, through the Take Care Clause, should prosecute, Congress cannot compel the president to prosecute outcomes taken pursuant to the president's own constitutional authority. If Congress could do so, it could control the president's authority through the manipulation of federal criminal law."[10] Now if the Framers truly intended the president or any federal official acting under his orders to enjoy blanket immunity from prosecution for federal crimes committed in the prosecution of a war or military campaign, then it would make little sense for them to have given the Senate sole power to try all impeachments, and it would not explain why any president convicted in an impeachment hearing continues to remain "liable and subject to indictment, trial, judgment, and punishment, according to law" (*Const.*, Art. 1, §3, ¶7).

Bush II administration OLC interpreters have fathered the concept that the President has constitutional authority to summarily suspend international treaties or portions of treaties that he happens not to like at his personal discretion without having to seek the advice and consent of the Senate, even though it is axiomatic that the powers that make a treaty are the only powers that may abrogate it.

OLC interpreters doggedly maintain that the President possesses unilateral authority to issue blanket determinations of POW-status for any individuals suspected of being members of al-Qaeda or the Taliban and detained amid hostilities in Afghanistan independently of case-by-case hearings before a competent military tribunal as explicitly required under GPW, Art. 5, ¶2.[11] The President's blanket determination of POW status was largely regarded throughout the administration as removing once and for all any Article 5 "doubt" that might arise as to whether a detainee qualifies as a POW according to GPW, Article 4 requirements. It remains bitterly ironic that under a Reservation originally entered by the United States with respect to GCP, Article 68, ¶2 in 1949, American military authorities could have legally applied the death penalty to any *duly convicted* al-Qaeda terrorist (as a violator of the laws and customs of war), participation in al-Qaeda being determined according to a tribunal operating under the principles of law and rules of evidence normally applicable to the prosecution of international war crimes.[12]

OLC interpreters have fathered the grotesque legal fiction of so-called "failed-state" doctrine as a strategy specifically invented to provide the Bush administration the color of law it needed to justify blanket denial of Geneva Conventions humanitarian protections to persons taken captive and detained during the war on terror, a war of indefinite duration. According to failed-state doctrine an entire nation of people (such as Afghanistan) may collapse or fail and thus lose its *sovereign authority* to exist before the international community as an independent entity whenever its "centralized governmental authority has almost completely collapsed, no central authorities are capable of maintaining government institutions or ensuring law and order, and violence has destabilized civil society and the economy."[13]

Once Afghanistan's statehood is removed its legal status as High Contracting Party to Geneva is thereby also removed, and so too any humanitarian provisions under Geneva normally protecting those taken captive amid hostilities. The purpose of failed-state doctrine is to obviate and neutralize the applicability of Geneva common Article 2 which says that "the Convention shall also apply to all cases of partial or total occupation of the territory of a High Contracting Party, even if the said occupation meets with no armed resistance." Under failed-state doctrine, common Article 2 can no longer constrict the President's authority to prosecute the war on terror, because Afghanistan (being no longer a state) no longer counts as a High Contracting Party to Geneva, even though its territory has recently come under United States and coalition occupation.

But even if Afghanistan had actually failed to exist as a state under Taliban rule (which it did not), and even if it thereby also failed to remain a High Contracting Party to Geneva (which it has been since September of 1956), captives taken in Afghanistan would still be protected under the GCP, Article 4, ¶1 requirement that "persons protected by the Convention [be] those who, at a given moment and in any manner whatsoever, find themselves, in case of a conflict or occupation, in the hands of a Party to the conflict or Occupying Power of which they are not nationals." This provision of Geneva protects any captive taken in the territory of Afghanistan regardless of civilian or combatant status (even assuming that Afghanistan had failed as a state) because the provision requires only that the United States be "a Party to the conflict" or a relevant "Occupying Power" in Afghanistan, while laying down no further reciprocal requirement for the "persons protected by the Convention."

The Bush administration wanted us to believe that Afghanistan ceased to exist as a state when the Taliban regime demonstrated its inability to control rampant internal discord and violence, and showed gross ineptitude when implementing basic humanitarian standards of justice in the treatment of its own people. But it makes no sense from a logical point of view to deny humanitarian protections to captives taken in Afghanistan on the grounds that the Taliban regime once denied the same protections to its own people. Failed-state doctrine simply has no grounding whatsoever under traditional standards of customary international law. Yet the doctrine continues to be recognized in some quarters of the Obama administration.

Hugo Grotius, the great Dutch jurist and statesman of the seventeenth century, considered by many authorities to be the father of modern international law, tells us, for instance, that

> neither a State nor a Republic ceases to exist, even when guilty of some injustice pervading the entire community; nor is an association of pirates or thieves a State, though perchance they recognize a certain equality among themselves without which no association could possibly subsist.[14] (*De Jure Belli ac Pacis*, Book 3, ch. 3, §2.1)

In a single stroke Grotius provides the legal solution to our quandry over Afghanistan's existence as a state and al-Qaeda's status as a non-state actor. On the one hand, Afghanistan's sovereignty can not simply fail because the Taliban happen to apply a cruel and repressive interpretation of Shari'a Law over a destitute and migratory population. Nor can al-Qaeda fighters be regarded as combatants in a conventional war, since acts of terrorism utilize unconventional tactics and serving in a terrorist brigade appears to compromise one's lawful status as a combatant, i.e., the targeting of non-belligerents runs contrary to the practices of civilized nations at war. Since Afghanistan has been engaged in a civil war for roughly thirty-five years, she arguably lost her soverign authority under failed-state doctrine and, thereby, her High Contracting Party status to Geneva *before* the Soviet invasion of 1979; but no one has ever advanced this argument, because failed-state doctrine did not exist before the late 1990's.

Now it is true that bandits, pirates, and terrorists, because they do not abide by the customs and laws of war in their targeting of non-belligerents, deserve criminal punishment that captured conscript soldiers in a conventional war would never be exposed to. But this punishment can only be meted out legally by a GPW, Article 5 hearing which affords these individuals full due process rights of access to legal counsel, the presumption of innocence, and the right to call forth evidence and witnesses of their own choosing and the right to review and weigh any evidence arrayed against them as grounds for their detention and confinement.

These basic rights are still denied systematically to suspects held at Guantánamo Bay, Cuba. And, even though the Department of Defense implemented the Combatant Status Review Tribunal (CSRT) system on July 7, 2004, these tribunals continue to suspend basic principles of law and rules of evidence normally applicable in a criminal court.

The mere suspicion that a person captured amid hostilities in Afghanistan post-9/11 is of al-Qaeda or Taliban membership does not, by itself, justify the use of cruel and inhumane treatment, or torture, but only makes the detainee eligible to be tried and convicted as a war criminal. The original orders of General Tommy Franks at CENTCOM for United States forces to abide by GPW, Article 5 requirements in the processing of captives of war was summarily rescinded a month later by Secretary of Defense Donald Rumsfeld in a Memorandum for the Chairman of the Joint Chiefs of Staff, dated 19 January 2002, according to which (suspected) al-Qaeda and Taliban individuals under the control of the Department of Defense "are not entitled to prisoner of war status for purposes of the Geneva Conventions of 1949."[15] Bush administration OLC officials have arrogated for the President the authority to unilaterally suspend the applicability of both positive *and* customary international law to *suspect* enemies of state in the war against al-Qaeda and the Taliban in Afghanistan, with the express purpose of placing captives of war beyond the territorial and jurisdictional reach of any U.S. court or international tribunal.

It has become increasingly clear, despite administration efforts to conceal documents from public scrutiny, that Bush II administration officials working in the Office of Legal Counsel, the Department of Justice, and the Defense Department knowingly conspired to extend the President's executive power well beyond expressly stated constitutional limits, unwarrantedly absorbing both plenary judicial *and* legislative power to define and punish offenses against the law of nations in America's new global war on terror, while deliberately watering down the legal definition of torture[16] so as to bypass strict humanitarian limitations explicitly prohibiting U.S. forces from using torture and other coercive interrogation techniques on captured persons of uncertain legal status in order to exact information from them. Prohibitions against torture and dehumanizing treatment of captives in war are spelled out in the Geneva Conventions,[17] the United Nations Convention Against Torture and other Cruel, Inhuman or Degrading Treatment or Punishment,[18] and the United Nations Universal Declaration of Human Rights of 1948.[19] These prohibitions are also given binding force in federal domestic law by the War Crimes Act 18 U.S.C. §2441 (*Appendix I*) and the anti-torture statute 18 U.S.C. §§2340-2340A (*Appendix H*).

Within months of September 11, OLC interpreters had already claimed for the President the right to make unilateral decisions regarding the applicability of existing Geneva Conventions to the conflict with the Taliban and al-Qaeda in Afghanistan, even though GPW, Articles 131 and 142, ¶s 2 and 3, specifically prohibit *any* High Contracting Party from absolving itself of liability in respect of grave breaches of the Conventions.[20] The administration's newly acquired judicial *and* legislative powers to conduct a global war on terror *indefinitely into the future* constitute nothing short of a bid for dictatorial imperium.

In Roman law "imperium" refers to the power of chief military command belonging to a highest magistrate such as a consul, the chief executive of state. Although there were two consuls holding office at any given time, power to command forces within a given jurisdiction was in the hands of only one. Imperium is the equivalent, under U.S. law, to the executive power the President has as Commander-in-Chief to lead military forces in time of war. But this presidential power to command does not constitute a dictatorship, for the President does not have the power to unilaterally declare war without congressional authorization, nor the power to suspend international agreements by his own authority, nor the specifically legislative power to craft new law by decree, nor the judicial power of final arbitration in the interpreting of existing federal laws.

Imperium approaches dictatorship in proportion as the chief executive succeeds in acquiring judicial powers to interpret law combined with new legislative powers to make law. The noted sixteenth century Belgian jurist Balthazar Ayala remarks that

> a Dictator duly appointed by [Roman] law was one who held supreme command in matters of war, peace, punishment, and reward, without appeal to any higher tribunal, so that, freed from all impediments, he might the more ably administer the weightiest matters of state.[21] (*De Jure et Officiis Bellicis et Disciplina Militari Libri III*, Book 2, ch. 3, §3)

The Romans appointed a dictator on extremely rare occasions for a limited term of office to manage matters of state in times of public crisis or national emergency. But the United States Constitution does not contain a provision for the emergency office of dictator; rather it vests the war initiating and war authorizing powers in Congress, placing the war-directing power in the hands of the President as Commander-in-Chief.

The framers clearly intended both the legislative and the executive arms of government to work *together* in a time of war. But this foundational principle of interbranch cooperation and concord was quickly jettisoned following the attacks of 9/11.

For instance, the President's November 13, 2001, Executive Military Order, although issued for the ostensible purpose of investigating suspected terrorists, is constitutionally unsound not only because it is based upon Section 836 of Title 10 of the United States Code, which is itself unconstitutional, but because the text of the Order utterly fails to ensure basic due process rights for detainees that are guaranteed explicitly to citizens and non-citizens alike under the Fifth and Fourteenth Amendments of the Constitution. Detainee processing by competent tribunal is guaranteed also under GPW, Article 5 requirements as well as under the Universal Declaration of Human Rights.[22]

The November 13 Order dispenses entirely with any presumption of innocence until proven guilty and it places in jeopardy fundamental Eighth Amendment protections against cruel and unusual punishment by clause 3(e)'s conferral, upon the Secretary of Defense, of arbitrary power to prescribe whatever conditions he happens to determine appropriate for any detainee or group of detainees he should choose without having to provide any reason for his decision.[23] By means of the November 13 Executive Order the President has appropriated to his executive power the authority properly belonging to Congress "to constitute tribunals inferior to the supreme court: to define and punish piracies and felonies committed on the high seas, and offenses against the law of nations" as well as the legislative power to "make rules concerning captures on land and water."[24]

In order to gain a broader perspective on the gravity and weight of the Bush administration's self-aggrandizing quest for plenary judicial and legislative power in the war on terror in the wake of 9/11, it is helpful to examine in some detail what I take to be the closest historic parallel we have to this constitutional crisis in American politics.

An Enemy Unlike Any They Had Ever Seen

The year was 68 BC when the senate and people of Rome were suddenly confronted with a grave threat to their national security from all quarters of the Mediterranean in an enemy unlike any they had ever seen. The trouble began when King Mithridates of Pontus, a self-styled warlord and enemy of the Roman people, subdued by military force the province of Asia (along the western coastal regions of modern day Turkey), and, after plundering the area and its inhabitants for several weeks, displacing the rule of law with anarchy and bloodshed, funded the construction of small skiffs and dispatched bands of pirates onto the high seas, who then plundered merchant vessels and commandeered civilian craft to grow their own fleet, using the porous seaside caves of Cilicia as safe-haven and base of operations.

With state sponsorship squarely behind them, these gangs of roaming banditti formed a secret brotherhood sealed with elaborate celebration rituals and strange religious sacrifices in honor of Mithras at Olympus.[25] They fell upon defenseless seaside towns, undermined or battered down the walls of others, seized and destroyed property, wantonly raped women,[26] and engaged in acts of random deadly violence against innocent life, often seizing hostages for ransom, only to behead them later aboard ships in cruel ceremonies of public humiliation. Rome truly fell into desperate straits as the seas were no longer safe for passage, and vital grain shipments from Egypt along with finished goods from the East began to dwindle to a halt. Famine slowly but inevitably crept in at Rome for the first time in recorded memory, as sporadic rapine and plunder nipped away at Italy's defenseless coastal hamlets.

The Roman people were desperate to end the violence and bring the pirates to justice. To this end the senate hastily conferred upon the most popular politician of the day, Gnaeus Pompey, unprecedented and plenary power to levy troops and ships-of-war for a space of three years, along with unlimited military power as commander-in-chief of operations over the entire Mediterranean within the Pillars of Hercules, and over land for a distance of up to 40 miles from the coast.[27] In addition to these new executive privileges (that went well beyond the powers of a consul), Pompey was granted plenary judicial power to determine the procedural rules and conditions of confinement governing the capture of enemy forces amid hostilities on the seas as well as on land.

Pompey was made by law the final arbiter over the detention, trial, and conviction (or acquittal) of all captives.[28] Pompey soon had the will of an entire nation united behind him, a unique state of affairs quite opposite the usual partisan wrangling and bitter infighting that defined the political topography of late republican Rome. Pompey's supporters dutifully sent patriotic letters and pamphlets across Italy to all coastal kings, rulers, peoples and cities, encouraging them to assist Pompey in every way they possibly could.[29] His supporters even deputized bands of private vigilantes to stand watch against any possible encroachments from without.

Pompey's newly enhanced executive power was made possible when his intimate friend and long-time supporter Aulus Gabinius drafted a proposal in the senate which, due to the widespread panic and public desperation following the attacks, was quickly rammed through without so much as a formal debate to become the *lex Gabinia* of 67 BC. It is reported[30] that even Julius Caesar supported the new measure, not because he cared at all for Pompey, but because he wanted to ingratiate himself with the people.

The Gabinian law granted Pompey not merely an admiralty, but a virtual monarchy with unchecked and irresponsible powers over all persons falling within his jurisdiction. For his service and dedication to Pompey, Gabinius was promoted to the office of Tribune of the People in the election of 66. He eventually attained the praetorship in 61, and the consulship in 58. A few years later, however, Gabinius was summarily recalled from his province of Syria by the senate, prosecuted for taking bribes, and banished from Rome in 55 for invading Egypt without senate authorization to do so, undertaking a war considered ill-omened by the Romans, as it was forbidden by the Sibylline books.[31] The jaded dealings of Gabinius finally caught up with him. And Pompey would come to be assassinated in Egypt by eunuchs under secret orders from Julius Caesar.

Pompey's arch-nemesis in his bid for enhanced power was a man named Gaius Calpurnius Piso, who used his own executive authority as consul in 67 to check Pompey from exercising his newly vested Gabinian powers too broadly.[32] Piso along with a small coterie of powerful but outnumbered senators quickly began to grow wary of such unchecked executive power in the hands of a relatively youthful and inexperienced politician. But as goods began to flow back into Rome once again in abundance, and new victories proclaimed on the high seas, Pompey's popularity soared to even greater heights. And this allowed his supporters all the political leverage they needed to remove Piso from office, and therewith the opportunity to remove all remaining political opposition to Pompey once and for all. At this critical juncture in history the Greek biographer Plutarch pauses to note that Gabinius already had the requisite draft-proposal to remove Piso from the consulship in hand and ready to go.[33] But Pompey prevented this proposal from reaching the senate, and thereby saved the republic from backsliding into a more permanent form of dictatorship.

It is undoubtedly the case that the Roman senate's conferral of unchecked executive power to conduct war, plenary judicial power of final arbitration over rules governing detention, trial, and sentencing of captives, along with plenary legislative power to levy troops, ships-of-war, and moneys as needed (to execute directives of strategy) onto the shoulders of Gnaeus Pompey, a fairly young and inexperienced chief magistrate, bears an uncanny resemblance to the vaguely broad and unchecked executive, judicial, and legislative powers unilaterally absorbed by President Bush and his Office of Legal Counsel in the days, weeks, and months following September 11. Yet Pompey succeeded in doing, amid circumstances of grave national peril similar to those in the United States immediately following the al-Qaeda attacks of September 11, three things that President Bush failed to do in the war on terror:

First, Pompey deliberately refrained from overextending his already heightened executive powers under the lex Gabinia by instinctively knowing when to reject patently unscrupulous legal advice from his closest advisors, e.g., by refusing to submit to the senate Gabinius's draft-proposal for the removal of Piso from the consulship.[34] *Second, Pompey guaranteed humane treatment for all captured suspects in the war on piracy,* treating them with mercy, and assuming them innocent until proven guilty by granting them a fair and regular trial to determine the lawfulness of their detention, acquitting the innocent, and sentencing only the worst offenders as war criminals, thereby keeping his prosecution of the campaign within the limits of customary international law, even though many of the individuals under his detention had not observed the laws and customs of war themselves. *Third, Pompey did not allow his captives to be brutalized or tortured in the process of acquiring intelligence information from them,* opting instead for humane treatment for all captives, granting clemency for the lightest offenders, and lengthy prison sentences for the worst among them. Pompey regarded clemency not as a quaint encumbrance, or a meaningless humanitarian formality, but as a strategic tool that allowed him to gain reliable intelligence information from captives, so that his forces could more quickly locate, capture, and prosecute the most dangerous offenders.

An Enemy Quite Like the One We Just Saw

The year was AD 2001 when, on the morning of September 11, bands of al-Qaeda terrorists commandeered commercial jetliners in mid-flight and deliberately crashed them into the World Trade Center complex in New York City, the Pentagon in Washington D.C., and a field in rural Pennsylvania, randomly killing over 3,000 innocent civilians. The trouble began when the Taliban, a self-styled reactionary Islamist regime and standing enemy of the United States and Israel, subdued by military force the territory of Afghanistan, and, after tormenting the region and its inhabitants for years, displacing anarchy with a form of Shari'a Law imposed with cruel alacrity, funded and harbored al-Qaeda, a paramilitary terrorist group led by Usama bin Laden, using the porous mountain caves of Afghanistan as safe-haven and base of operations. With Taliban state sponsorship squarely behind them, al-Qaeda formed a secret Islamic brotherhood sealed with elaborate celebration rituals and strange religious sacrifices in honor of fallen martyrs. In addition to previous terrorist attacks carried out successfully against U.S. embassies in Kenya and Tanzania (1998), as well as against the USS Cole (2000), al-Qaeda operatives occasionally seized civilians as hostages for ransom, only to behead them later in cruel ceremonies of public humiliation. America truly fell into desperate times as the skies appeared no longer safe for travel and international terrorists continued to elude authorities.

The American people were desperate to end the violence and bring the terrorists to justice. To this end, on September 14, 2001 the House and Senate immediately passed a Joint Resolution Authorizing the President to Use armed Military Force (AUMF) in hostilities directed specifically "against those responsible for the recent attacks launched against the United States on September 11, 2001." On September 25, 2001, Deputy Assistant Attorney General John C. Yoo released a memorandum aggressively expanding the scope of presidential war-directing power well beyond the range specified by the AUMF. A brand new Doctrine of Preemption emerged from the Office of Legal Counsel, one that arrogantly ignored both constitutional and AUMF limits to warmaking authority: "The President may deploy military force preemptively against terrorist organizations or the States that harbor or support them, *whether or not they can be linked to the specific terrorist incidents of September 11.*"[35] (Emphasis added.)

This new acquisition of executive war making power was heightened when President Bush's intimate friend and long-time supporter, Attorney General John Ashcroft, got what he and the Justice Department had been asking for for weeks, the almost immediate passage of the USA Partriot Act of 2001. This act introduces broad new changes to U.S. law designed to enhance the government's power of domestic surveillance regarding suspicious activities. Because of the widespread panic and public desperation caused by the attacks of 9/11, this piece of legislation was quickly rammed through both houses of Congress on October 23, 2001, without so much as a formal debate. Sections 213, 215, and 218 of the Patriot Act give the U.S. government unprecedented powers to access and surveil the personal electronic purchasing and communications records of American citizens, while watering down standards of evidence needed for authorization to conduct searches and seizures of information deemed relevant to an ongoing investigation relating to matters of foreign intelligence.

The act exhibits an utter disdain for the Fourth Amendment right of the people to be secure in their persons, houses, papers, and effects, against unreasonable searches and seizures by the government; it waters down the requirement of probable cause in the issuing of warrants for such searches, while bypassing, in many instances, the authority of a judge to issue such warrants.[36] It is well known, however, that even the President's sternest political opponents in the House and Senate supported the new measure, not because they cared at all for President Bush, but because they wanted to win the favor of the people by being seen as proactive against terrorism.

By early 2002 President Bush held consensus support in both houses of Congress with the will of a nation united behind him, a state of affairs quite opposite the bitter wrangling and partisan infighting so common to Washington politics. In January of 2002 the Justice Department announced the creation of the Terrorism Information and Prevention System (TIPS) with the vision of recruiting millions of American truckers, cable installers, letter carriers, train conductors, ship captains, utility employees, as well as private sector corporations housing vast data-mining networks as the new eyes and ears of a greatly expanded and privatized surveillance-industrial complex.[37]

Each of these measures, combined with the policy directives set forth in the September 25 Memorandum of John C. Yoo, gave President Bush not merely the power as Commander-in-Chief to direct the war effort against those responsible for the attacks of September 11, as outlined in the AUMF, but a virtual autocracy with unchecked and irresponsible powers to arbitrarily conduct preemptive attacks anywhere in the world at any time against terrorist *suspects* and states *suspected* of harboring them, regardless of whether or not they can be linked to the attacks of September 11.

On November 13, 2001, President Bush issued an Executive Military Order by which he claimed the exclusive power as President to capture, detain, and incarcerate without trial, under any conditions that he or the Secretary of Defense may prescribe, any non-U.S. citizen for which "there is reason to believe" that such a person is or was a member of al-Qaeda, or has engaged in, aided or abetted, or conspired to commit, acts of international terrorism, or has knowingly harbored such individuals, or any non-U.S. citizen with respect to whom the President unilaterally deems that "it is in the interest of the United States that such individual be subject" to detention pursuant to the terms of the order.[38] A non-U.S. citizen need not be a terrorist suspect nor one suspected of harboring terrorists to warrant detention under this order.

In the text of the Order the President claims it to be wholly within his statutory and constitutional power as Commander-in-Chief to appropriate not only exclusive *legislative* power to determine the procedural rules and conditions of confinement governing the capture of enemy alien combatants amid hostilities in Afghanistan and *anywhere else in the world*, but, by Subsection 3(e), the exclusive judicial authority to suspend GPW, Article 5 requirements of humane treatment for those awaiting trial to determine their POW status by a competent tribunal, if the Secretary of Defense feels the need to prescribe conditions other than the Geneva-style conditions of confinement outlined in Subsections 3(a)(b)(c)(d).

In claiming the unilateral power to determine procedural rules governing the detention and trial of suspected al-Qaeda and Taliban members captured in Afghanistan or elsewhere, President Bush had usurped a series of powers specifically assigned to Congress, not the president—namely the power to constitute tribunals inferior to the supreme court, to define and punish offences against the law of nations, to make rules concerning captures on land and water (in the context of wartime hostilities) and to make rules for the government and regulation of the land and naval forces.[39]

Executive Authority to Establish Military Commissions Does Not Confer Power to Suspend Geneva Requirements of Humanitarian Treatment for Those Awaiting Article 5 Hearings

Contrary to what is asserted in the November 13 Order, President George W. Bush does *not* have legal authority under the Constitution, the Geneva Conventions, or *Ex parte Quirin* 317 U.S. 1 (1942), to detain suspected enemies of the state indefinitely incommunicado without legal counsel, without trial, and without the benefits and protections of the principles of law and rules of evidence normally governing a criminal proceeding. While the Bush Order tracks closely the language of President Roosevelt's Proclamation of July 2, 1942, establishing military tribunals in the wake of the capture of seven German saboteurs planning an imminent attack against factories and installations in the United States, nothing in Roosevelt's Proclamation bars accused persons from access to civil courts for the purpose of determining the legality of their detention pursuant to the Proclamation. Yet the detainees held in confinement pursuant to the Bush Order "shall not be privileged to seek any remedy . . . or to have any such . . . sought on [their] behalf in any court of the United States, or any State thereof, or in any international tribunal."

Roosevelt's 1942 Proclamation was issued in order to try seven German saboteurs already held in U.S. custody, who specifically entered U.S. territory through coastal and boundary defenses, and were formally charged with committing or attempting to commit sabotage, espionage, hostile acts, or violations of the law of war. The November 13 Order, on the other hand, is a directive applying to some 18 million non-U.S. citizens with respect to any one of whom the President may determine that there is reason to believe that such person is or was a member of al-Qaeda. None of the foreign nationals detained pursuant to the Order has ever been charged and tried in court for committing or attempting to commit an act of terror, much less have they been tried by a competent tribunal as required by GPW, Art. 5, ¶2, where there is doubt as to a detainee's status as a Prisoner of War.

Article 5 hearings are designed to sort out persons properly detained as enemy prisoners of war from those who may have committed a crime of war. In cases where there is palpable reason to believe that a detainee is a terrorist, doubt arises concerning that detainee's Prisoner of War status. But, according to Article 5, "should any doubt arise as to whether persons, having committed a belligerent act and having fallen into the hands of the enemy, belong to any of the categories enumerated in Article 4, such persons shall enjoy the protection of the present Convention until such time as their status has been determined by a competent tribunal."

What was utterly amazing about the administration's unwillingness to properly interpret basic legal documents on international war crimes is that any captive of war who is found *by competent judicial process* to have partaken in al-Qaeda in Afghanistan would surely face charges for war crimes, and possibly the death penalty (pursuant to a U.S. Reservation entered to GCP, Art. 68, ¶2 in 1949).[40] Since the defendant's confirmed participation in a paramilitary transnational terrorist group could arguably render him a non-POW by failure to satisfy GPW, Art. 4(A)(2)(d) requirements of "conducting [his] operations in accordance with the laws and customs of war," there already existed (before 9/11) ample punitive tools in the body of both positive and customary international law[41] to put convicted terrorists behind bars for the protection of society. But such an application of law would have required slow, lengthy, deliberative, detailed, and laborious investigations that would not have produced the same dramatic headlines in the media as those produced by the actual Bush administration policy of smash, grab and conceal.

The case of suspects captured and detained pursuant to the November 13 Order is so radically different than the case surrounding the capture of German saboteurs on U.S. soil in 1942, that there exist serious doubts as to whether *Ex parte Quirin*, in which the Supreme Court reviewed the findings of a military commission—qualifies as a controlling precedent. In 1942 a group of German saboteurs (Messrs. Quirin, Haupt, Kerling, Burger, Heinck, Thiel, and Neubauer), one of whom (Mr. Haupt) was a U.S. citizen, disembarked from German U-Boats off the coasts of Florida and Long Island. Each donned civilian clothes to hide their identity, and proceeded with plans to destroy American war making facilities and infrastructure. All had received instructions and training in Germany. They were each directly ordered by members of the High Command to destroy war industries and infrastructure in the United States, for which they or members of their families were to receive a handsome monetary stipend from the German government.[42]

Fortunately, the saboteurs were arrested shortly after their landing, and President Roosevelt issued an Executive Proclamation appointing a military commission to try them for espionage and sundry violations of the laws of war and of the law of nations. The saboteurs were each charged with a crime and provided with competent legal counsel. They were even allowed to challenge the legality of their detention before the Supreme Court. And it is for these reasons that, as presidential historian Louis Fisher remarks, "nothing in *Quirin* justifies holding a U.S. citizen indefinitely without access to counsel or a trial."[43]

President Roosevelt issued his Proclamation on July 2, 1942, ordering that "all persons who are subjects, citizens or residents of any nation at war with the United States or who give obedience to or act under the direction of any such nation, and who during time of war enter or attempt to enter the United States . . . through coastal or boundary defenses, and are charged with committing or attempting or preparing to commit sabotage, espionage, hostile or warlike acts, or violations of the law of war, shall be subject to the law of war and to the jurisdiction of military tribunals."[44] But, in the opinion of Chief Justice Stone "neither the [President's] Proclamation nor the fact that [the detainees] are enemy aliens forecloses consideration by the courts of petitioners' contentions that the Constitution and the laws of the United States . . . forbid their trial by military commission."[45] In other words *no* President has unilateral authority to prevent U.S. Courts from considering the pleas of enemy aliens detained by U.S. authorities in time of war with regard either to the fact of their detention or to the conditions under which they are being detained; nor does the president have unilateral authority, according to the opinion of Chief Justice Stone, to remove detainees from the jurisdiction of U.S. Courts.

Despite these salient aspects of *Quirin*, the Bush administration, largely imitating the language of the Roosevelt Proclamation of 1942, summarily removed all suspected terrorists and harborers of terrorists under the November 13 Order from seeking any remedy and from having any remedy sought on their behalf before *any* court of the United States, or *any* state thereof, or of *any* international tribunal. Section VII(b)(1) of the Order gives the military tribunal exclusive jurisdiction over detainees, meaning that no other court anywhere on earth has power to review the decision of the tribunal, nor the power to order a retrial of the case. Section VII(b)(2) summarily removes any suspect non-citizen detained pursuant to the Order from the protection of due process in U.S. courts and equal protection under the laws guaranteed by the Fourteenth Amendment which grants due process rights to all persons (regardless of citizenship) who fall within the jurisdiction of U.S. courts.

Two months after President Bush issued the November 13 Order of 2001, Secretary of Defense Donald Rumsfeld issued a unilateral blanket determination that no al-Qaeda or Taliban individuals under the control of the Department of Defense would be entitled to POW status for purposes of the Geneva Conventions, even though Geneva unambiguously requires *all* detainees to be afforded full POW protection and treatment until such time as a competent tribunal can make a status determination on a case-by-case basis.[46] The administration was bedeviled by two recurring universal misconceptions in the days, weeks, and months following 9/11: (1) that the President's universal denial of POW status to detainees suspected of membership in al-Qaeda or the Taliban would somehow remove "any doubt" (under GPW, Article 4 criteria) as to their individual POW status, so as to remove the need for pesky case-by-case determinations of status as demanded by Article 5;[47] (2) that the President has constitutional authority as Commander-in-Chief conducting a military campaign to suspend any provision of Geneva he deems necessary or expedient in prosecuting the war against terrorism, in spite of the fact that both the suspension (i.e., partial abrogation) and the denunciation (i.e., total abrogation) of ratified treaties requires that (a) the treaty be suspended or denounced according to the terms of the instrument itself, and (b) the President seek the advice *and* consent of the Senate to make such alterations.

A number of key differences exist between these German saboteurs of 1942 and individuals detained after 9/11 pursuant to the November 13 Order on suspicion of being or harboring international terrorists.

First, the German saboteurs entered the territory of the United States as enemy belligerents, carrying explosives and specific plans of attack, while persons detained at Bagram airport, Afghanistan and transferred to Guantánamo Bay, Cuba did not.

Second, the German saboteurs were caught in the act of violating Articles 81 and 82 of the Articles of War (along with conspiring to do so), while many of the detainees denied due process at Guantánamo were not caught in the act of committing any war crime by U.S. forces, but were (in many cases) handed over to U.S. forces by third parties such as ordinary Afghans seeking to recover a generous bounty for their efforts,[48] or by members of the Northern Alliance, or by Pakistani intelligence operatives whose reports about the circumstances of capture were unclear from the beginning.

Third, the German saboteurs were immediately charged with violating the Laws of War before a military commission, while the detainees at Guantánamo were never charged with any crime.

Fourth, the German saboteurs were allowed to challenge the lawfulness of their detention and trial by military commission before the Supreme Court, whereas according to the text of the President's November 13 Order Subsection VII(b)(2) the individual detained shall not be privileged to seek *any* remedy or maintain *any* proceeding . . . in (i) any court of the United States, or any State thereof, (ii) any court of any foreign nation, or (iii) any international tribunal.

President Bush had arrogated to his office the exclusive authority to decide the guilt or innocence of captives of war once and for all, and in doing so he had placed his jurisdiction above that of the Supreme Court and of any international court of law! In the body of U.S. constitutional and international law, however, the President has no more authority to suspend the applicability of Geneva in reference to captured enemies of war than he has authority to suspend the laws of physics or mathematics in application to sensible or intelligible magnitudes.

Subsections VII(b)(1), (b)(2), and (c) of the November 13 Order make clear that the detained individual shall not have the right to seek *any* remedy to his detention. In *Rasul et al. v Bush et al.*, 124 S. Ct. 2686 (2004) the Supreme Court recently overturned the unilateral authority of the President to detain foreign nationals captured abroad in connection with hostilities in Afghanistan and incarcerated at Guantánamo Bay Naval Base by allowing them to petition U.S. courts for writ of habeas corpus so as to determine the legality of their detention. Petitioners in *Rasul* differed from petitioners in *Johnson v. Eisentrager*, 339 U.S. 763, in a number of respects.

Petitioners in *Eisentrager* were German nationals captured in Nanking, China for handing intelligence information on allied military movements to Japanese officials after the formal surrender of Germany but before the surrender of Japan. Six of the original 27 Germans were acquitted, and all were afforded a trial before a competent tribunal (an American military commission based in Nanking). Each was charged, tried, and convicted or acquitted for the precise acts for which they were originally detained. Once they were sentenced and sent to Landsberg penitentiary in American-occupied West Germany to begin their sentences they petitioned for writ of habeas corpus, alleging their imprisonment as violating Articles 1 and 3, as well as the Fifth Amendment of the Constitution. Their petition was originally dismissed, but the Court of Appeals reversed in *Eisentrager v. Forrestal*, 174 F.2nd 961 (1949) maintaining that rights guaranteed in the U.S. Constitution apply to anyone, citizen or non-citizen, detained by United States authorities *regardless of the territory in which this detention occurs*, and that petitioners are entitled to the writ if they can show their imprisonment to be illegal by reference to violations of their constitutional rights by detaining authorities.

The Court of Appeals in *Forrestal* further found that the petitioners failed to allege any fact showing lack of *military* jurisdiction in the respondents to accuse, try, and condemn the petitioners, and were unable to show that respondents acted in excess of their lawful powers. The *Eisentrager* court, however, reversed this appeals court decision holding that petitioners did not have a constitutional right to immunity from trial by military commission and subsequent punishment. In other words, the *Eisentrager* petitioners had 1. already been afforded trial, 2. were given the benefit of a presumption of innocence, 3. were also afforded competent legal counsel, and 4. were duly convicted before a military commission for violations of the law of nations punishable under the Constitution; whereas the Guantánamo detainees were given none of these privileges under the Bush administration, but were, in many cases, detained for months and sometimes years incommunicado, without trial, and often (but not always) subject to interrogations that often (but not always) violated GPW, Arts. 5 & 13.[49]

On February 6, 2006, Professor Mark Denbeaux completed a Report on Guantánamo Detainees in which he found that only 5 percent had been captured by United States forces, while 86 percent had been arrested by Pakistani or Northern Alliance forces and turned over to U.S. custody "at a time in which the United States offered large bounties for capture of suspected enemies,"[50] thus prompting many false abductions by Afghans and Pakistanis eager to collect large cash bounties of up to $5,000 for a Taliban fighter and $20,000 for an al-Qaeda fugitive. The Report found that as many as 55 percent of the detainees were *not* determined to have committed any hostile act against the United States or its coalition partners.

Since all captured al-Qaeda and Taliban suspects in America's ongoing war on terror must receive full Geneva protections as POWs unless (and until) this status can be reversed before a duly appointed competent tribunal—in which case the captive would face trial for war crimes, and, if convicted, could receive a prison sentence or even, in extreme cases, the death penalty—it follows by GPW, Art. 17, ¶4 that "no physical or mental torture, nor any other form of coercion, may be inflicted on prisoners of war to secure from them information of any kind whatever. Prisoners of war who refuse to answer may not be threatened, insulted, or exposed to unpleasant or disadvantageous treatment of any kind." Yet within a year and a month of 9/11 Lt. Col. Diane Beaver would formally request from the Commander of Joint Task Force 170 at Guantánamo Bay, Cuba formal legal permission to deploy "more aggressive interrogation techniques than the ones presently used" in order to obtain information from detainees that are "resisting interrogation efforts and are suspected of having significant information essential to national security."[51]

Lt. Col. Beaver reasoned exactly in the manner that then-White House Counsel Alberto R. Gonzales had months earlier in a memorandum opinion for the President. According to Gonzales, "since the detainees are not Enemy Prisoners of War, the Geneva Conventions limitations that ordinarily would govern captured enemy personnel interrogations are not binding on U.S. personnel conducting detainee interrogations at GTMO."[52] A group-think mentality combined with a "New Paradigm" urgency to prevent further terrorist attacks amid a state of declared national emergency led precisely to that rapid degeneration of military culture Gonzales specifically denied would arise as a result of a presidential blanket determination of non-POW status for captives suspected of Taliban and/or al-Qaeda membership.[53] In just a matter of weeks after 9/11 a torture culture emerged within the Bush II administration extending from the Office of Legal Counsel at Justice to the State Department and Department of Defense. What administration officials failed to understand was that no law can maintain its binding force as law if it be ignored or sidestepped whenever the exigencies of a crisis pressure authorities for immediate results.

GPW, Article 17's humanitarian provisions, for instance, were designed not only to protect captives of war, but also to prevent the forces of the detaining power from dehumanizing themselves in committing wanton acts of cruelty under the color of law. Torture as a method of extracting information simply does not work. Adrian Zuckerman, Fellow and Praelector in Jurisprudence at University College, Oxford, finds that "it can hardly be denied that a conviction that is founded on evidence obtained by torture or degradation is stripped of its moral validity in as much as it exploits the very practices that the criminal process sets out to eradicate."[54]

Aristotle of Stagira, tutor of Alexander the Great under Philip II of Macedon, admits that "those under compulsion speak the truth no less than lies, persistently refusing to tell the truth, but then easily inventing lies so as to make the torturing stop the sooner."[55] Examining the futility of torture the Italian jurist Cesare Beccaria notes that under coercive interrogation

> the impression made by pain may grow to such an extent that, having filled the whole of the sensory field, it leaves the torture victim no freedom to do anything but choose the quickest route to relieving himself of the immediate pain. Thus the criminal's replies are as necessitated [under torture] as are the effects of fire and boiling water. And thus the sensitive but guiltless man will admit guilt if he believes that, in that way, he can make the pain stop. All distinctions between the guilty and the innocent disappear as a consequence of the use of the very means which was meant to discover them.[56]

The sagacious Roman emperor Marcus Aurelius Antoninus taught in his *Meditations* that, in facing down a cruel and barbarous adversary, "the best method of defense is not to become like one's enemy."[57] From a logical point of view, the victim of torture either possesses or no longer possesses his senses. If he has lost his senses by being mentally or physically tortured to the point of oblivion, his information becomes useless gibberish. But if he has not yet been tortured to the breaking point, then he is still able to tell his interrogator whatever he thinks will put an end to his agony, or whatever he believes his torturer is likely to believe.

Cruelty is infectious because it vests the tormentor with a sense of absolute power over his victim. His sense of power is gained from draining his victim of worldly value. So, when the President and Secretary of Defense issued their respective blanket determinations not to count suspected al-Qaeda and Taliban captives as POWs under Geneva, their policy quickly expanded to include captives of conventional war taken during the U.S.-led invasion of Iraq and held at Abu Ghraib, Saddam's former torture prison. Did it occur to anyone in the OLC that a torture prison is an inappropriate place to house prisoners of war by GPW, Article 22's demand that captives of war "not be interned in penitentiaries . . . unhealthy areas, or [locations] where the climate is injurious for them"? Or Article 25's requirement that POWs be quartered "under conditions as favourable as those for the forces of the Detaining Power who are billeted in the same area"?

Iraqi captives who had nothing to do with al-Qaeda, the Taliban, or terrorism, but who were deemed to have intelligence value, or who were arrested in connection with suspected security offenses in Iraq were nonetheless treated as if they were, to use Rumsfeld's phrasing, "not entitled to prisoner of war status for purposes of the Geneva Conventions."[58]

According to a report issued in February of 2004 by the International Committee of the Red Cross (ICRC) on the treatment by Coalition Forces of prisoners of war and other persons protected under the Geneva Conventions in Iraq during arrest, internment, and interrogation:

> In certain cases, such as in Abu Ghraib military intelligence section, methods of physical and psychological coercion used by the interrogators appeared to be part of the standard operating procedures by military intelligence personnel to obtain confessions and extract information. Several

> military intelligence officers confirmed to the ICRC that it was part of the military intelligence process to hold a person deprived of his liberty naked in a completely dark and empty cell for a prolonged period and to use inhumane and degrading threatment, including physical and psychological coercion, against persons deprived of their liberty to secure their co-operation.[59]

Methods of ill-treatment most frequently alleged during interrogation by detainees at Abu Ghraib prison in Iraq included hooding, used to prevent captives from seeing their captors and to disorient them, and also to prevent them from breathing freely. Hooding was sometimes used in conjunction with beatings, thus increasing anxiety about when the blows would come. Handcuffing with flexi-cuffs, which were sometimes so tight and used for such extended periods that they caused skin lesions and long-term after-effects on the hands (nerve damage). Beatings occurred with hard objects (including pistols and rifles); slapping, punching, kicking with knees or feet on various parts of the body (legs, sides, lower back, groin); pressing the face into the ground with boots; threats of ill-treatment, reprisals against family members, imminent execution, or transfer to Guantánamo Bay, Cuba; being stripped naked for several days while held in solitary confinement in an empty and completely dark cell that included a latrine; being held in solitary confinement combined with threats, insufficient sleep, food or water deprivation, minimal access to showers (twice a week), denial of access to open air and prohibition of contacts with other persons deprived of their liberty; being paraded outside cells in front of other prisoners; acts of humiliation; exposure while hooded to excruciatingly loud noise or music, prolonged exposure while hooded to the sun over several hours, including during the hottest time of the day when temperatures could reach 50 degrees Celsius (122 degrees Fahrenheit) or higher; being forced to remain for prolonged periods in stress positions such as squatting or standing with or without the arms lifted.[60]

These allegations suggest that Iraqi detainees were not generally treated humanely, even though humane treatment is demanded by GPW, Article 13, ¶1 for POWs at *all* times. Nor were these detainees "protected particularly against acts of violence or intimidation and against insults and public curiosity," as specifically required by GPW, Article 13, ¶2. Abu Ghraib prison was both a penitentiary and a torture house used under the repressive regime of Saddam Hussein to punish political dissidents. The reasoning behind GPW, Article 21, ¶1's prohibition against internment in penitentiaries is that, as a matter of customary international law, it has not traditionally been considered a crime to take up arms for the defense of oneself or one's country amid foreign invasion, especially when pressed into service against one's will by a tyrant. It is easy to see how quickly a torture culture spread throughout a military and intelligence-gathering establishment no longer restrained by the "quaint"[61] encumbrance of tedious rules of international humanitarian law.

QUESTION ONE

DOES THE PRESIDENT HAVE CONSTITUTIONAL POWER AS COMMANDER-IN-CHIEF TO INITIATE A FOREIGN WAR WITHOUT CONGRESSIONAL AUTHORIZATION?

The Yoo-Flanigan Memo

The question whether the President of the United States has constitutional power to initiate a foreign war without congressional authorization might seem somewhat superfluous and out of place in our analysis of the Bush II war on terror given the congressional aegis contained in the Joint Resolution of September 14, 2001, Authorizing the President to Use Military Force (AUMF) against those he determines planned, authorized, or committed the attacks of September 11, 2001.[1]

In one fell swoop Congress entrusted President Bush with unprecedented and sweeping authority to single-handedly direct a global military and intelligence campaign against terrorism. Within three days of the attacks of 9/11 the Bush administration was operating at the full apogee of executive power, but in spite of that fullness of power, in spite of the overwhelming support of the American people and the generosity of the international community, the Office of Legal Counsel in the Department of Justice wanted still more; they wanted the power to engage even those terrorist groups *not demonstrably linked* to the attacks of 9/11.

The Bush administration's official position on executive war power was first laid out in the Yoo-Flanigan memorandum of September 25, 2001, according to which the Constitution, as interpreted by then-Deputy Assistant Attorney General John C. Yoo, "vests the President with the power to strike terrorist groups or organizations *that cannot be demonstrably linked* to the September 11 incidents, but that, nonetheless, pose a similar threat to the security of the United States and the lives of its people, whether at home or overseas."[2] (Emphasis added). The Yoo-Flanigan memo would come to define the official group-think position within the administration regarding the President's new-found constitutional latitude to conduct military operations against suspected terrorists and nations suspected of harboring or supporting them.

The idea that the President of the United States has legal authority to unilaterally suspend application of the Geneva Conventions with respect to the capture and detention of suspected members of al-Qaeda is a grotesque legal fiction borrowed directly from the Yoo-Flanigan interpretation of executive war power and subsequently built into the text of the President's February 7 Executive Order of 2002 regarding the treatment of al-Qaeda and Taliban detainees. Once the "New Paradigm" position on suspending Geneva became policy by means of Executive Order, it became the *only* position for the Bush White House, and the one unflinchingly accepted by almost all key members of the administration, remaining virtually unchallenged and unchanged by Congress to this day.

Note for instance how easily then-Secretary of State Colin Powell fell prey to the position that the President has authority to determine that GPW applies to the conflict in Afghanistan *while at the same time* determining universally for all captives (and independently of any Article 5 hearing) that detainees captured amid conflict are one-and-all *not* entitled to POW status. Powell notes in a memorandum from January 26, 2002, to Alberto Gonzales, then-Counsel to the President, that the advantages accruing from a determination that GPW does not apply "[w]ould result equally if the President determines that the GPW does apply but that the detainees are not entitled to POW status."[3]

On the one hand, Powell warns that a presidential decision that GPW does not apply to the conflict in Afghanistan against al-Qaeda and the Taliban would reverse over a century of U.S. policy and practice supporting the Geneva Conventions, in addition to causing a negative international reaction that could "undermine public support among critical allies" while possibly provoking foreign prosecutors to investigate and charge our officials and troops for crimes. On the other hand, Powell's logic is terribly flawed, since no President can both (1) determine that GPW does apply and (2) that detainees captured in conflict are *not* entitled to POW status, since, if GPW does apply, then GPW Article 5, ¶2 applies, which paragraph requires a "competent tribunal" to determine the POW status of every captive on a case-by-case basis, and so precludes any government official such as the President or Secretary of Defense from predetermining the POW status of any detainee prior to and independent of trial before a competent tribunal, should any doubt arise as to whether the detainee meets Article 4 criteria for POW status.[4]

Since we know by the Denbeaux Report of 2006 that about 1 in 20 detainees held at GTMO were actually apprehended by U.S. forces, there exists substantial reason to believe that administration officials failed to notice a salient Article 5 doubt about the true identity of persons held in custody. Until such time as a competent tribunal can conduct a hearing, the detainee is to be afforded full POW protection under Geneva; which means that "no physical or mental torture, nor any other form of coercion, may be inflicted on prisoners of war to secure from them information of any kind whatever" (GPW, Art. 17, ¶4).

The fog of war combined with the uncertainty of circumstances surrounding the capture and detention of persons brought into U.S. custody in Afghanistan creates precisely that shadow of doubt about the Article 4 status of the detainee that should have alerted members of the Bush OLC to the impending legal dangers involved in violating the humanitarian rights of persons falling under the legal jurisdiction of the United States. In his memorandum opinion for Timothy Flanigan, Yoo makes a number of claims that are, as I shall argue, inconsistent with the text and formative history of the U.S. Constitution. These claims also effectively expand the President's war making power beyond clear limits of accountability recognized for decades in the War Powers Resolution of 1973.

Objections to Positions Held in Yoo-Flanigan

Position 1.—Failing to notice, as a fundamental principle of law, that suspects are to be distinguished from criminals, the latter having been found guilty through due process of law, Deputy Assistant Yoo claims ill-advisedly that

> the President has constitutional power not only to retaliate against any person, organization, or State *suspected* of involvement in terrorist attacks on the United States, but also against foreign States *suspected* of harboring or supporting such organizations. (*TTP*, Memo 1, Introd., ¶ 2, p. 3, emphasis added)

On the Contrary, (*a*) suspects are never proper objects of retaliation under the rule of law as conceived in both Roman and Anglo-American traditions of jurisprudence, for such retaliation would negate any presumption of innocence on behalf of those held suspect. Perhaps this early confusion of suspect behavior for criminal behavior so soon after 9/11 was the very Archimedean point from which the Bush administration Office of Legal Counsel sought to undermine and systematically remove the terra firma of international humanitarian protection from those it labeled "unlawful enemy combatants." Had the administration followed military tradition, a thorough investigation leading to mandatory Article 5 hearings over each detainee's suspected role as an enemy combatant (as opposed to the mere fact of his detention in U.S. custody) would have determined the POW status of each captive case by case.

Yoo's statement fails to acknowledge the key fact that due process requires that we assume as not guilty (unless proven otherwise) any suspects accused of criminal activity. Yoo even expands his claim by saying that entire nations "suspected of harboring or supporting" terrorist organizations may become objects of United States retaliation overseas, if the President so deems it necessary.

Because the legal terms "harbor" and "support" remain undefined in the Yoo-Flanigan memorandum, it remains unclear whether countries such as Iran, Egypt, Jordan, or Syria could face retaliation by United States military forces on the grounds that certain of their citizens happen to provide physical sanctuary and financial support to international terrorist organizations which target the United States and its assets, even if their respective governments officially condemn and punish acts of international terrorism. And it is just this level of ambiguity between suspected harborers versus suspected practitioners of terrorism that gave President Bush almost unlimited latitude in initiating foreign wars and detaining suspects.

Yoo's blanket denial of any presumption of innocence on behalf of both individuals and states suspected of harboring or supporting terrorists came to be magnified and broadened in several subsequent Bush administration policy directives. The November 13 Military Order of 2001, for instance, denies non-U.S. citizens detained pursuant to the Order not only the presumption of innocence, but all manner of access to basic rights of due process (such as legal representation) according to traditionally accepted principles of law and rules of evidence. We shall examine the text of this Order in *Question Two* below.

(*b*) Retaliation understood as returning like for like is an unjust method of response to acts of terrorism; for such would require the United States to return random deadly violence for random deadly violence in response to the post-9/11 terrorist attacks in Bali, Madrid, London, Sharm el-Sheikh, and Mumbai—retaliation which is unacceptable because it would debase United States military culture. "Retaliation" is a word which derives from the Latin adjective "*talis*" meaning "of such a kind," "such like," or "equivalent to." To retaliate is to pay back another in like coin.

The so-called *lex talionis* is the law of reciprocating like for like: An eye for an eye, a tooth for a tooth. The term "retaliation" is used most appropriately in military contexts to describe symmetric force response to violent enemy attack, *i.e.*, if the enemy should engage you in the field, then you have the right of immediate self-defense by the laws and customs of war to engage him back.

"Retaliation," then, is an inappropriate term for describing the kind of legal relationship the United States ought to have with *suspected* international terrorists, or the states that sponsor them, because violence against suspects in any investigation short-circuits due process of law. It would have been far more appropriate for Deputy Assistant Yoo to have substituted the phrase "to apprehend and criminally prosecute" in place of "to retaliate against" to describe the manner in which the United States intends to deal with international terrorists.

Aristotle defined the law of returning like for like as the Law of Rhadamanthus:

> *If one should suffer what one did,*
> *Right justice would be met therein.*[5]

Retaliation is not justifiable under customary international law, nor under United States treaty law, if it takes the form of physical or mental coercion or torture used in order to extract information from suspect enemies of state detained in prison conditions incommunicado, without ever being charged for a crime, or permitted the advantages of legal counsel, or the right to view and weigh the evidence grounding their detention.

According to Grotius, the public desire for retaliation against perceived enemies of state does not justify killing them, even if retaliation be seen as a way of inspiring terror in one's enemies, and even if captives remain in obstinate defiance of their captors:

> Equity demands that those be spared who give themselves up to a conqueror unconditionally and in a suppliant manner. . . . Against these precepts of natural right and equity exceptions have often been made, none of them just, for instance, if retaliation be demanded [publicly], or if it be necessary in order to inspire terror, or if the adversary should prove especially obstinate in his resistance. . . . For no danger arises from persons who have been captured or from those who have surrendered themselves or desire to surrender themselves to us. Therefore, in order for someone to be justly put to death, a crime must first ensue, and one such that an impartial judge would reckon vindicated by penalty of death.[6] (*De Jure Belli ac Pacis,* Book 3, Ch. 11, §15, §16.1)

Position 2.—Yoo adopts as his central thesis the disturbingly broad claim that the President may deploy U.S. military force directly into foreign hostilities independently of congressional authorization, and that he may, if necessary, act contrary to, or outside the aegis of, an Act of Congress, specifically the Joint Resolution (AUMF) of September 14, 2001, which limits the horizon of the President's authority of military response to just those nations, organizations, or persons who planned, authorized, committed, or aided the terrorist attacks of 9/11. Not content with the broad powers already conferred upon President Bush in the AUMF, Yoo claims that

> the President may deploy military force preemptively against terrorist organizations or the States that harbor or support them, *whether or not they can be linked to the specific terrorist incidents of September 11.* (*TTP,* Memo 1, Introd., ¶3, p. 3, emphasis added)

On the Contrary, by the Joint Resolution (AUMF) of September 14, 2001,[7] Congress authorized the President to use military forces to retaliate only "against those responsible for the recent attacks launched against the United States," but not against those not responsible for such attacks. In enacting the Joint Resolution Congress clearly did not intend to hand the President a blank check to expand the war on terror beyond the al-Qaeda and Taliban nexus that harbored and supported bin Laden. While a new and more robust policy of preventative war was certainly in order after the attacks of 9/11, if we take Yoo at his word, the President has *de jure* authority, if he should deem it necessary, to preemptively attack Iran because many Iranians harbor and give physical sanctuary and financial support to Hezbollah, which currently operates out of Syria and Lebanon, and focuses its violence and rhetoric exclusively against Israel, yet has no perceivable connection to the attacks of September 11.

Yoo notes that the findings in the Joint Resolution include an express statement that "the President has authority under the Constitution to take action to deter and prevent acts of international terrorism against the United States" (S.J. Res. 23, Preamble, cl. 6), but fails to mention that this preemptive power applies only to al-Qaeda elements situated in various countries around the world, not to groups having nothing to do with the attacks of 9/11. The Deputy Assistant would have vastly strengthened his position had he addressed the question of the premissibility of preemption under international law as a separate inquiry within his draft opinion.

Position 3.—Yoo claims that the text structure and history of the Constitution establish that the Framers entrusted the President with the power to use military force in situations of emergency and that

> during the period leading up to the Constiution's ratification, the power to initiate hostilities and to control the escalation of conflict *had been long understood* to rest in the hands of the executive branch. By their terms, these provisions [*Const.* Art. 2, §§1-2] vest full control of the military focres of the United States in the President. (*TTP,* Memo 1, Part I, ¶4, p. 5, emphasis added)

On the contrary, (*a*) the debate at the Federal Convention of 1787 over which branch of government ought to hold the power of initiating hostilities in war, of controlling the escalation of a conflict, and of repelling a sudden attack remained quite unsettled right up to the very day of the final consensus draft of September 17, 1787. A working draft of the Constitution as it stood with the Convention in mid-summer 1787 originally assigned the Legislature the broad power "to make war" as opposed to the narrower power "to declare war" currently contained in Article 1, §8, ¶11. On Friday, August 17 a debate ensued on the floor of the Convention about whether to replace the term "make" with the narrower term "declare." A motion to strike "make" in exchange for "declare" was agreed to: Ayes–7; noes–2; absent–1. According to the Records of the Federal Convention compiled by James Madison, views differed so widely on the topic of assigning war powers, that there simply was no overarching consensus opinion among the Framers about which branch should hold the power of initiating and escalating an international conflict, contrary to what Yoo imagines. Mr.

Pinkney, for instance, opposed vesting the war making power in the legislature on the grounds that its proceedings were inherently too slow, and the House of Representatives too numerous in membership and diverse in interest to allow for speedy and informed deliberation on technical matters pertaining to war. Mr. Butler supported vesting the war making power in the President "who will have all the requisite qualities, and will not make war but when the Nation will support it."

Mr. Madison and Mr. Gerry moved to insert "declare," striking out "make" war; leaving to the Executive the power to repel sudden attacks. Mr. Sharman argued that the executive should "be able to repel and not to commence war" and that, in relation to the Legislature's war powers, the term "make" was preferable to "declare," the latter narrowing the power too much. Mr. Gerry, records Madison, "never expected to hear in a republic a motion to empower the Executive alone to declare war."

Mr. Elseworth, arguing for a material difference between making war and making peace, believed it should be easier to get out of war than into it, war requiring only an overt declaration, but peace attended with "intricate & secret negociations."

Mr. Mason believed that the Executive could not be trusted with the war power, and supported "clogging rather than facilitating war."[8] As these opinions attest, the Framers were highly mistrustful of executive power, and avoided vesting a single executive with unilateral war-initiating powers, while at the same time recognizing the need for unilateral executive power to command military forces to ward off sudden attacks and invasions.

(*b*) A consensus understanding on executive war making power did not fully emerge until the close of proceedings at the Federal Convention in September of 1787. This consensus position came to be elaborated through a series of *Federalist Papers* published by James Madison, John Jay, and Alexander Hamilton between October of 1787 and May of 1788. Arguing before a public ever-mindful of the dangers of unchecked monarchical power and skeptical of the corruption wrought by a hereditary crown committed to political absolutism and tyranny, Hamilton writes

> The most material points of difference [between the American President and the King of Great Britain] are these—First, the President will have only the *occasional command* of such part of the militia of the nation, *as by legislative provision* may be called into the actual service of the Union. The

> King of Great Britain and the Governor of New York have *at all times* the entire command of all the militia within their several jurisdictions. . . . Secondly, the President is to be Commander-in-Chief of the army and navy of the United States. In this respect his authority would be nominally the same as that of the King of Great Britain, but in substance much inferior to it. It would amount to nothing more than the supreme command and direction of the military and naval forces, as first General and Admiral of the confederacy: while that of the British King extends to the declaring of war and to the raising and regulating of fleets and armies; all which by the Constitution under consideration would appertain to the Legislature. (*The Federalist* No. 69, ¶6, emphasis added)

It is evident from the language of Hamilton that the initiation of foreign hostilities belongs to Congress and not the President, because it requires a declaration of war, except in cases of national emergency, foreign invasion, or repulsion of a sudden enemy attack.

In addition, the power to control the escalation of conflict (that Yoo claims as part of the President's plenary power to conduct war) often requires additional funding and heightened troop levels, both of which powers are unambiguously assigned to Congress and not the President under the Constitution. For instance, it is Congress that has the power to raise and support armies, to provide and maintain a navy, and to provide for calling forth the militia to execute the laws of the union, suppress insurrections, and repel invasions (*Const.*, Art. 1, §8, ¶s 12, 13, 15). But Congress has been lax in asserting these powers in recent decades.

The Framers' hesitancy to grant unchecked plenary power over the making and declaring of war to a single Chief reflected not only their personal aversion to the exercise of unbridled monarchical power vested in the King of Great Britain, but had precedent also in the writings of the ancient Greek historian of Rome, Polybius, who, in treating of the Roman constitution, noticed that the best commonwealth is one consisting of a mixed government containing elements of monarchy in the election of a chief magistrate or consul, of aristocracy in the selection of a senate, and of democracy or popular will in the election of a popular assembly. Each aspect of the Roman government was conceived by Polybius as providing a check against, or limit to, the exercise of the power of the others. Thus, a system of highly regulated consular war powers were the rule and not the exception for the Romans; and foreign wars initiated by consuls without authroization of the senate were illegal and censurable.

The celebrated Belgian jurist Balthazar Ayala notes in his discussion of treaties and truces that the Roman senate, but *not* the consuls, had the ultimate power to both begin and end war.

> And so, without a doubt, when the Roman consuls, in whom was vested the highest authority of state, took command of the army, they held the power to conduct war, and, by their own discretion, to harass and attack the enemy, and to control military discipline by their own will; but they did not have the power to begin or end a war without authorization from the senate and the command of the people.[9] (*De Jure et Officiis Bellicis et Disciplina Militari Libri III*, book 1, ch. 7, p. 79)

In other words, both popular assembly and senate were required to give the consuls authorization to make and conduct war against foreign enemies of the state.

(*c*) The power to initiate armed conflict overseas in defense of United States interests, along with the power to control the escalation of such conflict, does not rest in the hands of the executive branch. Certain emergency powers to deploy military forces in the wake of an attack rest in the hands of the executive. But the interpretation of emergency powers is constitutionally problematic, and requires deep consideration. During the Korean conflict, for instance, a looming nationwide strike in the steel industry was perceived by President Truman as a dire threat to national security. This perceived security threat prompted Truman to order his Secretary of Commerce to seize and operate most of the nation's steel mills. On June 2, 1952, in *Youngstown Sheet & Tube Co. v. Sawyer*, 343 U.S. 579, the Supreme Court upheld the decision of a federal district court which had issued a preliminary injunction restraining the Secretary of Commerce from carrying into effect Truman's executive order.

Justice Robert Jackson, concurring in the opinion of the Court, warned against possible abuses of executive war power amid perceived states of national emergency by noting that the Framers "knew what emergencies were, knew the pressures they engender for authoritative action, knew, too, how they afford a ready pretext for usurpation" and that, aside from temporary suspension of habeas corpus in time of rebellion or invasion (*Const.* Art. 1, §9, ¶2) the Framers "made no express provision for exercise of extraordinary authority because of a crisis" (*Id.*, 650).

The Bush administration essentially fell into the same error of judgment over the scope of presidential wartime power as was anticipated by Justice

Jackson more than half a century ago; namely, that "the opinions of judges, no less than executives and publicists, often suffer the infirmity of confusing the issue of a power's validity with the cause it is invoked to promote, of confounding the permanent executive office with its temporary occupant." *Id.*, 634. While we can be reasonably certain that international terrorism poses a grave and continuing threat to the national security of the United States, we must not confuse that certainty of danger with absoluteness of executive power in facing down that threat.

Position 4.—Deputy Assistant Yoo claims that some commentators

> argue that the vesting of the power to declare war gives Congress the sole authority to decide whether to make war. This view misreads the constitutional text and misunderstands the nature of a declaration of war. Declaring war is not tantamount to making war. (*TTP*, Memo 1, Part I, ¶6, p. 6)

On the contrary, (*a*) while it is unmistakably true that declaring war is not the same as making war, the commentators cited by Yoo say only that wars, big or small, officially declared or not officially declared, must receive congressional authorization at some point in time in order to be legal. None of the scholars cited by Yoo actually argues for *exclusive* congressional authority to decide *whether* to make war.[10] Instead the consensus position developed in the researches of these scholars indicates that Congress plays a central (but not exclusive) role in the making of war

1. *by declaring war, granting letters of marque and reprisal, and making rules concerning captures on land and water* (*Const.* Art. 1, §8, ¶11);

2. *by constituting tribunals inferior to the Supreme Court* (*Const.* Art. 1, §8, ¶9), which includes military tribunals constructed during a time of war for the purpose of *defining and punishing offences against the law of nations* (*Const.* Art. 1, §8, ¶10). Competent tribunals of this sort must be established by the United States (by requirement of GPW, Article 5) in order to determine the POW status of detainees captured in Afghanistan, who are held on suspicion of al-Qaeda or Taliban affiliation.[11] For instance, President Bush's issuance of the November 13 Executive Military Order of 2001 effectively precluded Congress from fulfilling its constitutionally designated role of establishing military tribunals and the rules governing pretrial, trial, and posttrial procedure, until the passage of the Military Commissions Act (MCA) on October 17, 2006 (Public Law 109-306, 120 Stat. 2601), almost five full

years after the issuance of the Order. However, the MCA merely reaffirms the unilateral executive authority to suspend international law at will originally asserted in the Executive Orders of November 13, 2001, and February 7, 2002. The MCA gives legislative weight and authority to the notoriously harsh system of Combatant Status Review Tribunals (CSRTs) established by Deputy Secretary of Defense Paul Wolfowitz on July 7, 2004,[12] merely nine days after the Supreme Court decision in *Rasul* held that prisoners (originally numbering Mamdouh Habib, Shafiq Rasul, Asif Iqbal, and David Hicks) could challenge the lawfulness of their detention in habeas proceedings in federal district court in Washington D.C. Messrs. Rasul and Iqbal had already been released by the time the Supreme Court decided *Rasul*; and Hicks had been referred for criminal prosecution before a military commission. In an attempt to neutralize the role of civilian courts in granting habeas relief to untold numbers of the detained, the Bush administration appears to have created the CSRT system as political cover to create the illusion and image of competent Article 5 tribunals taking place at Guantánamo.

This system is now being rethought under Obama; but no one ever came forward in the previous administration to explain why it was necessary to implement these procedures, or why it was necessary to alter Geneva Conventions protocol on military tribunals. We have seen, in the *Introduction*, how other nations and empires have encountered international threats of piracy and terrorism, and yet were successful in facing down those threats without compromising their own laws and treaties to do so.

Looming international threats have often been used by government officials throughout American history to curtail domestic freedoms. A quasi-war with France in 1798 was used by the Federalist Party to pass the Alien and Sedition Laws criminalizing any open-forum criticism of the Adams administration. The threat of communism in the 1920s and 1950s was used by Congress and the courts to suppress associations of intellectuals and artists. To what extent, then, are Americans willing to continue backing away from their international obligations and domestic liberties in order to obtain long-term security from an international terrorist threat the dimensions of which are neither clearly nor distinctly known? The fact remains that the current administration has quietly continued on with many of the executive-enhancing innovations of the Bush II OLC; and the civil liberties curtailed by congress shortly after 9/11 have never been fully restored.

Congress also plays a central (but not exclusive) role in war making

3. *by providing and maintaining a navy* (*Const*. Art. 1, §8, ¶13);

4. *by making rules for the government and regulation of the land and naval forces* (*Const*. Art. 1, §8, ¶14);

5. *by providing for the organization, arming, and disciplining of the militia, and for governing such parts of them as may be employed in the service of the United States* (*Const*. Art 1, §8, ¶16);

6. *by calling forth the militia to execute the laws of the union, suppress insurrections, and repel invasions* (*Const*. Art. 1, §8, ¶15).

(*b*) Rights of military preemption against an adversary exist under customary international law whenever the following four conditions obtain: Preemptive attack is an act of self-defense; the danger posed by the adversary is immediate and certain, imminent and deadly; the prospect of an attack is empirically verifiable through adequate intelligence; and there exists strong evidence that inaction is more dangerous than action.[13] These four conditions are established on the basis of legal interpretations authored by Grotius, Gentilis, and de Vitoria.[14] They four conditions are deliberately difficult to satisfy, since, were it permitted any nation to attack another for merely becoming adversarial, economically independent, or militarily and strategically stronger, interminable wars would proliferate throughout the world.

It is my opinion that, if these four conditions obtain against an al-Qaeda or Taliban adversary, then the President already has clear authority under the AUMF to launch a preemptive military assault. If these conditions are satisfied in relation to a dangerous terrorist group that is manifestly *not* connected with the attacks of September 11, but which is poised on the brink of launching an attack against the United States, its assets or possessions, the President has power to launch a preemptive attack, but is nonetheless bound under the War Powers Resolution of 1973 to seek congressional authorization to do so, unless the window of opportunity to strike be somehow too narrow in time to acquire such authorization.

The need for an executive fully able to respond to an emergency of foreign invasion was clearly felt at the Federal Convention of 1787, as Yoo acknowledges, when the Convention voted to change Congress's power to "make war" to a power to merely "declare war" (*Const*. Art. 1, §8, ¶11), leaving the President latitude to repel sudden invasions unilaterally by his own determination in cases where exigencies of time and circumstance do not allow for congressional authorization.

It appears to have been the Framers' intent, then, to separate the President's Commander-in-Chief power to conduct a foreign war from Congress's power to decide when, whether, and by how much the nation ought to go to war. James Madison wrote in 1793 that

> those who are to conduct a war cannot in the nature of things, be proper or safe judges, whether a war ought to be commenced, continued, or concluded. They are barred from the latter functions by a great principle in free government, analogous to that which separates the sword from the purse, or the power of executing from the power of enacting laws.[15] (*Helvidius*, No. 1, ¶39)

Five years later in 1798, with the Federalists in Congress passing sweeping executive-enhancing legislation during a quasi-war with France, Madison would write to Jefferson in a tone of anxiety that

> the constitution supposes, what the history of all governments demonstrates, that the Executive is the branch of power most interested in war, and most prone to it. It has accordingly with studied care, vested the question of war in the legislature. But the doctrines lately advanced [by the Adams administration] strike at the root of all these provisions, and will deposit the peace of the country in that department which the Constitution distrusts as most ready without cause to renounce it.[16]

Some constitutional scholars argue that the President must seek retroactive authorization from Congress after deploying military forces in emergency circumstances to meet sudden dangers abroad. Louis Fisher believes, for instance, that "even if a case could be made that the emergency facing Truman [in the wake of North Korea's invasion of South Korea] in June 1950 required him to act promptly without first seeking and obtaining legislative authority, nothing prevented him from returning to Congress and asking for a supporting statute for retroactive authority."[17] It is clear from these considerations that congressional powers to declare, finance, and sustain a foreign war far outweigh any temporary powers the President might have to unilaterally deploy United States military forces in contexts where congressional authorization cannot be obtained.

Position 5.—Using an obvious debater's trick to enhance the President's Commander-in-Chief power at the expense of diminishing Congress's role in authorizing, funding, and formally declaring war, Yoo distorts the historical record in claiming that

> the Framing generation well understood that declarations of war were obsolete. Not all forms of hostilities rose to the level of a declared war: during the seventeenth and eighteenth centuries, Great Britain and colonial America waged numerous conflicts against other States without an official declaration of war. . . . Given this context, it is clear that Congress's power to declare war does not constrain the President's independent and plenary constitutional authority over the use of military force. (*TTP*, Memo 1, Part I, ¶7, p. 7)

On the contrary, (*a*) Yoo neglects to inform us that President Jefferson both sought and received congressional authorization and financial support for his repeated deployments of naval forces against aggressive Barbary pirates that periodically issued forth from the shores of the Arab sheikhdoms of Morocco, Tunis, Tripoli, and Algiers to attack American merchant vessels sailing the Mediterranean during a period of sporadic skirmishes known as the Barbary Wars that lasted from 1801 to 1815, even though no state of war was ever formally declared by Congress. This fact, however, in no way implies that the Framing generation considered formal declarations of war to be obsolete; it does suggest, however, that President Jefferson viewed the piratic raids as criminal activity, against which it would have been inappropriate to formally declare a state of war. As a matter of national self-defense Congress quickly enacted legislation on February 6, 1802, authorizing President Jefferson to use military force in order to protect the free commerce of the United States against the pirates of the Barbary coast.[18]

Article 1 of the Constitution (§8, ¶11) grants Congress, in addition to the power of formally declaring war, the additional power of granting letters of marque and reprisal. Letters of marque and reprisal were granted on exclusive authority of Congress to private individuals to wage war overseas against the external enemies of the United States by use of their own privately financed and armed vessels. At a time in early American history when the only standing navy was the modest fleet of six vessels commissioned by President Washington in 1796 to protect U.S. merchant ships from attacks by pirates at sea, the power to grant a letter of marque was extraordinary, and the Framers were careful to assign this power to Congress alone, to the exclusion of the President. Congress was so careful to guard this power that it rejected an amendment in 1802 that would have empowered President Jefferson to grant letters of marque and reprisal on his own authority.[19]

The Barbary Wars involved the continual and repeated deployment of U.S. naval forces alongside privately funded armed vessels summoned into action by Congress over a period of several Presidential adminstrations to protect U.S. merchant shipping from piratic raids throughout the Mediterranean. Skirmishes on the high seas began on May 14, 1801, when the Pasha of Tripoli declared war on the United States for nonpayment of tribute. According to Louis Fisher,

> Jefferson told Congress that he had sent a small squadron of frigates to the Mediterranean to protect against the attack and then asked Congress for further guidance, stating he was "unauthorized by the Constitution, without the sanctions of Congress, to go beyond the line of defense."[20]

Given that the Barbary Wars stand as *the* premier example in early American history of conflict waged without an official declaration of war by Congress against a number of aggressive sheikhdoms threatening a state of jihad on the high seas, if certain conditions were not met, it is genuinely unfortunate that the Bush OLC managed to entirely ignore the role that jihadist ideology played in the Barbary Wars, when this ideology was openly documented with explicit references to jihad and holy war in the treaties that the United States concluded with Muslim rulers. According to Melvin E. Lee, representatives from Tunis and Algiers (the westernmost reaches of the Ottoman Empire) even described their territories to American envoys as "the frontier posts of jihad against European Christianity."[21] This description evokes an old tradition in Islam of the proud ghazi warrior, whose mission in life was to protect the frontiers of the dar al-Islam from foreign encroachment. In return for his years of military service to the Caliph, the ghazi warrior was provided with abundant farmland, moneys, and other assets to retire in peace, pride, and prosperity. Although the OLC could not have known of Lee's study in 2002, they could have easily accessed the text of treaties completed between the United States and the Arab sheikhs of the Barbary coast.

(*b*) The President's Commander-in-Chief authority over the use of United States military forces is neither independent of Congress and the courts, nor plenary, even during a war or some other state of national emergency.

First, the President's power to deploy military forces into foreign hostilities pursuant to a state of national emergency following an attack upon the United States is neither independent nor plenary according to Subsection 2(c)(3) of the War Powers Resolution of 1973, but limited to just sixty days after the issuance of a required Presidential report to the Speaker of the House and President pro tempore of the Senate. The President's report must set forth not only the circumstances necessitating the introduction of U.S. armed forces, but the constitutional and legislative authority under which such introduction took place, as well as the estimated scope and duration of the hostilities themselves. By these simple requirements the War Powers Resolution sought to ensure executive accountability to both Congress and the courts, so that even in a declared state of national emergency the President cannot wield his power to initiate war overseas independent of Congress and the courts. The Bush administration succeeded in finding loopholes in WPR standards of accountability to Congress. But, there is now a movement afoot in Washington to enact new war powers legislation requiring more stringent executive accountability.

Second, the Framing generation did *not* view formal declarations of war as obsolete, but proudly bound its conception of warfare to traditional and highly chivalric standards of customary international law according to which, as Cicero puts it, "no war is considered just unless it has been proclaimed and declared, or unless reparation has first been demanded."[22] In more recent times the U.S. Supreme Court has expressed serious concerns that the making of war without formal congressional declaration (as in the Korean conflict) could present an imbalance of war powers, with an increasingly powerful executive increasingly placing himself beyond the pale of accountability to Congress. In *Youngstown*, Justice Jackson noted that

> nothing in our Constitution is plainer than that declaration of a war is entrusted only to Congress. Of course, a state of war may, in fact, exist without a formal declaration. But no doctrine that the Court could promulgate would seem to me more sinister and alarming than that a President whose conduct of foreign affairs is so largely uncontrolled, and often even is unknown, can vastly enlarge his mastery over the internal affairs of the country by his own commitment of the Nation's armed forces to some foreign venture. (343 U.S., at 642)

Justice Jackson feared that as the President's Commander-in-Chief power naturally increases during a foreign war, it becomes increasingly easier for that same President to usurp expanded domestic powers as well, as for instance over the nation's economy, labor force, police and security focres, surveillance organs, etc.

Position 6.—In an attempt to expand the President's already congressionally inflated wartime authority as Commander-in-Chief under the Joint Resolution (AUMF) Yoo claims that

> the constitutional structure requires that *any* ambiguities in the allocation of a power that is executive in nature—such as the power to conduct military hostilities—*must be resolved in favor of the executive branch.* Article II, Section 1 provides that "[t]he executive Power shall be vested in a President of the United States." U.S. Const., Art. II, § 1. By contrast, Article I's Vesting Clause gives Congress only the powers "herein granted." *Id.* Art. I, § 1. This difference in language indicates that Congress's legislative powers are limited to the list enumerated in Article I, Section 8, while the President's powers include inherent executive powers that are unenumerated in the Constitution. . . . The purpose of the enumeration of executive powers in Article II was not to define and cabin the grant in the Vesting Clause. (*TTP*, Memo 1, Part I, ¶10, p. 8, emphasis added)

On the Contrary, (*a*) Yoo's Vesting Clause argument trots out almost verbatim an argument once deployed by Alexander Hamilton[23] in *Pacificus* No. 1 of June 29, 1793, to assert the existence of certain indefinite executive powers not enumerated in the Constitution, but which James Madison famously disparaged and lampooned two months later in *Helvidius,* No. 1, ¶50 by quoting Hamilton's words back from five years previous, *Federalist* No. 75, ¶2, where it is maintained that the powers of war, of peace, and of treaties are to be *shared* between the legislative and executive branches, and are not the domain of either branch to the exclusion of the other.[24]

The origin of all Vesting Clause arguments is Hamilton, *Pacificus* No. 1, ¶26 where he argues (in a tone diametrically opposite the Hamilton who penned *Federalist* No. 75) that the scope and reach of legislative power vested in Congress is *limited* to just those powers "herein granted" (Art. 1, §1), whereas the scope and reach of executive power vested in a President (Art. 2, §1, ¶1) is *unlimited,* indefinite, and includes powers not specifically enumerated in the Constitution at all. Both clauses *vest* the legislative and executive branches with certain powers specifically enumerated at various places in the Constitution, but Hamilton wants to go further and say that there exists a fundamental difference in the *essence* or *being* of the power assigned to each branch; legislative powers being inherently limited and finite in scope, executive powers unlimited and infinite.

The subtext here is that the Constitution specifically enumerates the functions of Congress, but does not limit executive authority to any specifiable list of powers. For instance, while the Constitution unambiguously stipulates that treaties can only be made by the President with the advice and consent of the Senate (Art. 2, §2, ¶2), Hamilton asserts at *Pacificus* No. 1, ¶39 that "their activity may be continued or suspended by the President alone"[25] even though treaty termination is nowhere defined in the Constitution.

Given that the Constitution stipulates a set of specific executive powers in Article 2, §2, albeit not "enumerated" or listed in serial succession as are the powers of Congress, this fact would indicate that the Framers clearly intended to create a *limited* executive just as they intended also to prescribe legally definable limits to the use of legislative and judicial power.

Despite these clear intentions, Hamilton maintains that the enumeration of executive powers found in the Constitution

> ought rather . . . to be considered as intended by way of greater caution, to specify and regulate the principal articles implied in the definition of Executive Power; *leaving the rest to flow from the general grant of that power,* interpreted in conformity to other parts of the constitution and to the principles of free government.[26] (*Pacificus* No. 1, ¶27, emphasis added)

It is interesting to note how Hamilton's distortion of the constitutional text is quickly masked with a blanket reassurance that his principle is both in conformity with the Constitution and does not contravene "the principles of free government," reassurances that would ring hollow just five years later in a period of grave Federalist authoritarianism that witnessed the passage of laws criminalizing everything from free and open-forum political expression to simply being a citizen of a nation against which the President has unilaterally and publicly proclaimed a wartime state of emergency. The Sedition and Enemy Alien Acts of 1798 were passed into law by a decidedly Federalist Congress amid thoughts of war with France which were bolstered by President John Adams.

Section 2 of the Sedition Act of July 14, 1798, decreed that any person could be fined or imprisoned (but not exceeding two years, or two thousand dollars) for writing, printing, uttering, or publishing any false, scandalous and malicious writing against any part of the federal government, including the President and Congress, with intent to defame said government.

Federalist proponents of the act who wanted to reassure their political opposition of the genuineness of their intentions could tout the fact that Section 3 allowed persons accused of seditious libel to give in evidence, in their own defense, "the truth of the matter contained in the publication charged as a libel." Section 4 of the Act even contained a sunset provision that removed its binding force on March 3, 1801.

Section 1 of the Alien Enemies Act of July 6, 1798, gave to President Adams, upon his own public proclamation of a state of national emergency due to a congressionally declared state of war *or* an invasion *or* some other predatory incursion against the United States, the unilateral power to "apprehend, restrain, secure, and remove" as an enemy alien any male fourteen years and up who happens to be a native, citizen, or subject of the nation designated as hostile by the President's proclamation. The broad latitude given to the President with these enactments was especially unfortunate since their authors sought to suppress free and open political dissent, the one ingredient vital to the existence and viability of any republic.

Power sharing between the various branches of government is a critical component of *any* republican constitution. As Madison himself knew, the power to bestow offices, and to approve or reject laws, to deliberate matters of war and peace, and to ratify treaties is fundamentally a matter of popular will and not of exeutive fiat, in a democratic republic. Madison borrowed his model for a mixed constitution directly from the writings of Polybius, Greek historian of ancient Rome, who tells us that under to the constitutional system of his day

> it is the People who bestow high office upon the deserving, the noblest reward of virtue in the State. The People have the power of approving laws, and most importantly, they deliberate on questions of war and peace. Further, in cases of alliances, terms of peace, and treaties, it is the People who ratify all these or the reverse. Thus here again one might plausibly say that the People's share in the goverment is greatest, and that the constitution is a democratic one.[27] (Polybius, *Histories*, book 6, ch. 14, §§9-12)

These words are highly relevant to contemporary discussions of the scope and reach of executive power under the U.S. Constitution, not merely because James Madison used Polybius's understanding of the Roman constitutional system as a springboard for his own ideas about the best form of government for America, but because ancient republican Rome was governed under a mixed constitution that contained a delicate framework of checks and balances governing all interaction between the executive, legislative, and judicial branches of government. The various branches were designed to work together as one, while avoiding internal factioning that would clog the legislative process. That any Chief of State, therefore, should seek absolute and indefinite war making powers not enumerated in the Constitution upsets the delicate system of checks and balances at precisely the point where that system is needed most, in exposing the lives of American men and women to mortal dangers overseas in foreign wars.

(*b*) Yoo's Vesting Clause argument also repeats the same recycled variant of Hamilton's original that was trotted out over a half century ago by the Solicitor General in his defense of President Truman's Executive Order 10340 bidding Secretary of Commerce Sawyer to seize and operate most of the nation's steel mills in an effort to avert an impending nationwide strike of steel workers in April of 1952 that threatened to significantly interfere with the nation's ability to produce armaments for the war effort in Korea.

Each of the Solicitor General's main arguments defending Truman's right to issue the Order on the basis of executive powers conferred by the Vesting clause (Art. 2, §1, ¶1), the Commander-in-Chief clause (Art. 2, §2, ¶1), and the Take Care clause (Art. 2, §3) is eloquently and sternly rebuked by Justice Robert Jackson in his concurrence in *Youngstown*—

> The Solicitor General seeks the power of seizure [over most of the nation's steel mills] in three clauses of the Executive Article, the first reading, "The executive Power shall be vested in a President of the United States of America." Lest I be thought to exaggerate, I quote the interpretation which his brief puts upon it: "In our view, this clause constitutes a grant of all the executive powers of which the Government is capable." If that be true, it is difficult to see why the forefathers bothered to add several specific items, including some trifling ones. The example of such unlimited executive power that must have most impressed the forefathers was the prerogative exercised by George III, and the description of its evils in the Declaration of Independence leads me to doubt that they were creating their new Executive in his image. . . . [I]f we seek instruction from our own times, we can match it only from the executive powers in those governments we disparagingly describe as totalitarian. (343 U.S., at 640, 641)

Youngstown is mentioned only twice in Yoo-Flanigan. The first mention occurs in Part III, ¶1 (*TTP*, p. 14) where an extract from the concurring opinion of Justice Frankfurter is used to establish the idea that "a systematic, unbroken, executive practice, long pursued to the knowledge of the Congress and never before questioned . . . may be treated as a gloss on 'executive Power' vested in the President by §1 of Art. II" (343 U.S., at 610-11, Frankfurter, J., concurring).

The Frankfurter quotation leads the reader of Yoo-Flanigan to believe that if previous Presidents have established the practice of stretching the limits of constitutional authority beyond provisions specifically enumerated in the instrument, or have established a pattern of subverting it outright, then it is also thereby entirely acceptable for then-President George W. Bush to do the same in the war on terror, which after all might involve the use of U.S. military forces in any number of unforeseeable overseas counterterrorist operations. Yoo cites the constitutionally problematic practices of previous Presidents like Harry Truman, who deployed U.S. troops in massive numbers to Korea in June of 1950 without any prior authorization from Congress, one day ahead of the U.N. Security Council Resolution requesting military assistance from U.N. member nations to repel North Korea's attack upon South Korea.

Whereas Truman sent United States military forces to Korea without congressional authorization and a full day ahead of the U.N. Security Council measure authorizing the use of force, Bill Clinton seems to have used U.N. and N.A.T.O. peacekeeping desiderata as substitute forms of legislative authorization.[28] For instance, Clinton acted under N.A.T.O. auspices in ordering air strikes in Bosnia in 1994, sidestepping the constitutional process of seeking congressional authorization, as required, absent an attack on the United States, under §2(c) of the War Powers Resolution of 1973. But any international aegis authorizing the United States to use military force must also be matched by congressional authorization, if proper constitutional process is to be preserved. Yoo mentions correctly that on March 24, 1999 "without any prior statutory authorization and in the absence of any attack on the United States" President Clinton ordered hostilities to be initiated against the Republic of Yugoslavia.[29]

What Yoo does not tell us, however, is that among the scholars cited in his memo, there is one Louis Fisher who has argued convincingly that both the Truman and Clinton deployments were unconstitutional.[30] Given that fact, what sense does it make to rely upon a list of historical examples of previous Presidential unconstitutionality as models of behavior for then-President Bush?

Since the twentieth century already contains a long-established pattern of American Presidents (from Truman to Clinton) who have deployed U.S. troops into foreign hostilities without first seeking congressional authorization (in contexts where the U.S. has *not* been directly attacked), the logical upshot of Yoo's citation of the Frankfurter concurrence must be that it is therefore permissible for the President to unilaterally deploy U.S. forces into foreign hostilities against international terrorist groups that are *not* in any way linkable to the attacks of 9/11.

Youngstown is mentioned a second time in Yoo-Flanigan at Part IV, ¶2 (*TTP*, p. 21) where the Jackson concurrence is deliberately twisted out of context to show that President Bush would be acting "at the apogee of his powers" in responding militarily under the AUMF of 14 September against those responsible for the attacks of September 11. Justice Jackson is quoted as arguing that when the President acts pursuant to an express or implied authorization of Congress, his authority is "at its maximum" (343 U.S., at 635). But astonishingly Yoo misses the central point of his own memorandum: He uses the Jackson concurrence to argue that President Bush's power as Commander-in-Chief is at its maximum after 9/11 because he has congressional authorization to respond to those responsible for the attacks of 9/11 *and* because those attacks have created a state of national emergency, which activates §2(c)(3) of the War Powers Resolution of 1973, allowing the President to *unilaterally* deploy U.S. military force in response to an attack without express authorization from Congress; but he fails to remember that his primary purpose was to prove that President Bush has the additional power (not authorized by Congress in the AUMF) to deploy military force preemptively against terrorist organizations and states that support them "whether or not they can be linked to the specific terrorist incidents of September 11." In other words, Justice Jackson's words only support the idea that President Bush remain within the AUMF, but they do not authorize the President to unilaterally transgress that authority by preempting perceived enemies of State not linkable to the attacks of 9/11. Yet this is exactly what unfolded with the invasion of Iraq in 2003. Saddam was allegedly giving safe-haven and refuge to al-Qaeda operatives, when in fact, he had no connection with the attacks of September 11, was not harboring terrorists, and did not possess WMD.

Position 7.—Reaffirming his belief in phantom executive powers not specifically enumerated or contained anywhere in the Constitution, Yoo contends that

> to the extent that the constitutional text does not explicitly allocate the power to initiate military hostilities to a particular branch, the Vesting Clause provides that it remain among the President's unenumerated powers. . . . [D]epriving the President of the power to decide when to use military force would disrupt the basic constitutional framework of foreign relations. From the very beginnings of the Republic, the vesting of the executive, Commander-in-Chief, and treaty powers in the executive branch has been understood to grant the President plenary control over the conduct of foreign relations. . . . As future Chief Justice John Marshall famously declared . . . "The President is the sole organ of the nation in its external relations, and its sole representative with foreign nations. . . . The [executive] department . . . is entrusted with the whole foreign intercourse of the nation" (10 Annals of Cong. 613-14 (1800)). (*TTP*, Memo 1, Part I, ¶s 11-12, p. 9)

On the Contrary, (*a*) it is not the case, as Yoo contends, that "the constitutional text does not explicitly allocate the power to initiate military hostilities to a particular branch" since the Constitution explicitly allocates to Congress, and not the President, the power to call forth the militia of the several states to execute the laws of the union, suppress insurrections, and repel invasions, along with the powers to both finance and formally declare war (Art. 1, §8, ¶s 11, 12, 13, 15). According to Madison, *Helvidius* No. 2, ¶13, "the power to judge of the causes of war, as involved in the power to declare war, is expressly vested, where all other legislative powers are vested, that is, in the Congress of the United States."[31] It is clear that the power to deliberate and judge of the causes of war are the necessary beginnings to making an informed decision about whether to engage the nation in warfare. The Framers intended to keep decisions of war and peace in the hands of the People, who are to bear the brunt of sacrifice in making war, and this requires legislative leadership in establishing advice and giving counsel to the President on foreign affairs, not maverick executive decision making.

(*b*) As already shown in response to *Position 6*, the Vesting Clause argument is an artificial smoke-screen designed to make us believe the President has indefinite, unenumerated, and irresponsible power over the nation's foreign affairs that are not specifically stipulated anywhere in the Constitution. Now, let there exist a set of all *x*, such that *x* is an executive power *not* enumerated in the Constitution. In other words, let *x* be any power flowing from some *general* grant of unenumerated powers to the executive. Now, let the executive powers that happen to be enumerated in the Constitution, Art. 2, §§1-4 contain the *specific* grant of powers to the executive. I maintain that the set of all *x* is an empty set, because any so-called unenumerated powers (derivable from some general grant of executive power) are actually ones that flow from the implementation of powers specifically given in the text. Just as there exist no ideal Platonic Forms in some supersensible eternal world beyond the particluar essences contained in the here and now, there exist no unenumerated executive powers existing beyond the ones specified in the constitutional text. Yoo maintains the set of all *x* to be full of infinitely broad and plenary powers which include the power to initiate military hostilities abroad independently of Congress. But he thereby misses the point that the specific rights and powers listed in the Constitution, as true of any statutory rights and powers, are meant to adapt themselves to the vicissitudes of future possible human circumstance, and that there is no need to posit a set of infinitely variable unenumerated powers, unless his intention was to provide legitimacy to the expansion of Presidential war powers beyond those stipulated in the Constitution.

The congressional authority to declare war and make peace already implicitly contains the parallel authority of judging of the causes of war, deliberating their dimension and scope, and making a final determination as to whether or not to deploy United States Armed Forces into the field of combat, so that the power of final arbitration in matters of war and peace cannot possibly be among the executive's unenumerated powers. Madison points out that Hamilton had already conceded that the right to declare war is vested in the legislature, and that the right to declare includes the right to judge whether the United States *ought* to be obliged to declare war or not:

> If the right to declare war be an exception out of the general grant to the executive power, every thing included in the right must be included in the exception; and, being included in the exception, is excluded from the grant.[32] (*Helvidius* No. 2, ¶6)

In other words, if the executive has not the authority to declare war, he has not the authority to determine whether or not the nation *ought* to declare war. The President must take any war or peace initiatives directly to the

Senate for debate and deliberation. President Washington's Neutrality Proclamation of June 1793, though strategically sound, is, in Madison's view, an exercise of executive power in excess of constitutional limits.

(*c*) The President does not have "plenary control over the conduct of foreign relations" as Yoo imagines him to have, since, for instance, the making of treaties belongs to foreign relations, but the Senate must first provide advice and consent to the President before any treaty can become federal law (*Const.* Art. 2, §2, ¶2) thus having, in effect, the same veto power over the fate of treaties negotiated by the President as the President himself has over the fate of legislation negotiated in Congress.

Plenary powers are the enemy of checks and balances. There exist only three plenary powers granted in the Constitution: the power of Congress to make law, the power of the Court to interpret it, and the power of the President as Commander-in-Chief to direct the course of strategy in a war authorized by Congress. The executive does not have plenary authority, however, to direct strategy in an unauthorized war, any more than he has the authority to suspend federal laws he happens not to like, any more than you or I have the legal authority to do whatever we will, to whomever we will, any time we will. The Framers deliberately designed the branches of our federal government to work together *cooperatively*, especially in time of national crisis or war, since wars require continuous funding, and the executive must appeal to Congress for such funding.

(*d*) The words of John Marshall quoted from a speech he once made as a Congressman on the floor of the U.S. House of Representatives at a time *before* he became Chief Justice of the Supreme Court can hardly be regarded as emblematic of the man's legal philosophy, especially as they have been wrenched embarrassingly out of context to imply a position that he never espoused. The Marshall quotation along with Yoo's assertion of Presidential "plenary control over the conduct of foreign relations" are drawn from the poorly reasoned and cryptically worded opinion of Justice George Sutherland in *United States v. Curtiss-Wright Export Corp.*, 299 U.S. 304, at 319, 320 without so much as the slightest indication, on the part of Yoo, that both contemporary scholars[33] and previous court desiderata have long since condemned the Sutherland opinion as an unreliable guide for ascertaining the proper balance of war powers under the Constitution.

While the Chief Executive may be "entrusted with the whole foreign intercourse of the nation," as Yoo's quotation from then-Congressman John Marshall suggests, the President is *not* the "sole organ" of the nation in its external relations, nor the "sole representative" of the nation in its foreign transactions in the manner of an absolute monarch. "The King of Great Britain is the sole and absolute representative of the nation in all foreign transactions" says Hamilton, so that

> the prerogative of making treaties exists in the crown in its utmost plenitude; and . . . the compacts entered into by the royal authority have the utmost complete legal validity and perfection, independent of any other sanction. . . . In this respect therefore there is no comparison between the intended power of the President, and the actual power of the British sovereign. The one can perform alone, what the other can only do with the concurrence of a branch of the Legislature. (*Federalist* No. 69, ¶7)

The Framers, it must be remembered, harbored a deep mistrust of unbridled executive power. They had recently risked their own mortal lives and political reputations in opposing the repressions of King George III. This mistrust is evident in the words of Hamilton where he claims that

> however proper or safe it may be in governments where the executive magistrate is an hereditary monarch, to commit to him the entire power of making treaties, it would be utterly unsafe and improper to entrust that power to an elective magistrate of four years duration. . . . An ambitious man might make his own aggrandizement, by the aid of a foreign power, the price of his treachery to his constituents. (*Federalist* No. 75, ¶3)

(*e*) Depriving the President of the power to decide when to use military force would not, as Yoo alleges, "disrupt the basic constitutional framework of foreign relations," because the constitutional framework to which Yoo refers does not vest the President with *unilateral* and *unqualified* power of decision, except, as is confirmed under the War Powers Resolution Subsection 2(c)(3), in response to a national emergency created by an attack upon the United States, its territories, its possessions, or its armed forces. Nor does the vesting of the Commander-in-Chief power grant the President "plenary control" over the conduct of foreign relations.

The epithet "Commander-in-Chief" indicates the President's exclusive and plenary control over the direction of strategy in a war authorized by Congress; it does not bestow upon him any occult powers that place him beyond the rule of law. According to the concurring opinion of Justice Jackson in *Youngstown*

> there are indications that the Constitution did not contemplate that the title Commander-in-Chief *of the Army and Navy* will constitute him also Commander-in-Chief of the country, its industries and its inhabitants. He has no monopoly of "war powers," whatever they are. While Congress cannot deprive the President of the command of the army and navy, only Congress can provide him an army or navy to command. It is also empowered to make rules for the "Government and Regulation of land and naval Forces," by which it may, to some unknown extent, impinge upon even command functions. (343 U.S., at 643, 644)

Position 8.—Relying upon the opinion of Justice Sutherland in *Curtiss-Wright,* Yoo contends that

> [the President's] foreign affairs power is exclusive: it is "the very delicate, plenary and exclusive power of the President as sole organ of the federal government in the field of international relations—a power which does not require as a basis for its exercise an act of Congress," *United States v. Curtiss-Wright Export Corp.,* 299 U.S. 304, 320 (1936). Conducting military hostilities is a central tool for the exercise of the President's plenary control over the conduct of foreign policy. There can be no doubt that the use of force protects the Nation's security and helps it achieve its foreign policy goals. Construing the Constitution to grant such power to another branch could prevent the President from exercising his core constitutional responsiblities in foreign affairs. Even in the cases in which the Supreme Court has limited executive authority, it has also emphasized that we should not construe legislative prerogatives to prevent the executive branch "from accomplishing its constitutionally assigned functions." (*Nixon v. Administrator of General Servs.,* 433 U.S. 425, 443 (1977)). (*TTP,* Memo 1, Part I, ¶s 13-14, p. 10)

On the Contrary, (*a*) Yoo quotes Sutherland's opinion out of context, for he cuts off the flow of words at midsentence and thereby fails to inform us that the President's power as "sole organ" of the federal government in the field of foreign relations is a power which, as Justice Sutherland continues, "like every other governmental power, must be exercised in subordination to the applicable provisions of the Constitution" (299 U.S., at 320).

(*b*) Justice Sutherland's opinion is riddled with logical and historical fallacies, and is not a reliable guide-post for determining the proper constitutional balance of power between the various branches; for immediately after Justice Sutherland tells us that Presidential foreign affairs power must be exercised in subordination to the Constitution, he turns back against his own stated position to argue that federal laws governing international treaties should not restrict the President's conduct of foreign affairs:

> It is quite apparent that if, in the maintenance of our international relations, embarrassment—perhaps serious embarrassment—is to be avoided and success for our aims achieved, congressional legislation which is to be made effective through negotiation and inquiry within the international field must often accord to the President a degree of discretion and *freedom from statutory restriction* which would not be admissible were domestic affairs alone involved. (299 U.S., at 320, emphasis added)

But what kind of international embarrassment would result to the nation from a maverick President who systematically fails to recognize, respect, and abide existing international agreements and ratified treaties that are intended to govern and restrict the implementation of United States foreign policy within universally recognized parameters?

Since international treaties become federal statutes as "supreme law of the land" upon ratification (*Const.* Art. 6, ¶2), freedom from statutory restriction is tantamount to freedom from restriction under existing international agreements. But flouting international agreements, especially at the Bush OLC in the Department of Justice, is not prudential foreign policy; for this invites our adversaries around the world to do the same.[34] Nor is it prudent to rely upon Justice Sutherland's convoluted logic. For instance, how can any President be reasonably expected to exercise his foreign relations power "in subordination to the applicable provisions of the Constitution" and yet be given, at the same time, "freedom from statutory restriction" that would allow him to ignore or suspend the application of provisions of extant ratified treaties he happens not to like?

Under the Constitution, Art. 2, §3, the President is to "take care" that federal laws be faithfully executed. The President enforces law; he does not create it, for this is a legislative function. Nor does he stand as final arbiter in interpreting the law, for this is a judicial function. Nor is it part of the President's power as Commander-in-Chief to subvert the law as he sees fit, nor to undermine, by grave breaches, extant international treaties. In other words, if the President does not agree with the tenor, purpose, or wording of certain provisions of a treaty, he must seek to change them by persuading the Senate to ratify a new treaty, or seek to abrogate the existing treaty altogether by going to the Senate and requesting this. The President is only free to act within the provisions of a ratified treaty; and he is at no leisure (in interpreting applicable federal laws) to alter or suspend them in order to carry out his foreign policy directives.

(*c*) It is not an indubitable truth, as Yoo suggests, that the use of U.S. military force around the world "protects the Nation's security and helps it achieve its foreign policy goals," since some uses of military force are, and have been proven to be, either detrimental to the realization of United States foreign policy aspirations, or ineffectual in reaching desired political outcomes. Perhaps the guiding tenet of neo-conservative political philosophy at the Bush OLC was the mistaken belief that the sheer use of overwhelming military force will have a universally curative effect of winning friends and influencing people around the world toward accepting United States hegemony in regions deemed necessary for purposes of long-term peace and security.

Perhaps this optimism in the effectiveness of military force is gathered from America's success as a long-standing member of N.A.T.O. in ensuring peace in Europe. But Western military involvement in the Islamic world has had historically one overriding and dominant effect: It draws jihadists from all quarters of the Middle East who creep across borders, through layers of security, and into virtually any logistical context to disrupt military activities and, where possible, to strike at the heart of operations. This cause-and-effect pattern has existed between the Christian and Islamic worlds since Western military involvement in the Middle East began in the Levant after the Council of Clermont sanctioned the First Crusade in 1095,[35] merely two decades after the Byzantine loss to the Seljuks at Manzikert in 1071. It is likewise becoming increasingly evident that a large and continuing Western military presence in Afghanistan is eliciting a growing insurgency from the Pashtun tribal areas along the Pakistan-Afghanistan border to join the Taliban as a resistance movement. In other words, post-9/11 military involvement appears to be exacerbating the same pre-9/11 social disorders that initially led to military involvement to counter Taliban support of al-Qaeda. The British faced the same dangers of a Wahhabi-inspired foreign jihadist uprising in the hills of Afghanistan and northern Pakistan in the 1870s as coalition forces face currently. A *New York Times* article dated February 13, 1872, tells of "a mischevous nest of fanatical conspiracy" creating havoc by disseminating the "bigoted propaganda of the Wahabees . . . among the thirty millions of Mohammedan subjects" of north-west British India.

If terrorists follow no law but the law of suicide revenge, then intimidating them by conventional military means will not work. Far better it is for the United States to use force more sparingly in targeted micro-operations focused around disrupting several regional terrorist threats simultaneously as they emerge, and, when apprehension of individuals proves to be impossible, to militarily preempt targeted groups or cells in the planning or training statges of an attack. The recent rise to power of al-Shabbab in Somalia may present several such simultaneous terrorist threats as militants seek to export violence abroad.

Position 9.—Although Congress handed President Bush sweeping powers of response to the attacks of 9/11 merely eleven days prior the issuance of the Yoo-Flanigan memo, and absent any congressional interference with the President's execution of strategy as Commander-in-Chief in the War on Terror, Yoo nevertheless asserts that

> as we read the WPR, action taken by the President pursuant to the constitutional authority recognized in Section 2(c)(3) *cannot be subject to the substantive requirements of the WPR*, particularly the interrelated reporting requirements in Section 4 and the "cut off" provisions of Section 5, 50 U.S.C. §§1543-1544. Insofar as the Constitution vests the power in the President to take military action in the emergency circumstances described by Section 2(c)(3), we do not think it can be restricted by Congress through, e.g., a requirement that the President either obtain congressional authorization for the action within a specific time frame, or else discontinue the action. Were this not so, the President could find himself unable to respond to an emergency that outlasted a statutory cut-off, merely because Congress had failed, for whatever reason, to enact authorizing legislation within that period. (*TTP*, Memo 1, Part IV, ¶5, p. 22, emphasis added)

On the Contrary, (*a*) military deployments ordered by the President pursuant to Section 2(c)(3) of the WPR are those ordered in the wake of a national emergency created by an attack upon the United States, its territories, its possessions, or its armed forces;[36] but John Yoo thinks that *any* executive deployment of force into hostilities ordered pursuant to Subsection 2(c)(3) automatically allows the President to wriggle out of legal accountability to Congress (and thereby the people) under Sections 4 and 5(b)(c). Yoo contends that President Bush's military response to those he deems responsible for 9/11 does not need to be accompanied by an Official

Report to Congress setting forth the circumstances, constitutional authority, or estimated scope and duration of hostilities *at any point in time*. This bald assertion of executive branch independence from Congress is especially troubling in a democratic republic, since Congress is charged with the responsiblity of funding and authorizing U.S. military deployments, and reporting kept from Congress is information blocked from the people.

Deputy Assistant Yoo claims that Congress no longer has its authority under Section 5(c) to order President Bush to withdraw troops deployed in response to the attacks of 9/11 *in general*; and this may have been intended to include the campaign that was eventually to be undertaken against Saddam Hussein in Iraq a year and half after the memo's release, since the *casus belli* (the occasion precipitating war) against Saddam was alleged to be his development of WMD along with his suspected harboring of al-Qaeda fugitives and his flouting of U.N. directives, all three of which were vital to the sustenance and continued life of that state-of-declared-national-emergency that gave the President his Yooian right not to account to Congress for his decision-making process in the first place.

This phantom loophole concocted by Yoo means that *any* deployment of U.S. military force into foreign hostilities that the President deems linkable to 9/11 is a deployment that Congress need not know about, cannot order terminated at any point in time, nor one for which the President need give any legal and strategic rationale. The loophole may been created by the Bush II policy need to link Saddam with al-Qaeda and WMD after 9/11 as a pretext for invasion, since both allegations (terrorist collusion combined with dangerous weapons) were now vital to linking Saddam's recalcitrance in Iraq with the President's officially declared state of national emergency.

(*b*) The Bush military deployments in connection with the attacks of 9/11 are unambiguously subject to the substantive requirements of the WPR (in spite of what Yoo says) because Section 4 of the WPR applies to any deployment ordered "in absence of a declaration of war" and the AUMF constitutes no such formal declaration, but represents only a specific statutory authorization. And Congress intended it this way. A formal Declaration of War against Terrorism would be legally inappropriate under customary international law because sovereign states traditionally declare war only against other sovereign states, but never against bands of criminals, be these pirates, brigands, or terrorists. At the same time, a formal declaration of war would have also exempted the President's decision-making authority from the reporting requirement of Section 4(a). This requirement is crucial to maintaining an appropriate congressional check against presidential deployments in absence of a formal declaration of war.

(*c*) Central to the Yoo opinion is the idea that the President has plenary authority to deploy force against those he deems responsible for 9/11 pursuant to WPR Section 2(c)(3)'s state-of-emergency requirement, when really the President is authorized pursuant only to Section 2(c)(2)'s specific statutory authorization requirement, statutory authorization in the AUMF trumping any situation where authorization cannot otherwise be had (as congressional authorization places the President at the apogee of his war-making power). Section 2(c)(3) gave President Bush only a brief window of congressionally unauthorized military response time between the morning of September 11, 2001, and late Friday evening September 14, when the House passed S.J.Res. 23 (AUMF). Yoo seems to have preferred the (by then inoperative) state-of-emergency clause, WPR 2(c)(3), because emergency situations instill the sense of animal desperation and fear that make people more willing to relax normal accounting procedures. But oddly enough the strategy selected at the OLC makes backward sense from a legal perspective, because presidential deployments pursuant to a state-of-emergency still qualify as subject to Section 4's Reporting requirement, since Section 4 applies "in absence of a formal declaration of war."

Position 10.—Deputy Assistant Yoo concludes his memorandum opinion with a bizarre twist of logic, wherein he claims that

> the Joint Resolution is somewhat narrower than the President's constitutional authority. The Joint Resolution's authorization to use force is limited only to those individuals, groups, or states that planned, authorized, committed, or aided the attacks, and those nations that harbored them. It does not, therefore, reach other terrorist individuals, groups, or states, which cannot be determined to have links to the September 11 attacks. Nonetheless, the President's broad constitutional power to use military force to defend the Nation, recognized by the Joint Resolution itself, would allow the President to take whatever actions he deems appropriate to preempt or respond to terrorist threats from new quarters. (*TTP*, Memo 1, Part IV, ¶10, p. 23)

On the Contrary, (*a*) the Joint Resolution of September 14, 2001, is decidedly *not* narrower than the President's constitutional authority to direct strategy against those responsible for 9/11, because the AUMF *is* the horizon of the President's constitutional authority to do so. In fact, this authorization officially ends the brief three-day window of opportunity from 9/11 to 9/14, 2001, during which the President had authority under WPR Section 2(c)(3) to respond to 9/11 without congressional restriction.

(*b*) How can it be the case that the AUMF is narrower than the President's constitutional authority to respond to 9/11, yet permissive enough to allow the President to respond to "terrorist threats from new quarters" that need not be linked to 9/11? The answer, says Yoo, is contained in a single clause from the preamble to the AUMF (S.J.Res 23): "the President has authority under the Constitution to take action to deter and prevent acts of international terrorism against the United States." Yoo seems to think that this clause gives the President those plenary and unenumerated executive powers that he has been arguing for throughout. The clause, however, has more the appearance of formality than of a substantive grant of power, since it simply activates the President's constitutional function as Commander-in-Chief without stipulating what the horizon of that power may be.

(*c*) Yoo cites a bevy of previous Presidential deployments of military force (some authorized by Congress, others not) as precedent for touting vast executive war making powers post-9/11. These deployments of United States military force I place under four general categories,

1. Those commenced under U.N. or N.A.T.O. auspices for purely protective or peace-keeping purposes;
2. Those commenced under U.N. or N.A.T.O. auspices for combat purposes in contexts where hostilities are imminent;
3. Those commenced (independent of U.N. or N.A.T.O. auspices) to specifically target (via precision air strikes or other limited ground assault operations) persons, groups, or installations which have attacked the United States, its territories, possessions, or armed forces, or are threatening to imminently do so;
4. Those commenced (independent of U.N. or N.A.T.O. auspices) as offensive combat operations broader in scope than precision air strikes and limited ground assault operations.

Under category (1) may be placed President Bush I's deployment of substantial U.S. military forces to Saudi Arabia in Operation Desert Shield on August 8, 1990, for purely peacekeeping purposes as a direct response to the Iraqi invasion of Kuwait, with the ostensive purpose of protecting the vast oil fields of eastern Arabia. Saddam Hussein was given the peaceful option of withdrawing Iraqi troops from Kuwait, but he stubbornly refused, and Operation Desert Shield became Operation Desert Storm.

Offensive military operations commenced in early 1991, for which President Bush I sought and received congressional authorization pursuant to WPR. Presidential permission to use force was required from Congress since no attack on the United States causative of a state of national emergency had then taken place. Operations Desert Shield and Desert Storm stand as two exceptional cases of post-War II presidential deployment consistent with both U.S. constitutional and international law.

Under category (2) may be placed Truman's emergency deployment of troops to Korea in June of 1950 one day ahead of U.N. Security Council authorization, and independent of any congressional approval or a declaration of war. One may also place under category (2) President Clinton's initiation of hostilities against the Republic of Yugoslavia on March 24, 1999 which took place without any prior congressional authorization and independent of any attack on the United States, its territories, possessions, or armed forces.

Clinton's foreign policy practice seems to replay a theme developed in the previous administration by then-Bush I Defense Secretary Cheney, who once suggested that U.N. Security Council authorization for the use of force in Operation Desert Storm was sufficient warrant by itself, independently of what Congress decided to do. This philosophy of bypassing Congress in the execution of presidential foreign policy objectives appears to have carried over into the administration of George W. Bush in terms of the OLC's readiness to bypass ratified treaty provisions perceived as limiting the President's range of policy opitions in conducting a counterterrorist military campaign.

As Yoo correctly points out (*TTP*, p. 17) President Bush I appended a statement upon signing Public Law No. 102-01, 105 Stat. 3 (1991) officially declaring that his request for congressional authorization is not to be taken as a surrender of presidential authority to call armed forces into action:

> My request for congressional support did not, and my signing this resolution does not, constitute any change in the long-standing positions of the executive branch on either the President's constitutional authority to use the Armed Forces to defend vital U.S. interests or the constitutionality of the War Powers Resolution. (*Statement on Signing the Resolution Authorizing the Use of Military Force Against Iraq*, 1 *Pub. Papers of George Bush* 40, 1991)

In the window of time between Operation Desert Shield and actual combat operations in Desert Storm, then-Secretary of Defense Dick Cheney testified before the Senate Armed Services Committee on December 3, 1990 that President Bush did not require "any *additional* authorization from Congress" prior to the initiation of offensive operations in Operation Desert Storm.[37] Cheney's phrase "additional authorization" suggests that he believed U.N. Security Council Resolutions (which contained an ultimatum for Saddam to exit Kuwait) to be sufficient warrant for the President to send U.S. troops into combat. The day following Cheney's comments the House Democratic Caucus drafted a resolution calling for the President to seek congressional authorization prior to the beginning of combat operations in Desert Storm. The resolution passed 177 to 37.[38]

Under category (3) may be placed several examples:

> α. President Reagan's unilateral order of April 14, 1986, to conduct targeted air strikes against the government of Colonel Gadhafi of Lybia. Selected targets included sites in Tripoli and Benghazi, Lybia.
>
> β. President Clinton's order of June 26, 1993, for limited air strikes against Iraqi Intelligence Service (IIS) headquarters in Baghdad. As Yoo points out, the IIS had planned an unsuccessful attempt to assassinate former President Bush in Kuwait in April of 1993. A total of 23 missles were launched against IIS headquarters from U.S. Navy surface ships.
>
> γ. President Clinton's order of August 20, 1998, for limited air strikes targeting terrorist cells in Afghanistan and the Sudan. Clinton cited as justification for these strikes the fact that he had "convincing evidence" that the groups he had targeted played a significant role in the U.S. Embassy bombings in Kenya and Tanzania in 1998 killing some 12 Americans and nearly 300 Kenyans and Tanzanians.

Under category (4) would be placed any *substantial* deployment of United States armed forces wholly independent of U.N. and N.A.T.O. authorization. Although the United States successfully acquired U.N. support to lead a military campaign to oust Saddam Hussein from Iraq in 2003, this authorization does not ameliorate the Bush administration's false allegations of WMD development and links between Saddam, international terrorism, and the al-Qaeda attacks of 9/11.

A significant gray area not discussed in Yoo-Flanigan deals with non-congressionally authorized air strikes ordered by a President against an adversary in anticipation and prevention of some imminent deadly danger, but absent any actual attack on the United States. What if a terrorist group with a proven track record of violence in Syria or Lebanon or Egypt, but which has no history of attack on the United States, its possessions, or its armed forces, but which, for purposes of this example, is now suddenly threatening to launch such an attack? Does the President have authority to preempt this threat militarily without congressional authorization? I must accede that he most certainly does, but I also admit that he must seek concurrent or (if time does not permit) retroactive congressional authorization to do so.

A President may preemptively strike a terrorist cell not affiliated with bin Laden or the attacks of 9/11, while staying within the requirements of the WPR and customary international law, as long as he or she seeks concurrent or retroactive authority from Congress, and as long as the following four conditions are met: Preemptive attack must be an act of self-defense; the danger posed by the adversary must be immediate and certain, imminent and deadly; the prospect of an adversary's attack must be empirically verifiable through adequate intelligence; and there must be substantial evidence that inaction is more dangerous than action.

None of the examples Yoo provides under each category of deployment offer sufficient precedent or weight to justify expanding the President's wartime authority to respond to 9/11 *beyond* the scope of the AUMF. If a non-al-Qaeda affiliated terrorist cell threatens to strike, or if there is adequate intelligence that danger is on its way to the United States, the President may unilaterally order preemptive strikes, but he or she must explain in the Report to Congress the reason why authorization could not be had.

To understand why this is the case we need to distinguish what is permissible under customary international law and treaty law, from what is permissible under U.S. constitutional law. Both Bush I and Clinton seem to have relied heavily, and in ostensibly laudible ways, on international process to establish legitimacy for their decisions to commence hostilities, yet both administrations were reluctant to seek congressional approval for their deployments of U.S. forces, but for markedly different reasons.

I have argued elsewhere that the President has a right under customary international law to preempt imminent deadly dangers to the United States, its possessions, or armed forces from non-al-Qaeda linked international terrorists in the planning stages of an attack, but I disagree with Yoo's conclusion that the President may take whatever actions he deems appropriate to preempt future possible attacks, because he neglects to lay out *any* conditions under which preemptive action would be permissible under customary international law, while seeking to remove the President from any role of accountability before Congress, as required by the War Powers Resolution. President Bush's attorneys at the OLC appear to have salted away for him a host of unenumerated, exclusive, and plenary war-making powers which run roughshod over America's long-standing humanitarian treaty committments, and War Powers Resolution limits to the exercise of executive power.

QUESTION TWO

DOES AN EMERGENCY OF WAR PERMIT THE PRESIDENT TO USURP JUDICIAL AND LEGISLATIVE POWERS TO INTERPRET LAW AND DEFINE AND PUNISH OFFENCES AGAINST THE LAW OF NATIONS?

The November 13 Executive Order

On November 13, 2001, for the ostensible purpose of protecting the United States and it citizens from further terrorist attacks following the tragedy of 9/11, and for the effective conduct of military operations to combat international terrorism, President Bush issued an Executive Military Order[1] requiring the detention and possible trial[2] of any non-U.S. citizen whom he, as President, has reason to believe is or was a member of al-Qaeda, or has engaged in, aided or abetted, or conspired to commit, acts of international terrorism, or acts in preparation therefor, or who has knowingly harbored one or more such individuals. This Order represents an unconstitutional delegation of judicial and legislative power to the executive.

The President's November 13 Order explicitly and unambiguously sidesteps the Fifth and Fourteenth Amendments of the Constitution of the United States, subverts the rule of law by abrogating rules of evidence and principles of due process traditionally applicable in criminal investigations and trials, and transgresses federal law by flouting twenty-three separate provisions of the International Covenant on Civil and Political Rights (ICCPR), a treaty ratified by the United States Senate on April 2, 1992.[3]

In spite of these embarrassing legal infidelities, the November 13 Order has flourished surreptitiously under United States federal law in both the Detainee Treatment Act (DTA) of 2005 and the Military Commissions Act (MCA) of 2006. On July 7, 2004, just nine days after the Supreme Court ruling in *Rasul*,[4] Deputy Secretary of Defense Paul Wolfowitz issued an Order

Establishing Combatant Status Review Tribunals (CSRTs)[5]—a contemptuous gesture in the face of the court's decision in *Rasul,* since the CSRT system establishes only the veneer of due process, but is, in reality, a sham system of procedural rules that ignore requirements to establish competent tribunals explicitly required as a matter of law by GPW, Art. 5, ¶2, with a host of specific rules governing the trial process spelled out in GCP, Arts. 71, 72, 73, 74, 75. And both the GPW and the GCP apply to any person (combatant or non-combatant) who is captured amid hostilities in Afghanistan or Pakistan on suspicion of terrorist collusion, because, by common Article 2, the Geneva Conventions

> shall apply to all cases of partial or total occupation of the territory of a High Contracting Party, even if the said occupation meets with no armed resistance.

Afghanistan has been a High Contracting Party to Geneva since September of 1956. And the current presence of United States and coalition military forces on the ground in Afghanistan constitutes a partial occupation of Afghanistan. GCP, therefore, applies to captured foreign nationals in U.S. custody suspected of being or harboring terrorists because GCP Article 4 defines protected persons as those who,

> at a given moment and in any manner whatsoever, find themselves, in case of a conflict or occupation, in the hands of a Party to the conflict or Occupying Power of which they are not nationals.

By conducting military operations inside the territory of Afghanistan the United States represents a Party to an ongoing conflict with al-Qaeda and Taliban elements, while constituting one of many Occupying Powers in Afghanistan.

The November 13 Order exempts from humanitarian and other legal protections under Geneva and the ICCPR any non-U.S. citizen with respect to whom the President has reason to believe "it is in the interest of the United States" that such person be detained pursuant to the Order, subsection II(a)(2). The Order itself, however, is patently unconstitutional because it is based in part on section 836 of Title 10 of the United States Code, subsection (a), which is itself unconstitutional, because this subsection allows the President to prescribe rules governing pretrial, trial, and post-trial procedures, including modes of proof, for cases triable in courts-martial, military commissions and other military tribunals, and this power to prescribe procedural rules for tribunals inferior to the Supreme Court is strictly congressional domain by *Const.*, Art. 1, §8, ¶9, not an executive privilege.

By enacting 10 U.S.C. §836(a) Congress unwarrantedly delegated to the President not one but several of its legislative powers under the Constitution, for it is Congress, and not the President, that has the power to define and punish offenses against the Law of Nations (Art. 1, §8, ¶10), and to make rules for the government and regulation of the land and naval forces (Art. 1, §8, ¶14), land and naval forces being regulated by a system of military laws which require courts-martial and military tribunals to be established and enforced properly. Since Congress has the power to make rules for the government and regulation of the nation's military forces, Congress must also have the concomitant power to make rules governing legal procedures for courts-martial and other military tribunals, since these tribunals are indispensable for the government of land and naval forces.

Subsection 836(a) also allows the President to violate international law by applying "so far as he considers practicable" the principles of law and rules of evidence generally recognized for the trial of criminal cases in United States district courts. This means that, if the President deems it practicable to prescribe new trial rules for detainees that dispense with any presumption of innocence on behalf of the accused, he may do so under §836(a), even though this violates Article 14(2) of the ICCPR: "Everyone charged with a criminal offence shall have the right to be presumed innocent until proven guilty according to law." We have a statute in subsection 836(a) that allows any president to *unilaterally* suspend key provisions of ratified U.S. treaties. Subsection 836(a) is, therefore, unconstitutional.

If the President deems it practicable to deny a detainee the right to appeal, he may do so under §836(a), contrary to GCP, Article 73, ¶1: "A convicted person shall have the right of appeal provided for by the laws applied by the court."

If the President wishes to hold suspects incommunicado and without legal counsel, he may do so under §836(a), contrary to ICCPR, Article 14(3)(d): "[Everyone shall be entitled] to be tried in his presence, and to defend himself in person or through legal assistance of his own choosing . . . and to have legal assistance assigned to him, in any case where the interests of justice so require."

If the President wishes to allow into evidence against the detainee, a confession of guilt that was extracted by means of torture or other coercive interrogation techniques, he may do so under §836(a), contrary to ICCPR 14(3)(g): "[Everyone shall be entitled] not to be compelled to testify against himself or to confess guilt."

If the President wishes to prevent a detainee from presenting evidence necessary for his own exoneration, he may do so under §836(a), contrary to GCP, Art. 71, ¶1: "Accused persons shall have the right to present evidence necessary to their defence and may, in particular, call witnesses."

By the November 13 Order the President did what Subsection §836(a) already allowed him to do: He systematically suspended for non-U.S. citizens detained under the Order the generally recognized principles of law and rules of evidence applicable to citizens *and* non-citizens alike by the Fourteenth Amendment, simply because he deemed it practicable to do so. In other words, by issuing a unilateral Executive Order that deprives non-U.S. citizens detained on suspicion the right to petition for writ of habeas corpus,[6] the right to be presumed innocent until proven guilty, the right to appeal to any higher court, the right to humanitarian treatment free from cruel and unusual punishment, the President has denied non-U.S. citizen detainees, who fall within the jurisdiction of the United States by the fact of their detention, the equal protection under the law due them by the Fourteenth Amendment. But the human rights guaranteed in the Constitution extend to *all* persons falling under the jurisdiction of the United States regardless of their nationality or territorial location, because these rights extend to them *by means of the operational functioning of United States officials*.

The Fourteenth Amendment containing the equal protection clause was adopted in 1868, three years after the adoption of the Thirteenth Amendment that freed the slaves. Since the Fourteenth Amendment grants full citizenship and equal protection under the law to recently freed African-American slaves living in the South, who had been denied basic citizenship rights to that point, the Amendment makes clear that "no state" shall make a local law that abridges the *constitutional* rights of its denizens, regardless of their citizenship status. The Fourteenth Amendment was worded in a deliberate attempt to apply constitutional protections to traditionally *non*-U.S. citizen African-American slaves who, post-Reconstruction, lived in contexts where state laws in the South systematically failed to protect their life, liberty, property, or interests.

But let us suppose the following: The Fourteenth Amendment says that *no state* shall deny to any person within its jurisdiction the equal protection of the laws. The amendment applies only to laws enacted by the several states, and not to any other instruments of law. Since the Fourteenth Amendment applies only to laws enacted by *state* governments, it does not apply to the November 13 Order, because the November 13 Order is not a law enacted by any state of the United States. On the contrary, if federal law prohibits the several states from doing *x*, then federal law is asserting itself as the *instrument* guaranteeing the prohibition of *x*. The federal government is, in the Fourteenth Amendment, ordering the several states to do what it had already been doing under the Constitution, namely, ensuring Fifth Amendment due process rights to *all* persons falling within the jurisdiction of the United States.

Here are ten specific objections I have to President Bush's November 13 Executive Order:

Objection 1.—It is not quite clear whether the November 13 Order actually envisions establishing Article 5 hearings at any point in time to determine whether persons detained in U.S. custody pursuant to the Order were actually engaged in or conspiring to commit acts of terrorism, since Subsection II(b) can only guarantee that "*if* the individual [detained pursuant to the Order] is to be tried, that such individual is tried only in accordance with Section 4," and Section 4 fails systematically to implement the structure of an Article 5 hearing that would have guaranteed the "full and fair trial" that the Order claims to be implementing at Subsection IV(c)(2).

Persons detained pursuant to the November 13 Order receive no guarantee that a trial will even be held to determine the legality of their detention, or whether they are guilty of any criminal offence by violating the laws and customs of war. Just eight weeks after the tragedy of 9/11 the Bush administration had already allowed its gloves-off approach in Afghanistan to compromise the kind of deep investigating that would have led to real convictions of international terrorists (based on irrefutable evidence) presented before properly constitututed Article 5 tribunals. By dispensing with customary international law and sidestepping Geneva the administration made it unnecessarily more difficult for America to win international support for its campaign against global terrorism.

Objection 2.—The President has no constitutional authority to unilaterally determine rules of procedure governing trials and prosecutions of possible international war crimes committed by persons detained pursuant to the Order, because it is Congress, not the President, that has the power to define and punish offences against the law of nations. Congress did not fulfill its constitutional obligation of defining and punishing such offences until the passage of the Military Commissions Act (MCA) on October 17, 2006.[7]

The MCA simply implements the exact structure of the Wolfowitz Order establishing CSRT, which Order in turn implements the inquisition-like procedural setting envisioned by President Bush and Secretary of Defense Rumsfeld in the original draft of the November 13 Order. For instance, the Military Commissions Act formally recognizes as an unlawful enemy combatant *any* detainee held in U.S. custody and already "determined to be an unlawful enemy combatant by a Combatant Status Review Tribunal, or another competent tribunal established under authority of the President or the Secretary of Defense" (MCA §948a(1)(ii)). Notice the delicate addition of the phrase "or other competent tribunal" used here in order to attach Article 5-like legitimacy to the CSRT system, as if that system fulfilled, or was ever really intended to fulfill, any of the due process requirements of a true Article 5 tribunal, and in spite of the fact that no Article 5 hearing worthy of the name would predetermine a defendant's legal status as "unlawful enemy combatant" before a single witness was ever called to testify, or a single piece of evidence presented at trial against him.

The Military Commissions Act is disturbingly riddled with deliberate legal misdirection and self-contradictory doublespeak. Subsection §948b(f), for instance, establishes military commissions which afford

> all the necessary "judicial guarantees which are recognized as indispensable by civilized peoples" for purposes of common Article 3 of the Geneva Conventions.

But then, in the very next paragraph, the act rescinds this humanitarian promise of decency by withdrawing all protections of the Geneva Conventions for *any* alien non-U.S. citizens captured in Afghanistan and held in U.S. custody on the presumption of being an "unlawful enemy combatant," since Subsection 948b(g) stipulates that

> no alien unlawful enemy combatant subject to trial by military commission under this chapter may invoke the Geneva Conventions as a source of rights.

By Subsection 949d(f)(C)(2)(B) of the act, U.S. government officials may, if the president of the tribunal deems it necessary for national security reasons, conceal from the detainee the body and source of evidence being used to justify his detention:

> The military judge, upon motion of trial counsel, shall permit trial counsel to introduce otherwise admissible evidence before the military commission, while protecting from disclosure the sources, methods, or activities by which the United States acquired the evidence if the military judge finds that (i) the sources, methods, or activities by which the United States acquired the evidence are classified, and (ii) the evidence is reliable.

In the Article 5 hearings actually required by federal law and international protocol an alien accused of being an unlawful enemy combatant would normally be afforded the right not only to contest the reliability of the evidence arrayed against him, but, for this very purpose, to have disclosed to him the body and source of the evidence, so that he may have an opportunity to refute each point in turn.

With such procedural disadvantages facing the detainee, it is all the more grievous that Paragraph (*c*) of the Wolfowitz Order Establishing CSRT does not even afford the accused competent legal counsel. Instead the detainee is given a "personal representative" who is blocked from sharing any evidence with the detainee that the government may actually be using to justify their detention, if that evidence is deemed classified by the Department of Defense. By Paragraph *g*(8) the detainee is allowed to call into witness on his behalf only persons "reasonably available," and "the Tribunal shall determine the reasonable availability of witnesses." Since Guantánamo Bay, Cuba is removed thousands of miles away from the region of South Asia where suspects were initially apprehended, any witnesses or physical evidence that could weigh in on their behalf are simply too far away to be considered reasonably available. The Department of Defense is hardly likely to spend its budget whisking destitute migrant herdsmen from Afghanistan into and out of GTMO base for purposes of trial, to testify that they remember seeing this or that detainee at a certain time or place several weeks before the detainee was captured, etc. GTMO base was selected by the Bush administration precisely because it appeared to be the ideal location for a prison beyond the law.

But, as I have argued previously, constitutional rights of due process extend to non-US citizens at GTMO base through the *operation* of U.S. Government officials, to all human beings who happen to fall within the custody of the United States for any reason whatsoever, but especially by reason of captivity in a zone of combat, since possessing human rights has nothing to do with the rights-holder's physical location or citizenship status, but with whether or not that person falls within the jurisdiction of the United States. And, as is evident from even a cursory reading of *Const.* Art. 3, §2, ¶1, the judicial power of the United States was conceived by the Framers as *routinely* extending its jurisdiction to places and events located well beyond the territorial confines of the United States, while at the same time protecting the trial rights of persons of non-U.S. citizenship in their legal transactions with the United States. In essence, applicable Geneva protections in the context of Article 5 hearings would afford detainees, through the operation of U.S. military tribunals relocated to South Asia, about nearly the same palate of rights they would have under constitutional protection in U.S. criminal courts, minus jury selection and media publicity, thus raising the bar on the quality of evidence required for convictions beyond hearsay evidence.

When United States military operations began in Afghanistan General Tommy Franks originally issued orders from CENTCOM to ensure that Geneva humanitarian guarantees would be extended by U.S. military personnel to all persons captured and held in custody, but Secretary of Defense Rumsfeld intervened on January 19, 2002, to remove those guarantees from suspected members of the Taliban and al-Qaeda. Subsequently, no constitutional guarantees are afforded GTMO detainees under the CSRT, since

> the Tribunal is not bound by the rules of evidence such as would apply in a court of law. Instead, the Tribunal shall be free to consider any information it deems relevant and helpful to a resolution of the issue before it. At the discretion of the Tribunal, for example, it may consider hearsay evidence, taking into account the reliability of such evidence in the circumstances. (*Order Establishing Combatant Status Review Tribunal,* ¶*g*(9))

So, even if the detainee's personal representative possesses classified information revealing the *source* of evidence weighing against him, he cannot share that information with the detainee, because "the Tribunal does not have the authority to declassify or change the classification of any national security information it reviews" (¶*g*(9)).

According to the Denbeaux Report on the Guantánamo Detainees released in February of 2006, and based exclusively upon the U.S. Government documents, 5 percent of the detainees were captured by United States forces, while 86 percent were arrested by either Pakistan or the Northern

Alliance and turned over to United States custody.[8] This statistic raises serious Article 5 doubt about the Article 4 POW status of detainees held at GTMO. Nevertheless the CSRT system expresses no doubts whatsoever about the identity of persons detained, since it presupposes in Paragraph (*a*) that "each detainee subject to this Order has been determined to be an enemy combatant *through multiple levels of review* by officers of the Department of Defense" even though none of those levels of review have involved hearings of any kind.

Justice Anthony Kennedy sharply criticizes several constitutional inadequacies inherent to the CSRT system in a recent opinion delivered in *Boumediene v. Bush*, 553 U.S. ___ (2008), at Section IV.C.¶3 as well as Section V.B.¶s 6, 7, 8. Justice Kennedy notes, for instance, that although the detainee is allowed to present "reasonably available" evidence before the military tribunal, (¶*g*(7)), "his ability to rebut the Government's evidence against him is limited by the circumstances of his confinement and his lack of counsel at this stage."[9]

While the CSRT guarantees detainees the right to seek habeas relief in United States courts, (¶*b*), "the habeas court," writes Kennedy, "must have sufficient authority to conduct a meaningful review of both the cause for detention and the Executive's power to detain."[10] However, since there are seemingly no limits to the admission of hearsay evidence—the tribunal being free to consider *any* information it deems relevant and helpful (¶*g*(9))—and since the detainee is allowed to call witnesses, but only if they are "reasonably available," Kennedy concludes that the detainee's opportunity to question witnesses is "likely to be more theoretical than real."[11]

Objection 3.—Subsection III(a) of the November 13 Order delegates to the Secretary of Defense the power to forcibly relocate individuals captured in Afghanistan to bases located thousands of miles away for purposes of interrogation, because it stipulates that any individual subject to the Order shall be "detained at an appropriate location designated by the Secretary of Defense outside or within the United States"; but this language unhesitatingly flouts the GCP, Art. 49, ¶1 prohibition on individual or mass forcible transfers of protected persons from occupied territory (such as Afghanistan) to the territory of the Occupying Power (the United States) or to that of any other country occupied or not "regardless of their motive."

Objection 4.—Subsection III(e) of the November 13 Order delegates to the Secretary of Defense unilateral and irresponsible power to suspend, alter, or revoke, for any reason and in any manner he may prescribe, the humanitarian conditions of detention seemingly guaranteed detainees by Subsections III(b)(c)(d).

Any talk of humanitarian treatment in the November 13 Order is useless finery given that individuals subject to the Order may be (and in fact have been) detained indefinitely on suspicion and held incommunicado without legal representation, or any semblance of due process in places undisclosed and far removed (through individual or mass forcible transfers) from the occupied territory where they were originally apprehended.

Article 9, ¶5 of the International Covenant on Civil and Political Rights provides that "anyone who has been the victim of unlawful arrest or detention shall have an enforceable right to compensation." The ICCPR was negotiated under President George H.W. Bush and ratified by the Senate to become federal law—a historically significant accomplishment. But someone at the Bush II OLC should have raised the alert that violations of this provision of the ICCPR could result in highly embarrassing civil damages litigation in U.S. federal courts brought against administration officials.

Objection 5.—Subsection IV(a) of the November 13 Order stipulates that individuals subject to it may be punished in accordance with penalties provided under applicable law, but it is difficult to know, from the perspective of the administration's "New Paradigm" policy, which renders obsolete Geneva's strict limitations on the questioning of enemy prisoners, just what the phrase "applicable law" could possibly mean in the Order, given that so many applicable laws were already subverted under the very Order in which they were supposedly to be *applied* to the punishment of prisoners.

Objection 6.—In Subsection IV(b) of the November 13 Order the President delegates to the Secretary of Defense a purely legislative power, that even he as President does not have, to define and punish offences against the law of nations by *Const.* Art. 1, §8, ¶10:

> [T]he Secretary of Defense shall issue such orders and regulations, including orders for the appointment of one or more commissions, as may be necessary to carry out Subsection (a) of this Section.

The constitutional provision assigning to Congress the exclusive power to define and punish offences against the law of nations also envisioned the same "piracies and felonies committed on the high seas" as the ones actually committed against American merchant vessels throughout the Mediterranean by Barbary pirates issuing from the sheikhdoms of Morocco, Tunis, Algiers, and Tripoli. These sheikhdoms sought nominal cash tribute from the United States in exchange for peaceful passage on the high seas. But Presidents Washington, Adams, Jefferson, and Madison each rejected this option out of hand as humiliating defeat, since safe passage at sea was a universally recognized custom among the civilized nations of the world. Thus the so-called "New Paradigm" concept is really not new at all, since the practice of pursuing, apprehending, and defeating rogue Arab Muslim and Middle Eastern non-state actors waging campaigns of jihad against American commercial interests on the high seas was common throughout the earliest days of the republic.

Objection 7.—Subsection IV(c)(3) of the November 13 Order provides that the Secretary of Defense shall issue rules for the conduct of proceedings of military commissions that provide for the "admission of such evidence as would, in the opinion of the presiding officer of the military commission . . . have probative value to a reasonable person." This provision of the subsection, however, fails to define what it means for evidence to have "probative value" to a reasonable person. In effect, Subsection IV(c)(3) empowers the presiding officer of the military tribunal to jettison from proceedings any evidence that the detainee might claim in his own defense, such as hearsay evidence—the only kind of evidence likely to be available to anyone held incommunicado and prevented from accessing the means to his own defense—if the presiding officer determines the evidence to lack probative value to a reasonable person, yet the CSRT system constructed directly from the blueprint of the November 13 Order readily admits the thinnest hearsay evidence available into proceedings against the detainee, so long as the officers on the commission deem the information to be "relevant and helpful to a resolution of the issue before it" (*Order Establishing Combatant Status Review Tribunal,* ¶*g*(9)).

Objection 8.—For the ostensible purpose of protecting classified or classifiable information, Subsection IV(c)(4)(A) of the November 13 Order provides that the Secretary of Defense may conclusively determine not only the *manner* in which relevant materials and information about the activities of an alleged terrorist are handled in trial, but also the question as to *whether or not* such materials and information shall be entered into evidence at all, in addition to the question as to *whether or not* the detainee shall have access to such materials and information at trial, yet sensitive information is routinely entered into evidence in trials involving the prosecution of key members of organized crime syndicates without compromising the tactics of law enforcement or the safety of government witnesses.

Subsection IV(c)(4)(B) amplifies this power still further to include the power to decide whether or not a detainee shall even have "access to [trial] proceedings" in the first place. The Secretary of Defense can, pursuant to Subsection IV(c)(4)(B), indefinitely delay the trial of any detainee for any reason he sees fit, even though GCP, Art. 71, ¶2 specifically stipulates that accused persons "be promptly informed, in writing, in a language they understand, of the particulars of the charges preferred against them, and shall be brought to trial *as rapidly as possible*." (Emphasis added)

Objection 9.—Under Subsection IV(c)(8) of the November 13 Order President Bush arrogates to himself, or the Secretary of Defense, powers of final judicial review over any decision arrived at by military commission over the conviction, sentencing, or acquittal of individuals detained pursuant to the Order. But questions involving possible offences against the law of nations are federal questions, and federal courts have exclusive jurisdiction over all federal questions, not the President.

By this subsection the President has usurped powers of final arbitration over federal questions arising as a result of verdicts reached by military commissions, yet the Supreme Court holds exclusive and plenary power of final arbitration over *all* federal questions. The Supreme Court is also the final interpreter of federal statutes. Thus, had the Constitution been upheld in the post-9/11 rush to war, and had the trials of suspected al-Qaeda and Taliban fugitives been legitimate Article 5 affairs, the Supreme Court would have served as the court of final appeal, and would, in such a context, entertain petitions for writ of habeas corpus, but only in circumstances where petitioners could show their constitutional rights had been infringed. Note that detainees in *Eisentrager* were denied their petition for the writ because they could not show any infringement of constitutional liberties. They had already received due process of law by being tried, sentenced, and convicted. They were serving out their sentences at Landsberg penitentiary in

American-occupied West Germany. They were afforded legal counsel, competent tribunals, and rules of evidence consistent with a spirit of procedural fairness; and six of the *Eisentrager* detainees were acquitted.

Objection 10.—Subsection VII(b)(2) of the November 13 Order supplies the legal corollary to Subsection IV(c)(8) by removing one further check to the President's newly acquired judicial power of final arbitration over federal questions pertaining to offences against the law of nations:

> [Individuals subject to this Order] shall not be privileged to seek any remedy . . . or to have such remedy . . . sought on the[ir] behalf, in (i) any court of the United States, or any State thereof, (ii) any court of any foreign nation, or (iii) any international tribunal.

Perhaps it was the confusion accompanying a nation's haste that caused the President to carelessly misapply the provisions of his own November 13 Order when he detained U.S. citizens Yasser Esam Hamdi and Jose Padilla as "enemy combatants" and held them incommunicado and without access to legal counsel, while simultaneously refusing to charge them with any specific crime—Hamdi having been handed over to U.S. authorities in Afghanistan by Northern Alliance personnel in late 2001, Padilla arrested in Chicago by federal marshals on May 8, 2002.

The President's blunt refusal to consider the legality of the detentions of Hamdi and Padilla represented a gross violation of their Fifth and Fourteenth Amendment rights to due process and equal protection under the law. The searing mistrust held by the Bush White House and Justice Department officials for prominent *liberals* and so-called "activist" federal judges before 9/11 quickly devolved, after the attacks, into an open contempt for the very principles of political *liberalism* that foundationalize our constitutional republic. Absent from the Order is any reference to the term "person" to describe the being and the legal standing of the detainee. The Order speaks only of "individuals subject to this Order" and refuses to acknowledge the humanity of those it considers to be irredeemably blank vessels devoid of any uniqueness, character, or inherent natural value *qua* living.

QUESTION THREE

DOES CUSTOMARY INTERNATIONAL LAW ACKNOWLEDGE BUSH II OLC "FAILED STATE" DOCTRINE?

The Yoo-Haynes II Memo

Soon after the terrorist attacks of September 11, Bush administration attorneys in the Office of Legal Counsel, at the United States Department of Justice, set about the herculean task of addressing the following question: Does the President of the United States have authority under law to unilaterally suspend application of customary international law norms in addition to various provisions of positive international treaties, such as the Geneva Conventions, in regard to those suspected of al-Qaeda or Taliban affiliation captured amid hostilities in Afghanistan and placed in United States custody?

The Bush OLC position on this matter was defined by then-Deputy Assistant Attorney General John C. Yoo in a memorandum opinion dated January 9, 2002, for William J. Haynes II, General Counsel at the Department of Defense. In that opinion, Yoo postulates that the President undoubtedly does have such authority to unilaterally and temporarily suspend the Geneva Conventions, because neither the federal War Crimes Act (WCA) nor the Conventions themselves apply to the detention conditions at Guantánamo Bay, Cuba, nor do they apply to trials by military commission of suspected al-Qaeda or Taliban prisoners. The Yoo-Haynes II opinion also establishes the policy position that customary international law does not have any binding legal effect on either the President or the military because it is not federal law.[1]

These OLC positions are extremely troubling, however, not only because they reverse two centuries of United States military practice in upholding the customary law of nations, but because they also place the Commander-in-Chief on radically unstable legal ground while fighting a war against bands of international terrorists who can only be defeated by means of the continuing support and cooperation of an international law-enforcement community that had, for the space of two Presidential terms, become increasingly wary of America's abandonment of Geneva.

On January 16, 2002, the United Nations High Commissioner for Human Rights issued a formal Statement on the Detention of Taliban and al-Qaeda Prisoners calling for all detainees to be treated humanely, and consistent with the provisions of the International Covenant on Civil and Political Rights (ICCPR) and the Geneva Conventions Relative to the Treatment of Prisoners of War. The High Commissioner's Statement also called upon the United States to provide detainees the principles of a fair trial before a competent Article 5 tribunal.[2]

Two months later, on March 12, 2002, the Inter-American Commission on Human Rights issued a Decision on Request for Precautionary Measures regarding the Guantánamo Bay detainees pleading with the United States government "to take urgent measures necessary to have the legal status of the detainees at Guantánamo Bay determined by a competent tribunal. But none of these international pleas swayed the administration from turning its back on Geneva. Nor did the European Parliament's insistence on a resolution adopted on January 30, 2003, that the fight against terrorism "should in no way endanger the protection of fundamental human rights and must be based on international humanitarian law."[3]

The Bush administration fell deaf to the pleas of the United Nations Special Rapporteur on the independence of judges and lawyers, Dato' Param Cumaraswamy, who, on March 12, 2003, issued a press release warning that "the war on terrorism cannot possibly be won by denial of legal rights, including fundamental principles of due process of those merely suspected of terrorism."[4]

Nor did the Bush administration heed the warning of international legal expert Johan Steyn that "what takes place today [at Guantánamo Bay] in the name of the United States will assuredly, in due course, be judged at the bar of informed international opinion."[5]

The position I wish to advance here is that *no* President has authority to temporarily suspend Geneva's humanitarian protections regarding the detention and interrogation of persons suspected of Taliban or al-Qaeda affiliation in the War on Terror, because

> (*a*) No Article 5 tribunal has ever determined such affiliation, with the result that it is unclear whether suspects in captivity have actually done anything to violate the laws and customs of war; and even if they had, Geneva extends protection to all persons convicted of crimes of war.
>
> (*b*) Temporary or partial suspension of Geneva is nowhere allowed in the instrument, but only total and permanent withdrawl through GPW, Article 142's denunciation clause, ¶2.
>
> (*c*) Any denunciation sought in the context of hostilities in Afghanistan cannot take effect until after hostilities between U.S. and Taliban/al-Qaeda forces have ceased, peace has been concluded, and captives repatriated to their countries of origin (GPW, Art. 142, ¶3).
>
> (*d*) Denunciation does not impair the obligations which the Parties to the conflict are still bound to fulfil "by virtue of the principles of the law of nations" as they result from the usages established among civilized peoples (GPW, Art. 142, ¶4).

In addition to these limits, a notification of denunciation must be formally submitted to the Swiss Federal Council in writing (Art. 142, ¶2), and one year must elapse before the denunciation takes effect (Art. 142, ¶3). And, even if the denunciation has taken effect, and even if this denunciation allows a loophole for the implementation of a policy of coercive interrogation, Article 142, ¶4 says that humanitarian obligations would still apply "by virtue of the principles of the law of nations." These principles are norms of customary international law (CIL), but such norms are jettisoned as inapplicable in Yoo-Haynes II because they are not encoded as federal laws. Thus, in spite of these salient restrictions in Geneva, a newer and more imaginative method for removing captive suspects from the rule of law was invented by administration lawyers at the Office of Legal Counsel.

Objections to Positions Held in Yoo-Haynes II

Position 1. —Upon the request of General Counsel Haynes to be informed as to whether or not the laws governing armed conflict, including international treaties and federal laws, apply to conditions of detention and procedures for trial of suspect members of al-Qaeda and the Taliban, Deputy Assistant Yoo sets forth the position that

> we conclude that these treaties do not protect members of the al-Qaeda organization, which as a non-State actor cannot be party to the interna-

tional agreements governing war. We further conclude that these treaties do not apply to the Taliban militia. (*TTP*, Memo 4, Introd., p. 38)

On the Contrary, (*a*) laws governing armed conflict between nations exist either by positive (treaty) law or by custom, and neither aspect of law allows for inhumane treatment of captives of war for any reason regardless of alleged crimes. Although customary international law traditionally distinguishes legitimate "enemies" (Lat., *hostes*) as those who publicly declare war against us, or we against them, from illegitimate brigands (*latrones*), pirates (*piratae*), and thieves (*praedones*), this distinction only suggests that the latter are prosecutable for crimes of war, while the former are not. A remnant of this customary international law distinction between legitimate and illegitimate methods of war is found in the GPW requirement that Prisoners of War *not* be interred in penitentiaries (Art. 22, ¶1). The idea behind this restriction is that a legitimate enemy (*hostis*) has not committed a crime in taking up arms to defend his country, and so ought not be housed like a criminal during the period of his captivity.

(*b*) The Geneva Conventions do not require that a captured individual be a citizen or subject of a High Contracting Party in order to derive the humanitarian protections and legal status of a person protected under the Treaty, since GCP, Article 4 applies without any further distinction to "those who, at a given moment and in any manner whatsoever, find themselves, in case of a conflict or occupation, in the hands of a Party to the conflict or Occupying Power of which they are not nationals."

(*c*) While it is true, as Yoo contends, that the al-Qaeda organization is a non-state actor, since al-Qaeda has no sovereign authority to declare and conduct war, nevertheless the Taliban regime was the *de facto* sovereign authority of the state of Afghanistan at the time hostilities began with U.S. forces post-9/11.

Although the Taliban constitutes a ruthlessly inhumane regime that conscripts innocent young men into its service against their will, while enforcing an especially coercive form of Shari'a Law over its subjects, that regime nevertheless constituted, before 9/11, a centralized government authority capable of administering law and maintaining rudimentary institutions of state.[6]

(*d*) The legal question which ought to have concerned Yoo the most was not whether al-Qaeda or the Taliban was a state actor, but whether the State of Afghanistan was a High Contracting Party to Geneva, which indeed she has been since September of 1956. And perhaps it was just the realization of this inescapable fact of Afghanistan's signatory status that caused Yoo to plunge headlong into the so-called "failed-state" doctrine. As Yoo puts it:

> A State has failed when centralized government authority has almost completely collapsed, no central authorities are capable of maintaining institutions or ensuring law and order, and violence has destabilized civil society and the economy. (*TTP*, Part III, §B, ¶7, p. 54)

On the contrary, Yoo's definition is logically convoluted because a state need only be *on the brink* of anarchy and, in his words, "almost completely collapsed" in order for it to lose its statehood, even though it still exhibits the very centralized government authority that makes it a state. What the definition lacks in the way of logic it makes up for in political convenience. Yoo's definition allowed the Bush administration to display the veneer of international legitimacy it needed to single out Afghanistan as a "failed-state," even though the Taliban regime still possessed enough centralized government apparatus in September of 2001 to stand as the sovereign authority of an existing state. That power is sovereign which holds *de facto* control of the administration of a state, regardless of how ruthless or unjust, beneficent or kind, this sovereign power may be.

Position 2.—Having just asserted his thesis that neither the Geneva Conventions nor the War Crimes Act of 1996 (18 U.S.C. §2441) regulate the detention of al-Qaeda prisoners captured during the Afghanistan conflict, Yoo lays bare the still broader claim that

> the Geneva Conventions do not apply for several reasons [to the treatment of Taliban militia]. First, the Taliban was not a government and Afghanistan was not—even prior to the beginning of the present conflict—a functioning State during the period in which they engaged in hostilities against the United States and its allies. Afghanistan's status as a failed State is ground alone to find that members of the Taliban militia are not entitled to enemy POW status under the Geneva Conventions. Further, it is clear that the President has the constitutional authority to suspend our treaties with Afghanistan pending the restoration of a legitimate government capable of performing Afghanistan's treaty obligations. (*TTP*, Memo 4, Introd., ¶4, p. 39)

On the Contrary, (*a*) the Geneva Conventions *do* apply to the treatment of Taliban and al-Qaeda militia, precisely because the Taliban *was* a functioning government authority, and Afghanistan a sovereign state and High Contracting Party to Geneva. A nation's statehood does not slowly ebb out of existence over time simply because the regime in power ceases to exist, or because it poorly administers government, or because its laws become unjust. If this were so, Soviet Russia under the cruel hand of Stalin and Germany amid the imminent collapse of the Weimar Republic would most certainly have counted as failed states.

We must distinguish, then, between a state and its *de facto* sovereign government or regime. Customary international law has long recognized states to endure all changes in government or regime, as shown in (b). Thus, a change in the regime governing Afghanistan creates no change in the obligations the United States has toward protected persons captured and detained amid hostilities as part of her partial occupation of Afghanistan.

James Madison was keen to distinguish between a state and its *de facto* government when he recognized that United States treaty obligations to France (in 1793) survived in tact despite changes in the French government that began in 1789 with the violent overthrow of the absolute monarchy of the Bourbons—

> As a change of government then makes no change in the obligations or rights of the party to a treaty, it is clear that the executive can have no more right to suspend or prevent the operation of a treaty, on account of the change, than to suspend or prevent the operation, where no such change has happened. Nor can it have any more right to suspend the operation of a treaty in force as a law, than to suspend the operation of any other law.[7] (*Helvidius* No. 3, ¶19)

Madison recognizes two questions at play here: Does a nation lose its statehood upon the sudden mutation or death of its sovereign government? And, of equal importance, Does the President of the United States have constitutional authority to suspend the operation of a treaty when that treaty has been ratified by the Senate and exists as federal law? The answer to both questions appears to be resoundingly "no."

Federal case law further buttresses the idea long established as custom among civilized nations that even radical changes in the government of a state do not put an end to treaty obligations vis-à-vis that state. The United States Supreme Court held in *Clark v. Allen*, 331 U.S. 503 (1947), for instance, that "the outbreak of war does not necessarily suspend or abrogate treaty provisions" and, in particular, that "there is no evidence that the political departments of the Government have considered that the collapse and surrender of Germany [in 1945] put an end to such provisions of the 1923 Treaty as survived the outbreak of war or the obligations of either party in respect of them" (331 U.S. at 508, 514—Justice Douglas delivering the opinion of the court). Thus, even though Germany underwent tumultuous political upheaval including radical and sudden changes in sovereign government between 1923 and 1945, these developments do not alter the existence of Germany as a sovereign state on an existentially equal footing with other nation-states in the world.

Clark is a case concerning whether or not the provisions of Article IV of a 1923 Treaty between Germany and the United States survive in tact despite the complete collapse of the German government in 1945. The court is very well within its jurisdiction in deciding this delicate and politically charged case because judicial power extends to *all* cases in law and equity arising under ratified treaties (*Const.* Art. 3, §2, ¶1). But Yoo sees *Clark* in as a decision about the scope of executive treaty power that demonstrates only

> the Supreme Court's sanction for the Executive's constitutional authority to decide the "political questions" whether Germany had ceased to exist as a Nation State and, if so, whether the 1923 Treaty with Germany had become inoperative. Equally here, the executive branch should conclude that Afghanistan was not "in a position to perform its treaty obligations" because it lacked, at least throughout the Taliban's ascendancy, all the elements of statehood. (*TTP*, Memo 4, §A, ¶5, p. 52)

But *Clark* has nothing to do with whether or not the President may decide questions of statehood, because the case is not really about the scope of executive power at all. Nor is the court abdicating its power to determine the political question of whether states abide changes in regime. The court holds only that the political departments (i.e., the executive and legislative branches of government) have not considered the collapse of Germany as putting an end to the 1923 Treaty, but not that they are the *only* departments of government vested with authority to decide such questions.

The deliberate misrepresentation of federal court cases is common fare throughout the Bush administration OLC memoranda, a symphony of frustrating non-sequiturs providing ornament for what was actually part of a much broader "permanent campaign" mentality of deliberate public misdirection and propaganda to guide the nation into a series of wars the White House deemed necessary for purposes of national security.[8]

Given such iridescent beacons of authority and precedent weighing against "failed-state" doctrine as Madison, Grotius, and *Clark*, the policy desideratum set forth in the Yoo-Haynes II opinion appears all the more adrift. Yoo argues that Afghanistan's High Contracting Party status to Geneva be removed because she is no longer a state. She is no longer a state because her government has been poorly administered by the Taliban regime for some time, and the Taliban shows no willingness whatsoever to honor its treaty obligations, and is itself perched on the brink of total collapse. Yet the regime of President George W. Bush had been poorly administering the laws of the United States for eight years, had repeatedly shown no willingness to abide or honor its treaty obligations under Geneva, the ICCPR, and the CAT, and was itself perched on the brink of total collapse come January 21, 2009. But no one would argue that the United States had, by a change of regime, compromised its own statehood, or that she should have her High Contracting Party status to Geneva removed because of the administration of one ill-advised President.

(*b*) Yoo's "failed-state" doctrine not only lacks precedent among the customs and practices of nations, it is contradicted *toto caelo* by Grotius:

> Neither a State nor a Republic ceases to exist, even when guilty of some injustice pervading the entire community; nor is an association of pirates or thieves a State, though perchance they recognize a certain equality among themselves without which no association could possibly subsist.[9] (*De Jure Belli ac Pacis Libri Tres*, Book 3, ch. 3, §2.1)

Grotius is saying the same thing inside-out: States are permanent entities which abide social upheaval; they neither come-to-be nor pass away regardless of whether good unions of people (i.e., republics) turn bad, or bad unions of people (i.e., pirates and thieves) turn good.

(*c*) It is far from "clear" that the President has constitutional authority to suspend our treaties with Afghanistan, since the President cannot make a treaty except by advice and consent of the Senate (*Const.*, Art. 2, §2, ¶2), and it is axiomatic in both Roman and Anglo-American legal tradition that the parties which make a treaty are the only parties legally entitled to break it. If the President requires the advice and consent of the Senate to make a treaty, he requires the same in suspending or abrogating it, since otherwise he would operate outside the scope of his constitutionally vested powers.

Proponents of the view that the President does *not* need the advice and consent of the Senate in order to terminate a treaty "fail to consider," writes constitutional historian David Gray Adler, "the Framers' paramount concerns surrounding the treaty power, and their intention to resolve sectional disputes and state jealousies. One primary goal at the Philadelphia Convention was to restore the reputation of the country with respect to its international agreements."[10] The Framers intentionally made the executive less autocratic that the King of Great Britain, less able to act unilaterally and unchecked, an executive empowered to carry out or *execute*, but not *make* law, precisely in order to allow the United States to become more steadfast in honoring its treaty commitments than it had under the *Articles of Confederation*. Adler suggests they did this so as to prevent an executive with strong regional bias from upending United States commercial treaty law in order to give favor to his region of preference. The Framers sought a strong executive to be Commander-in-Chief in times of national crisis, but not one so powerful as to ignore the advice and counsel of the Senate.

Position 3.—Having just differentiated the al-Qaeda terrorist network as a *non-state* entity from the Taliban regime as a *state* entity unable to administer government in a country on the brink of failure, Yoo turns against his own stated position and proceeds to lump both groups together as if distinguishing them meant nothing as a matter of law:

> It appears from the public evidence that the Taliban militia may have been so intertwined with al-Qaeda as to be functionally indistinguishable from it. To the extent that the Taliban militia was more akin to a non-governmental organization that used military force to pursue its religious and political ideology than a functioning government, its members would be on the same legal footing as al-Qaeda. (*TTP*, Memo 4, Introd., ¶4, p. 39)

On the Contrary, (*a*) the Taliban and al-Qaeda *are* distinguishable not only because the former is a State actor while the latter is not, but because the former harbors the latter, and not vice-versa. Not only had the Bush administration refused throughout the Afghanistan campaign to offer captives of war legitimate Article 5 hearings to determine who they are and whether they really did what they were alleged to have done, the Yoo-Haynes II opinion seems to encourage the practice of conflating prisoners together and confusing their identity as if there were no difference in criminal law between committing a violent act versus harboring someone who had, as if it made no difference to the quality and direction of the investigation then being conducted on the ground by coalition forces in search of bin Laden.

On September 11, 2001, President Bush proclaimed: "We will make no distinction between the terrorists who committed these acts and those who harbor them."[11] Few Americans could have imagined, at the time, that these words would go on to shape the President's *entire* approach toward international terrorism: If any distinction of law (including any provision of a ratified treaty) should interfere with the President's ability to carry out his function as Commander-in-Chief of the Armed Forces of the United States, that law is to be jettisoned and deemed unconstitutional because it diminishes the power constitutionally vested in the Executive as Commander-in-Chief to conduct the nation's war on terror in a "New Paradigm" context where terrorist attacks could mean mass civilian casualties.

(*b*) In customary international law, however, the practice of carelessly lumping captives of war together without distinction is the hallmark of a reckless conqueror, not of a just sovereign. Grotius tells us, in fact, that

> Demosthenes, in his *Epistle* for Lycurgus's children, praises Philip II of Macedon, who refused to make all among his enemies slaves, "For he did not assess the same rights and privileges for everyone, but weighing the merits of each person, Philip II conducted himself with the dignity of a Judge."[12] (*De Iure Belli ac Pacis Libri Tres,* Book 3, ch. 14, §1.2)

Position 4.—Having summarily removed suspect al-Qaeda and Taliban captives from humanitarian protection under Geneva, Yoo concludes that

> customary international law, whatever its source and content, does not bind the President, or restrict the actions of the United States military, because it does not constitute federal law recognized under the Supremacy Clause of the Constitution. The President, however, has the constitutional authority as Commander-in-Chief to interpret and apply the customary or common laws of war in such a way that they would extend to the conduct of members of both al-Qaeda and the Taliban, and also to the conduct of the U.S. Armed Forces towards members of those groups taken as prisoners in Afghanistan. (*TTP,* Memo 4, Introd., ¶5, p. 39)

On the Contrary, (*a*) the President of the United States most certainly ought to be bound by customary international law, because this law derives from a body of *de facto* customs and practices pertaining to war, peace, and diplomacy long accepted by the civilized nations of the world. Following these standards is tantamount to preserving good faith in our dealings with the world at large, good faith (*bona fides*) being the *a priori* foundation for the possibility of peace among nations, as it signifies a basic trust in one's fellow man, a belief in the goodness of the human spirit, and a genuine desire to live in harmony with one's neighbors. But the OLC argued from an entirely opposite perspective. The President, in their view, ought never to have his command hindered in a time of war by considerations of customary international law, since this law is not standing federal law.

Now while it is true that customary international law forms no part of federal law, the Geneva Conventions do, since they were ratified by Senate Resolution on July 6, 1955.[13] Geneva was given additional force in federal law by the War Crimes Act of 1996, 18 U.S.C. §2441, which penalizes with heavy fines, imprisonment, and even death, if death results to the victim, the commission of any war crime defined as a "grave breach in any of the international conventions signed at Geneva" on August 12, 1949, regardless of whether or not that crime occurred inside or outside United States territory.

"Grave breaches" as defined in GPW, Art. 130 include the following acts, if committed against persons or property protected by the Convention: "Wilful killing, torture or inhuman treatment . . . wilfully causing great suffering or serious injury to body or health . . . or wilfully depriving a prisoner of war of the rights of fair and regular trial prescribed in this Convention." Since the War Crimes Act does not contain an immunity clause, there is reason to suspect that high Bush administration officials might be called to account over documentation of grave breaches by United States military and intelligence personnel during their tenure of office.[14] The President's appointees at the OLC appear to have told him only what he wanted to hear without alerting him to alternative legal interpretations.

(*b*) It is not even true to say that customary international law does not exist as federal law, since its principles are *written into the text* of ratified treaties, and ratified treaties are federal laws. In addition, CIL has been assigned the force of federal law by the Supreme Court in those cases where the relevant legal question at issue cannot be decided by reference to any controlling executive proclamation, legislative act, or judicial decision. One such case upholding the binding force of CIL is *The Paquete Habana*, 175 U.S. 677 (1900), where the Court held that

> [customary] international law is part of our law, and must be ascertained and administered by the courts of justice of appropriate jurisdiction as often as questions of right depending upon it are duly presented for their determination. For this purpose, where there is no treaty and no controlling executive or legislative act or judicial decision, resort must be had to the customs and usages of civilized nations, and, as evidence of these, to the works of jurists and commentators, not for the speculations of their authors concerning what the law ought to be, but for trustworthy evidence of what the law really is. (175 U.S., at 700)

The question at issue in *The Paquete Habana* concerns whether or not peaceful coastal fishing vessels are exempt from capture as prize of war. The Court held the United States Navy's capture as prize of two civilian fishing smacks owned by Cuban nationals to be both unlawful and without probable cause. (The fishing smacks had set out on an expedition *before* the outbreak of the Spanish-American War, and before the U.S. blockade of Cuba began, and were apprehended only upon their return to Cuba.) Such capture was not in accordance with what the court called "the general consent of the civilized nations of the world." And it is important to see that many legal questions arise in international affairs that are not transparently resolvable by appeal to the terms of positive instruments of law, though they may be resolvable by appeal to the customs and practices of nations.

Second, in *Murray v. The Schooner Charming Betsey*, 6 U.S. (2 Cranch) 64, 118 (1804), the court held that "an act of Congress ought never to be construed to violate the [customary] law of nations if any other possible construction remains, and consequently can never be construed to violate neutral rights or to affect neutral commerce further than is warranted by the law of nations as understood in this country." The Charming Betsey Canon effectively prevents federal law from being interpreted (or distorted) in such a way as to violate or contradict the customary law of nations. Applying the canon to the current context, the Joint Resolution AUMF of September 14, 2001, and the Military Commissions Act of 2006 ought not to be construed so as to violate universally recognized laws of war, such as the right of prisoners not to be mistreated during their captivity, the right of diplomatic immunity, the right of return of prisoners to their home countries (i.e., postliminy) upon the cessation of hostilities, and so on.

Third, in *Banco Naçional de Cuba v. Sabbatino*, 376 U.S. 398 (1964) the court held that the Cuban government's expropriation of Compania Azucareara Vertientes-Camaguey de Cuba (C.A.V.), a Cuban company owned largely by U.S. residents contracted with an American commodities broker to purchase Cuban sugar, was *not* protected by the Act of State Doctrine, which precludes judicial inquiry in the United States respecting the public acts of a recognized foreign sovereign power committed within its own territory, although Cuba's expropriation of C.A.V. had violated other norms of customary international law pertaining to individual property rights.

The Cuban government's expropriation of C.A.V. took place under Cuban Law No. 851 in direct response to an act of the U.S. Congress on July 6, 1960, which lowered the sugar quota from Cuba. Mr. Justice Harlan, delivering the opinion of the court, noted that

> law [No. 851] gave the Cuban President and Prime Minister discretionary power to nationalize by forced expropriation property or enterprises in which American nationals had an interest. . . . Our State Department has described the Cuban law as "manifestly in violation of those principles of international law which have long been accepted by the free countries of the West. It is in its essence discriminatory, arbitrary and confiscatory." (376 U.S., at 402, 403)

The State Department's comments here highlight the fragility of customary international law, whose binding force quickly evaporates in contexts where civilized nations choose to ignore it.

(*c*) Customary international law has been assigned force and weight in the Preamble to the Vienna Convention on the Law of Treaties (1969) which affirms that "the rules of customary international law will continue to govern questions not regulated by the provisions of the present Convention."[15] In the conduct of the nation's foreign affairs, customary international law has traditionally played an important policy-formative role in solving disputes between nations where there exists no controlling treaty provision or guiding protocol. Dispensing with customary norms makes no sense from either a strategic or legal perspective, as it invites our adversaries around the world to do the same.

Position 5.—In spite of the fact that GPW, Art. 131 forbids any High Contracting Party (such as the United States) from absolving itself of liability for committing grave breaches, and in spite of the Deputy Assistant's awareness of that provision, he nevertheless provided the President a convenient backdoor justification for deplorable conditions of confinement at camps X-Ray[16] and Delta at Guantánamo Bay by arguing that

> the WCA does not criminalize all breaches of the Geneva Conventions. Failure to follow some of the regulations regarding the treatment of POWs, such as difficulty in meeting all of the conditions set forth for POW camp conditions, does not constitute a grave breach within the meaning of [GPW], Art. 130. Only by causing great suffering or serious bodily injury to POWs, killing or torturing them, depriving them of access to a fair trial, or forcing them to serve in the Armed Forces, could the United States actually commit a grave breach. (*TTP*, Memo 4, Part I, §A, ¶4, p. 43)

On the Contrary, it is irrelevant, from a logical point of view, that the WCA does not criminalize *all* breaches of the Geneva Conventions, since failure to follow non-breach requirements, even the most basic restrictions on camp conditions or conditions of confinement, can quite easily lead over time to permanent physical and/or psychological impairment in the captive that would constitute a grave breach under WCA. The vicissitudes of war inevitably bring death and destruction to the innocent, but success in Afghanistan depends, in part, on minimizing these consequences, while securing tribal cooperation with U.S. and coalition efforts to root out the Taliban.

The job of the Deputy Assistant Attorney General is not to describe for the President the law as the President would like it interpreted, but the law as the international community is bound to interpret it.

For instance, GPW, Art. 22's prohibition on the use of penitentiaries to house POWs may seem downright quaint and overly demanding when dealing with captives whom Secretary Rumsfeld once described as "the worst of the worst,"[17] but for persons not charged with any crime, whose belligerency against the United States often exists on hearsay grounds, maximum security confinement in a penitentiary located on a distant penal colony in Cuba or at Abu Ghraib prison in Iraq is tantamount to a criminal conviction and sentence. In late 2006, Joseph Margulies, lead attorney for petitioners in *Rasul*, described the maximum security environment at Camp Delta in these terms:

> Each prisoner lives in a six-foot-eight-inch by eight-foot cell twenty-four hours per day, except for twenty to thirty minutes' individual exercise five days a week (up from two), followed by a five-minute shower. Shackled whenever they leave their cells, the prisoners exercise in a twenty-five by thirty-foot cage on a concrete slab. Bright lights shine in the cells around the clock. Guards constantly patrol the rows, with each cell observed by a guard at least once every thirty seconds.[18]

Although prisoners at Camp Delta are allowed basic comfort items as well as a copy of the Koran and although they are provided a place to defecate and are given regular meals, such genuinely worthy efforts on the part of the administration to accord with Geneva become minimized once we add in the year-round summer heat of Guantánamo Bay, along with the prospect of indefinitely long detention, interrogation, and examination faced by the detainee.

Position 6.—Although Deputy Assistant Yoo does well to recognize that common Article 3 of Geneva may require the United States as High Contracting Party "to follow certain rules even if other parties to the conflict are not parties to the Conventions," he nevertheless negates this moral high-ground position by removing common Article 3 from applying to the conflict with the Taliban and al-Qaeda on the grounds that

> it appears . . . the drafters of the Conventions had in mind only the two forms of armed conflict that were regarded as matters of general international concern at the time: armed conflict between Nation States (subject to Article 2), and large-scale civil war within a Nation State (subject to Article 3). (*TTP*, Memo 4, Part I, §C, ¶7, pp. 44-45)

On the Contrary, (*a*) since the conflict in Afghanistan involves the United States, and is international in scope, Yoo infers that common Article 3 cannot apply. But exempting suspected al-Qaeda and Taliban members from humanitarian protections under Geneva is a legal decision less ungrounded than it is foolhardy. What possible strategic value can there be in depriving captives of war common Article 3 humanitarian protections? What actionable intelligence is a detainee held in isolation from the outside world for a year or more likely to possess? Common Article 3 protects persons *taking no part in active hostilities,* including members of armed forces who have *laid down their arms.*

Common Article 3 protects captives of war from violence to life and person, murder, mutilation, cruel treatment and torture, outrages upon personal dignity, humiliating and degrading treatment, as well as the passing of sentences and the carrying out of executions without previous judgment. What possible motivation, then, could the OLC have had in stripping detainees of humanitarian protections, unless it was deliberately conspiring with high-echelon Bush administration officials to create a viable legal pretext for the post-9/11 formation of a torture culture within the military and intelligence community for the ostensible purpose of gleaning high-value information from detainees captured in Afghanistan and suspected of high-level terrorist collusion?

On October 11, 2002, Lt. Col. Diane Beaver requested formal permission from the Commander of Joint Task Force 170 to implement "more aggressive interrogation techniques" than the ones then being used at GTMO base, as groups of detainees had begun to develop their own resistance techniques to interrogators.[19] On January 15, 2003, Secretary of Defense Donald Rumsfeld ordered the establishment of a Working Group within the Department of Defense to assess the legal, policy, and operational issues relating to interrogations of detainees held in U.S. custody.[20]

Secretary Rumsfeld expected the Working Group Report to be completed and delivered to him within 15 days, an unrealistic expectation given the legally problematic nature of many of the enhanced counter-resistance techniques then under discussion. The two-week demand also suggests how little value the Secretary of Defense placed in the investigation of the legal, ethical, and policy implications of enhanced interrogation. On March 3, 2003, nearly three months after Rumsfeld issued his original Order, the Working Group completed its first draft Report on Detainee Interrogations in the Global War on Terrorism. In the final version of the Working Group Report issued a month later—a report Rumsfeld originally ordered classified for 10 years—the group recommended for approval by the Secretary a select category of ten "more aggressive" counterresistance techniques to be used during the interrogation of intransigent suspects. These techniques include 1. threatening to transfer the detainee to a third country (e.g., Egypt, Syria, Jordan, etc.) for further interrogation, in a process known as extraordinary rendition (which is illegal under GCP, Art. 49, ¶1); 2. isolation, with a recommended 30-day limit; 3. use of prolonged interrogations; 4. forced grooming; 5. prolonged standing in so-called "stress positions"; 6. sleep deprivation; 7. physical training; 8. face or stomach slap; 9. removal of clothing; 10. increasing anxiety by use of aversions.[21]

(*b*) Now even if the OLC's strategy in suspending common Article 3 was to create a legal loophole for coercive interrogations at bases far removed from the rule of law, such a maneuver is puzzling given that the removal of common Article 3 does not impair the operation of other provisions to the Treaty, such as common Article 1 which ensures that all High Contracting Parties "undertake to respect and to ensure respect for the present Convention in *all* circumstances."

(*c*) While it is arguably the case that common Article 3 describes only conditions of civil war, and so does not apply to cases of *international* conflict, as between the United States and Afghanistan, nevertheless the pre-existing conflict between the Taliban and Northern Alliance was precisely that picture of widespread civil strife and confusion envisioned in the OLC reading of common Article 3. If common Article 3 applied between these opposing forces before American involvement, as the OLC reading would lead us to expect, then why would the article suddenly cease operation after the introduction of United States and coalition forces?

Position 7.—In order to hedge his bets against anyone who might construe Geneva common Article 3 as applicable to America's involvement in Afghanistan, Deputy Assistant Yoo claims that

> if we were to read the Geneva Conventions as applying to *all* forms of armed conflict, we would expect the High Contracting Parties to have used broader language, which they easily could have done. . . . Given due weight to the State practice and doctrinal understanding of the time, it seems to us overwhelmingly likely that an armed conflict between a Nation State and a transnational terrorist organization, or between a Nation State and a failed State harboring and supporting a transnational terrorist organization, could not have been within the contemplation of the drafters of common Article 3. These would have been simply unforeseen and, therefore, not provided for. (*TTP*, Memo 4, Part I, §C, ¶s 11, 12, pp. 46-47, emphasis added)

On the Contrary, (*a*) nowhere in the text of common Article 3 does it say that the cases of armed conflict to which it shall apply be limited to conflicts between state actors. Nor does the text exclude application of the article to conflicts between a state versus a non-state actor. From Yoo's perspective the drafters of common Article 3 were dominated by what he calls a "state-centered view of international law" which would have rendered them unable to countenance wars involving non-state adversaries. But only a year before the conclusion of Geneva in 1949 a people that would become the state of Israel in 1948 were fighting for their own independence and statehood in a guerilla campaign of attrition that involved the use of highly asymmetric and unconventional means of warfare.

These unconventional means would have been borrowed, in many cases directly, from the French Resistance to the Nazi occupation of France by means of underground paramilitary guerilla fighters grouped into cells, and feared for their surprise attacks and ability to penetrate deep within enemy fortifications. The French Resistance and the Israeli War for Independence of 1948 may very well have formed a fresh template of armed conflict "not of an international character" envisioned by the drafters of common Article 3. If so, the drafters would have countenanced unconventional armed conflict involving revolutionary groups operating within, and often against, a larger functioning state regime. If so, common Article 3 would apply to conflict between a state versus a non-state actor.

(*b*) If the Deputy Assistant is correct in his assertion that common Article 3 is limited to cases of civil war, then, by definition of "civil war," common Article 3 must apply to conflicts that involve at least one *non*-state actor. For, in any case of civil war it must be the case that either: 1. the preexisting state *ceases to exist*, so that civil war arises between two non-state actors battling for ultimate sovereignty, or 2. the preexisting state *continues to exist*, with a significant portion of it divided off in an independent secessionist revolutionary movement, whose assertion of state sovereignty is the very issue of dispute in the war. If it is true, as Yoo maintains, that the drafters of Geneva common Article 3 espoused a purely state-centered view of international law, then why did they spend their time drafting an article to account for cases of civil war involving at least one (or more) non-state actors? It is problemmatic to assert that common Article 3 excludes war between states, but that the drafters of Geneva were dominated by a state-centered approach to international law.

Position 8.—Yoo claims that the WCA represents an unconstitutional congressional infringement on the President's discretion to direct the military:

> The WCA regulates the manner in which the U.S. Armed Forces may conduct military operations against the enemy; as such, it potentially comes into conflict with the President's Commander-in-Chief power under Article II of the Constitution. As we have advised others earlier in the conflict, the Commander-in-Chief power gives the President plenary authority in determining how best to deploy troops in the field. Any congressional effort to restrict presidential authority by subjecting the conduct of the U.S. Armed Forces to a broad construction of the Geneva Convention, one that is not clearly borne by its texts, would represent a possible infringement on presidential discretion to direct the military. We believe that Congress must state explicitly its intention to take the constitutionally dubious step

> of restricting the President's plenary power over military operations (including treatment of prisoners) and that unless Congress clearly demonstrates such an intent, the WCA must be read to avoid such constitutional problems. (*TTP*, Memo 4, Part I, §C, ¶13, p. 47)

On the Contrary, Yoo is arguing that for Congress to interpret common Article 3 in such a broad fashion as to restrict the President's field of strategic options by confining him, say, to rules of humane treatment for captive al-Qaeda suspects, would be an infringement on the President's constitutional authority as Commander-in-Chief to conduct the war on terrorism.

But the Constitution (Art. 1, §8, ¶s 9-16) delegates to Congress quite a number of war powers that often infringe upon the President's power as Commander-in-Chief. For instance, had Congress stood up and fulfilled its function in 2001 by defining and punishing piracies and offences against the law of nations (*Const.* Art. 1, §8, ¶10), it could have prevented President Bush from suspending the Geneva Conventions, and from locating prisoners of war thousands of miles from the zone of conflict through a system of mass forcible transfers; it could have stopped the President from instituting a torture culture within the military and intelligence community; it could have also established rules governing trials, detentions, and treatment for captives of war in the Afghanistan conflict.

Nowhere does the Constitution allow the President to suspend, revoke, or otherwise violate the law of nations or standing federal law in order to more effectively carry out his vision as Commander-in-Chief of the Armed Forces in time of war. If this were so, the command role of the President would conflict with and even, in the current context, negate his role as chief executor of the laws of the land. But since the President must carry the laws into effect, he is not allowed thereby to alter or amend them in order to achieve his foreign policy objectives.

Position 9.—On the basis of his foregoing assertions Yoo claims that

> members of the al-Qaeda terrorist organization do not receive the protections of the laws of war. Therefore, neither their detention nor their trial by the U.S. Armed Forces is subject to the Geneva Conventions (or the WCA). . . . First, al-Qaeda's status as a non-State actor renders it ineligible to claim the protections of the Geneva Conventions. Second, the nature of the conflict precludes application of common Article 3 of the Geneva Conventions. Third, al-Qaeda members fail to satisfy the eligibility require-

> ments for treatment as POWs under Geneva Convention III. . . . Therefore, the military's treatment of al-Qaeda members captured in that conflict is not limited either by common Article 3 . . . or 18 U.S.C. §2441(c)(3), the provision of the WCA incorporating that Article. (*TTP*, Memo 4, Part II, ¶1-2, p. 48)

On the Contrary, (*a*) by Yoo's own admission common Article 3 countenances humanitarian protection for prisoners captured amid civil strife or revolutionary uprising, who may be members of non-state militias (for instance, members of splinter groups vying for power in conflicts *not* of an international character). In other words, the drafters of Geneva already foresaw in common Article 3 the very scenarios of unpredictable non-state behavior that Yoo believes prevent suspected al-Qaeda participants from claiming protections under Geneva.

(*b*) Even if the "novel" nature of the present conflict in Afghanistan precluded the application of common Article 3, that novelty would not thereby preclude application of common Articles 1 and 2 to the present conflict, nor would it preclude application of the Geneva Convention Relative to the Treatment of Prisoners of War (GPW), Articles 5; 13.1, 13.2, 13.3; 14.1, 14.3; 17.4; 18.3; 20.1, 20.2; 21.1; 22.1; 25.1; 84.2; 85; 87.3; 99.2, 99.3; 104.2(3); 105; 106; 126; 130; 131; 142, nor application of the Geneva Convention Relative to the Protection of Civilian Persons in Time of War (GCP), Articles 4; 27.1, 27.2, 27.3; 31; 32; 33; 49.1, 49.2; 71; 72; 73; 75; 93; 94; 95; 96. The Bush administration has both openly infracted and publicly ignored, as a point of official policy, each of the foregoing provisions of Geneva in its prosecution of the global war on terrorism.

(*c*) When Yoo claims that al-Qaeda members fail to satisfy "eligibility requirements" for treatment as POWs under GPW he is referring to standards of conduct in battle (stipulated in GPW, Article 4) that all captives must satisfy in order to derive full protection as Prisoners of War. Since an actual member of al-Qaeda would never, if tried, qualify as a POW under GPW, Article 4(A)(2)(d)'s requirement for conducting his operations in accordance with the laws and customs of war, Yoo concludes that all captives suspected of al-Qaeda affiliation fail to meet the eligibility requirements for treatment as POWs. But he misses the fact that POW status is conferred, not in a blanket manner over an entire population of captive suspects by Presidential decree, but by competent military tribunals on a case-by-case basis. Theoretically speaking, if solid criminal investigation determined that a certain captive was an al-Qaeda member, and these facts were presented at a legitimate Article 5 tribunal hearing, that captive could face a lengthy prison sentence or perhaps, depending upon the severity of his crime, even death. So, there never really existed any need to deprive suspects of their human rights, since Geneva already provides for criminal trials of suspected members of international terrorist organizations at war with the United States.

(*d*) Yoo's motivation for wriggling out of Geneva common Article 3 (as opposed to common Article 2 or common Article 1) at last becomes transparent: The WCA definition of "war crime" at 18 U.S.C. §2441(c)(3) includes conduct which "constitutes a violation of common Article 3 [of Geneva]." If common Article 3 no longer applies in the new paradigm of global counterterrorism, then the President is not really committing federal war crimes, as defined under Subsection 2441(c)(3), by, for instance, granting blanket approval for the use of coercive interrogation techniques, cruel treatment, along with forced transfers and renditions of terrorist suspects to third countries for purposes of interrogation, all while denying captives of war access to regularly constituted courts.

Position 10.—Any legal argument in favor of applying Geneva to captured Taliban suspects depends, says Yoo,

> on assumptions that [1] during the period in which the Taliban militia was ascendant in Afghanistan, the Taliban was the de facto government of that nation, that [2] Afghanistan continued to have the essential attributes of statehood, and that [3] Afghanistan continued in good standing as a party to the treaties that its previous government had signed. We think that all of these assumptions are disputable, and indeed false. . . . It is clear that, under the Constitution, the Executive has the plenary authority to determine that Afghanistan ceased at relevant times to be an operating State and therefore that members of the Taliban militia were and are not protected by the Geneva Conventions. (*TTP*, Memo 4, Part III, Introd., ¶2 and §A, ¶1, pp. 50-51)

On the Contrary, (*a*) Yoo's requirement [3] that Afghanistan, in order to be counted a state, must continue "in good standing as a party to the treaties that its previous government had signed" is a bogus claim phrased in deliberately subjective terms that would exclude from statehood any nation, such as the United States, that has recently failed to live up to its own international agreements. Requirement [3], if applied to the Bush policy and practice of ignoring international protocol in the war on terror, would place the United States perilously close to a temporary condition of "statelessness," as Yoo calls it, that would effectively suspend her High Contracting Party status to Geneva.

In addition, requirement [3] is nowhere contained among the criteria for statehood enumerated at §201 of *Restatement (Third) of the Foreign Relations Law of the United States*, which provides a convenient threefold test to determine whether an entity constitutes a state:

i. Does the entity have a defined territory and population?
ii. Are the territory/population under the control of its own government?
iii. Does the entity engage in or have the capacity to engage in formal relations with other States?

We know that prior to 9/11 Afghanistan possessed a defined territory with a migratory population, but that she had been in a state of civil war for roughly a quarter century going back to a time before the Soviet invasion. We know that, by the late 1990s, this population was under the control of its own government, since it was forcibly subjected to a radical and brutally repressive form of Shari'a Law administered by the Taliban regime. At the same time, this eagerness to impose Shari'a meant the return of law and order for many Afghans after years of widespread civil war, corruption, and anarchy. For these reasons, Afghanistan satisfied criteria (i) & (ii). We also know that the Taliban regime satisfied criterion (iii), since it had in fact been the recipient of, and subsequently rejected, President Bush's ultimatum to hand over members of al-Qaeda that it was harboring before and after the attacks of 9/11.

The Taliban, while clearly a focus of evil in the modern world, nevertheless exhibited the capacity to engage in formal relations with other states on a rudimentary level.

Nor is Requirement [3], as formulated by Yoo, anywhere to be found among the State Department's four chief criteria for statehood,

α. Does the entity have effective control over a clearly defined territory and population?
β. Is there an organized governmental administration of the territory?
γ. Does the entity have the capacity to act effectively to conduct foreign relations and to fulfill international obligations?
δ. Has the international community recognized the entity?[22]

State Department criteria (α) & (β) essentially repeat U.S. Foreign Relations Law criteria (i) & (ii) using different words. Criterion (γ) also repeats criterion (iii)'s requirement that the entity have a capacity to conduct or engage in foreign relations. But (γ) only requires an entity to possess the *capacity* to fulfill international obligations, which is a question of fact, and not that the entity also *be in good standing* as a party to the treaties its previous government had signed, which is a question of value. Under Yoo's "good standing" requirement, any state having temporary problems meeting its international agreements due to poorly administered government would be in jeopardy of compromising its status as a state actor, which is absurd.

(*b*) It is *not* at all clear that the President has plenary constitutional power to determine that Afghanistan had failed as a state, and that, therefore, members of the Taliban regime are not to be protected under Geneva, because there is no provision in the Constitution that would allow the President to unilaterally suspend, alter, or abrogate existing treaties independently of advice and consent from the Senate. Nor did the Framers, in making treaties the supreme law of the land, intend for them to be repealable ad libitum by any one member of the compact, but only so far as *all* parties responsible for their creation may think proper. John Jay, for instance, warned that those who would oppose making treaties the supreme law of the land

> would do well to reflect that a treaty is only another name for a bargain; and that it would be impossible to find a nation who would make any bargain with us, which should be binding of them *absolutely*, but on us only so long and so far as we may think proper to be bound by it. . . . But still let us not forget that treaties are made not by only one of the contracting parties, but by both, and consequently that as the consent of both was essential to their formation at first so must it ever afterwards be to alter or cancel them. (*Federalist* No. 64, ¶11)

(*c*) Yoo quotes Hamilton's *Pacificus* No. 1 to posit the existence of an open set of nondescript executive powers which somehow "flow from the general grant of that power" contained in Article 2 of the Constitution.[23] But there exists no such *general* grant of executive power anywhere in the instrument, but a series of *specific* powers are already enumerated of the executive at Article 2, §2. Even if Yoo's arguments for expansive executive power allowed the President, in time of national crisis, to legally abrogate treaties (or other federal statutes) at will, his function as Chief *Executive* would prevent him from doing so, since as Hamilton aptly points out in the same *Pacificus* essay, "the Executive is charged with the *execution* of all laws, the laws of Nations as well as the Municipal law, which recognizes and adopts those laws" (*Pacificus*, No. 1, ¶34).[24] Hamilton countenanced a robust Chief Executive who boldly assumes plenary power in times of national crisis. But he never envisioned an executive who would neglect his most fundamental duty of *executing* the laws.

Position 11.—According to Yoo, the President has constitutional power to *interpret* GPW in such a manner as to prevent it from applying to captured Taliban and al-Qaeda suspects because

> part of the President's plenary power over the conduct of the Nation's foreign relations is the interpretation of treaties and of international law. Interpretation of international law includes the determination whether a territory has the necessary political structure to qualify as a Nation State for purposes of treaty implementation. In *Clark v. Allen*, 331 U.S. 503 (1947), for example, the Supreme Court considered whether a 1923 treaty with Germany continued to exist after the defeat, occupation and partition of Germany by the victorious World War II Allies . . . the Court held that "the question whether a State is in a position to perform its treaty obligations is essentially a political question. *Terlinden v. Ames*, 184 U.S. 270, 288 [(1902)]. We find no evidence that the political departments have considered the collapse and surrender of Germany as putting an end to such provisions of the treaty as survived the outbreak of the war or the obligations of either party in respect to them." Thus, *Clark* demonstrates the Supreme Court's sanction for the Executive's constitutional authority to decide the "political questions" whether Germany had ceased to exist as a Nation State and, if so, whether the 1923 treaty with Germany had become inoperative. (*TTP*, Memo 4, Part III, §A, ¶s 4 & 5, p. 52)

On the Contrary, (*a*) the President does *not* have constitutional authority to interpret ratified treaties and customary international law concepts as final arbiter of their meaning, scope, or applicability in the implementation of foreign policy, since power to say what the law is is emphatically the province and duty of the Judicial Department, *Marbury v. Madison*, 5 U.S. 137, 177 (1803), not the Chief Executive, whose essential function is to execute existing law. Federal courts possess exclusive jurisdiction over federal questions "arising under the Constitution, the laws of the United States, and treaties made, or which shall be made, under their authority" (*Const.* Art. 3, §2, ¶1). The phrase "shall be made" means that the federal judiciary has the power to interpret whether or not a *proposed* treaty, one not yet ratified, violates the Constitution, or runs counter to an existing treaty, or other laws of the United States. And the power to interpret law clearly has implications in the political domain because it sets legal boundaries as to what the President and Congress may do relative to the implementation of an existing treaty. The President and Senate together create and dissolve treaties. But insofar as a treaty is federal law it is inviolable by either department of state without the other's consent.

(*b*) Whatever power the executive may have to *interpret* law, it most certainly does not include the power to *determine* it; if it did, the President could suspend, alter, or abrogate ratified treaties at will. Nor does the President have legal authority to determine that Afghanistan, or any other sovereign nation, is a "failed-state" and, as a consequence, no longer a High Contracting Party to Geneva, both because the judiciary exercises exclusive jurisdiction over such questions (i.e., questions pertaining to treaties and to customary international law), and because the Constitution limits the executive to carrying treaties (and all other federal laws) into effect, even if he finds them distasteful. Yoo's vision of a robust Executive with enhanced powers to interpret and suspend ratified treaties[25] without advice or consent of the Senate revives a thesis once advanced by Alexander Hamilton in defense of President Washington's Neutrality Proclamation of 1793, that

> the power of determining . . . upon the operation of national Treaties as a consequence of the power to receive ambassadors and other public Ministers is an important instance of the right of the Executive to decide the obligations of the Nation with regard to foreign Nations.[26] (*Pacificus* No. 1, ¶38)

Hamilton is saying that the executive power of determining whether a treaty is operative or inoperative in a given context is a consequence or natural outgrowth of the executive's power to receive foreign ambassadors. But even were this so, it does not establish unilateral executive power to nullify or amend extant treaties.

Countering Hamilton's defense of executive privilege in deciding the nation's obligations in regard to foreign nations, Madison contends that although

> a suspension of treaties might happen from a *consequential* operation of a right to receive public ministers, which is an *express right* vested by the

> constitution; it could be no proof, that the same or a similar effect [i.e., a treaty's being suspended] could be produced by the direct operation of a constructive power.[27] (*Helvidius* No. 1, ¶32)

Madison claims here that the President's right to receive or not receive foreign ambassadors could place an existing treaty in virtual suspension, but that no treaty can come to be formally suspended merely because the President construes the treaty text in such a way as to find the instrument inoperable. No inference in favor of an executive right to unilaterally suspend the operation of a treaty can be drawn from the Constitution based upon the express right to receive public ministers and to recognize foreign governments, since neither of these formalities involves altering or suspending existing treaty laws.

(*c*) *Clark* does *not* demonstrate the Supreme Court's sanction or endorsement of executive authority to decide so-called "political questions." Yoo quotes *Clark* entirely out of context to suggest a position opposite the opinion actually delivered by Justice Douglas. Yoo contends that *Clark* delegates the power to interpret treaties and questions of statehood to the political departments (and thus to the President), when in reality the Court exercised its own interpretative powers in *Clark*, as it did in *Terlinden v. Ames*, 184 U.S. 270 (1902), by maintaining the premise that the outbreak of war does *not* necessarily suspend or abrogate treaty provisions, and that, as a result, the Treaty of 1923 with Germany continued in tact between 1923 and 1947 in spite of tumultuous changes in the political landscape of Germany. The *Clark* court had interpreted that a state had not failed, and that a treaty had not ceased operation. The court's *deference* to the political departments on questions of international law and treaties (*Id.*, 331 U.S., at 514) appears to have been hastily misread by Yoo as a *delegation* of interpretative power to the political departments, which *Clark* clearly does not support.

Position 12.—"Traditional legal analysis makes clear," claims Yoo,

> that Afghanistan was a failed State during the period of the Taliban militia's existence. A State has failed when centralized government authority has almost completely collapsed, no central authorities are capable of maintaining government institutions or ensuring law and order, and violence has destabilized civil society and the economy. A failed State will not satisfy some or all of the three tests for "statehood" under international law. (*TTP*, Memo 4, Part III, §B, ¶7, p.54)

On the Contrary, traditional legal analysis does *not* make clear that Afghanistan was a failed-state under Taliban rule, because traditional legal analysis includes consideration of customary international law notions, which are to be acquired by an examination of the opinions of classical jurists, philosophers, historians, and statesmen, according to which, there has already long existed a consensus position that a state does not cease to be a state simply because its ruling element backslides into tyranny or unmitigated violence. Grotius, for instance, chides Cicero as crude for not realizing that states abide even fundamental changes in the shape and character of a regime.

> Cicero, therefore, spoke too unpreparedly in *De Rep.* 3 in asserting that when a King becomes unjust, or when the nobles become so, or the People, there no longer exists a corrupt republic, but none at all. Augustine corrects Cicero's opinion in saying, "Neither shall I therefore affirm that a People is not a People, nor a State a State, so long as there remains the union of a rational multitude associated in a harmonious community for the things they love." A diseased body is still a body, and a State, however gravely ill, still a State, so long as there remain laws and judgments and all the other things necessary to ensure that foreigners no less that private citizens are able to enjoy rights among themselves. And it was Dio Chrysostomus who rightly said that law (especially the law of nations) exists in a State the way the mind exists in a human body, for, upon the removal of the law, a State no longer exists.[28] (*De Iure Belli ac Pacis Libri Tres,* book 3, ch. 3, §2.2)

The Taliban's utter refusal to ensure basic rights to its subjects made the *state* of Afghanistan "gravely ill" to be sure, but a state nonetheless. President Bush's ultimatum to the Taliban established a momentary state-to-state relationship between the United States and Afghanistan. The Taliban regime's intransigence in refusing to hand over members of al-Qaeda per the President's demand served as *just cause* for the commencement of U.S. military action to topple the regime. This being said, no President can both issue an ultimatum to the Taliban regime *and* refuse to recognize Afghanistan's statehood.

Statehood was removed from Afghanistan by the OLC weeks *after* the commencement of hostilities in South Asia. Had the President removed statehood from Afghanistan (as a failed entity) in the hours immediately after the attacks, he would have thereby also removed the crucial diplomatic mechanism of appealing to the Taliban leadership to hand over members of al-Qaeda. Afghanistan remained a state even under Taliban rule, as she continued to maintain a defined territory with a self-governed population that maintained formal relations with other states via the Taliban.

Position 13.—According to Deputy Assistant Yoo, the President remains free to suspend provisions of Geneva in the Afghanistan conflict, regardless of whether or not Afghanistan be considered a failed state.

> Even if Afghanistan under the Taliban were not deemed to have been a failed State, the President could still regard the Geneva Conventions as temporarily suspended during the current military action. As a constitutional matter, the President has the power to consider performance of some or all of the obligations of the United States under the Conventions suspended. [Note:] The suspension of a treaty is distinct from the denunciation or termination of one. Suspension is generally a milder measure than termination, often being partial, temporary, or contingent upon circumstances that can be altered by the actions of the parties to the treaty. Moreover, at least in the United States, suspension of a treaty can be reversed by unilateral executive action, whereas termination, which annuls a treaty, and which is therefore more disruptive of international relationships, would require Senate consent to a new treaty in order to be undone. (*TTP*, Memo 4, Part III, §E, ¶1, p. 64, and n. 81, pp. 65-66)

On the Contrary, (*a*) Geneva contains no provision recognizing the right of any High Contracting Party to temporarily *suspend* application of the Conventions vis-à-vis another High Contracting Party. Nor does Geneva recognize any distinction between a party's temporary *suspension* of the treaty versus a full and total *denunciation* of it, as if there were one article providing for suspension, and another for denunciation.

Article 142 of GPW allows High Contracting Parties to remove themselves from the treaty by denouncing the treaty at any time. But Article 142 lays down a lengthy one year delay *after* the Swiss Federal Council has been notified for denunciation to take effect. And, if notice to denounce is given while the denouncing power is involved in a conflict, the denunciation can not take effect until peace has been concluded *and* prisoners of war repatriated to their countries of origin. Yoo fabricates the existence of a suspension option to Geneva because he wants to create a portal out of the instrument, a way of wriggling out of the cumbersome requirements of Article 142.

Yoo correctly observes in footnote 81 that "a decision to regard the Geneva Conventions as suspended would not, of course, constitute a 'denunciation' of the Conventions, for which procedures are prescribed in the Conventions" (*TTP*, p. 65). Since no formal process for *suspending* Geneva is any-where stipulated in the text, it makes little sense to appeal, as does Yoo, to Article 60 of the Vienna Convention on the Law of Treaties (1969), which allows for "termination or suspension of the operation of a treaty *as a consequence of its breach.*" (Emphasis added.)

This article of the Vienna Convention—if it did apply to the present conflict—would apply only if Afghanistan could be proven to have committed grave breaches of Geneva against United States forces. Secondly, the Vienna Convention on the Law of Treaties is a distillation of norms and standards imported from customary international law, but, by Yoo's own admission, such norms must be placed outside the horizon of legal consideration due to the novel nature of the present conflict, since "importing customary international law notions concerning armed conflict would represent a direct infringement on the President's discretion as the Commander-in-Chief and Chief Executive to determine how best to conduct the Nation's military affairs."[29]

(*b*) Deputy Assistant Yoo does well to cite David Gray Adler's discussion of President Franklin D. Roosevelt's claims to heightened executive power to unilaterally terminate treaties in his termination of the London Naval Treaty of 1936, but fails to tell us of Adler's cautionary conclusion to the effect that

> there has been no predominant method of termination, or even a discernable trend. . . . The argument that an action, if repeated often enough, gains currency is representative of an "adaptive theory of constitutional interpretation that substitutes usage for constitutional mandates." This gloss-of-life contention has found frequent expression in the area of foreign affairs; the effect has been to create a presidential monopoly of foreign relations.[30]

(*c*) The administration's marginalization of positive treaty law sets a dangerous precedent, which, if accepted, means that a single individual occupying one office of state can alter existing federal law at will without being checked. We must now inform the nations and peoples of the world with whom we transact business or have treaty commitments that our Commander-in-Chief has unilateral authority to suspend any agreement or any provision thereof that he happens not to like on a temporary or indefinite basis, with respect to any party he chooses, and that this executive privilege of unilateral suspension cannot be checked, reversed, or altered by any other power of state.

Position 14.—Borrowing a page from the work of Professors Bradley and Goldsmith,[31] Yoo criticizes the so-called "modern position" established by both legal precedent and scholarship after *The Paquete Habana* that customary international law is part of United States federal law[32] by arguing that

> allowing customary international law to rise to the level of federal law would create severe distortions in the structure of the Constitution. Incorporation of customary international law directly into federal law would bypass the delicate procedures established by the Constitution for amending the Constitution or for enacting legislation. . . . In other words, customary international law has not undergone the difficult hurdles that stand before enactment of constitutional amendments, statutes, or treaties. (*TTP*, Memo 4, Part IV, §A, ¶3, p. 72)

On the Contrary, (*a*) customary international law (CIL) has indeed undergone several difficult judicial hurdles on its way to being incorprated as federal common law post-*Sabbatino*. Yoo wants to prevent so-called "activist judges" from freely interpreting customary international law in a way that recognizes natural human rights *in cases where positive statutes or treaties do not apply*. Neo-conservative legal philosophy does not want to bind the foreign policy of the President of the United States to norms and standards not specifically contained in any positive statute. But the Bush administration had seven years to implement this maverick philosophy, and it has led only to America's reckless estrangement from the international community.

(*b*) Given that CIL is only applicable in cases where positive laws do not apply, Yoo's contention that "severe distortions" in the Constitution would result from recognition of CIL norms is baseless. The Constitution even recognizes the currency of CIL, by delegating to Congress the power to define and punish offences against the law of nations (*Const*. Art. 1, §8, ¶10). But since CIL has never been interpreted by United States courts as *supplanting* existing federal law, it seems odd that Yoo would want to tie the hands of judges by preventing them from recognizing human rights in cases where positive laws are silent.

(*c*) Customary international law (the law of nations) has been traditionally seen as derivable from rights people have *by nature in virtue of their hu-*

manity, prior to and independent of their socio-economic position and political standing in the society in which they live. According to Grotius

> a natural right is a dictate of right reason, indicating for any act, from its agreement or disagreement with the rational and social nature of mankind, that it contains either a moral baseness or a moral necessity, and consequently that such an act is forbidden or commanded by God, the Author of nature.[33] (*De Jure Belli ac Pacis Libri Tres*, book 1, ch. 1, §10.1)

Customary international law, as viewed by Grotius, is grounded *a priori* on the existence of *natural* human rights, which give to it an importance in law *above* that of positive statutes. There exists overwhelming juridical precedent for the distinction between natural versus legal human rights, the very distinction whose existence and significance is called into question by the Bradley, Goldsmith, and Yoo rejection of customary international law as federal law.[34] Not only is their legal argument a smokescreen, given that ratified U.S. treaties are federal laws, and customary international law norms are written into the text of such positive instruments, but their philosophical position amounts to out-and-out nihilism, because, in denying the existence of a natural and objective basis for human rights, they say "no" to the existence of inherent natural value in all life, a value that exists even in the simplest creature, a value that ought to preclude reasonable persons from using coercion and torture to dehumanize perceived enemies.

The prevailing consensus position in the Western philosophical tradition recognizes that some rights exist *independently* of the structure or word of any positive human decree, so that, moral judgments asserting rights-claims can be true or false based upon the disposition of ambient naturalistic facts. Aristotle encapsulates this idea in distinguishing natural from legal political justice:

> Of political justice part is natural, part legal: Natural, that part which everywhere has the same force, and does not exist by people thinking this or that; legal, that part which is originally indifferent one way or the other, but when laid down, is not indifferent, e.g., that a prisoner's ransom shall be a mina, or that a goat is to be sacrificed, but not two sheep, as well as laws enacted on the grounds of particular circumstance, (e.g., that sacrifice be made in honor of Brasidas) and proposals passed in popular assemblies.[35] (*Nicomachean Ethics*, book 5, ch. 7, 1134b18-34; cf. *Magna Moralia*, book 1, ch. 33, 1194b30-1195a8)

According to Cicero, right (*jus*) and justice (*justitia*) originate primarily from nature, and only secondarily from written laws, cultural customs, and social norms, which establish *de facto* positive rights. If the judgments of men were always in accord with nature, then justice would be observed by all, i.e., unjust positive laws would simply not exist. Cicero also argued that law (*lex*) is not primarily the product of human thought, but of something eternal ruling the universe by its wisdom in command and prohibition.[36]

According to the celebrated Roman constitutional jurist Lucius Domitius Ulpianus all humans are free and autonomous *by nature*; but, by the customs and practices of peoples throughout the ages, there arose the institution of slavery,

> which institution took its origin from the right of nations, seeing that by the right of nature all were born free, and manumission was not yet known, since slavery itself was unknown. But afterwards slavery burst on the scene by the right of nations; then followed the benefit of manumission. And, while all of us were once called by one natural name "human," by the right of nations three classes of people came into existence: freemen, slaves, and freedmen who had ceased being slaves.[37] (*The Digest of Justinian,* first part, book 1, title 1, §4 (extract from Ulpian's *Institutes*)

These words mark a revolutionary statement at law: No slavery of any kind whatsoever is just or appropriate among humans, for by nature all persons are born free and autonomous *qua* human.

Thomas Aquinas even remarks that because humans are imperfect and prone to stray from the good, positive justice in the State is not always in sync with natural political justice.

> Were human nature always upright this requirement [that positive justice be in accord with natural political justice] would always have to be met. Yet since, as sometimes happens, it is wrong-willed, there are cases when a deposit should not be restored, lest a man make criminal use of it, as when one beside himself with rage or an enemy of State demands the immediate return of his weapons.[38] (*Summa Theolog.* II. II. q. 57, art. 2, obj. 1)

Aquinas points out that although *positive* justice may order one to return a deposit of weapons to the person to whom they are contractually owed, *natural* political justice may require that one withhold them from an individual out of his mind with rage.

(*d*) The activist "modern position" of incorporating customary international law notions into cases where positive laws are silent is actually a more staid and conservative interpretation of law than the neo-conservative abandonment of the customs and practices of nations. And there is ample precedent in United States case law for the legitimacy and standing of customary international law. The 1842 decision in *Swift v. Tyson* subsumed customary international law under general common law, applicable in both federal and state courts, but not exclusively federal in character.[39] General common law is customary law derived from the unwritten laws of England, and is "generally derived from principles rather than rules; it does not consist of absolute, fixed, and inflexible rules, but rather of broad and comprehensive principles based on justice, reason, and common sense."[40]

To begin with, §34 of the Judiciary Act of 1789 hands to the several states the power to determine rules of procedure in trials at common law in cases where the Constitution, treaties, or statutes of the United States do not strictly apply. The act set up a system whereby state and local courts could freely interpret both local *and* international customary law on a state-by-state basis.[41] But *Tyson* acknowledges that §34 of the act "does not extend to contracts or other instruments of a commercial nature, the true interpretation and effect whereof are to be sought not in the decisions of the local tribunals, *but in the general principles and doctrines of commercial jurisprudence.*" (Emphasis added.)[42] *Tyson* set up a system whereby both state and federal courts could freely interpret customary international law in cases where positive laws were silent.

The "modern position" of incorporating CIL as federal common law emerged from two cases decided on the same day. First, in *Erie Railroad Co. v. Tompkins*, 304 U.S. 64, 70 (1938) the court held that the liability of a railroad company for injury caused by negligent operation of its equipment depends "in the absence of a federal or State statute" upon the unwritten laws of the state wherein the accident occurred. Just as nations share customs in common, so each state in the Union recognizes its own local customs as common to that state. But Justice Brandeis was concerned only with unwritten state and local customs, not with international law, when he delivered the opinion of the court. According to Philip C. Jessup's take on *Erie*, "any question of applying [customary] international law in our courts involves the foreign relations of the United States and can thus be brought within a federal power."[43] And, as Jessup notes, this is indeed already the case according to *Const.*, Art 1, §8, ¶10 which grants Congress the power to define and punish offences against the law of nations." This stipulation clearly implies that powers of final arbitration in matters involving the application and interpretation of customary international law rests in federal, and not state or local, hands. "It would be as unsound as it would be unwise" says Jessup, "to make our state courts our ultimate authority for pronouncing the rules of international law."[44]

In the second case, *Hinderlider v. La Plata River & Cherry Creek Ditch Co.*, 304 U.S. 92, 110 (1938) Justice Brandeis concluded that the question whether the water of a stream must be apportioned between two states in contention for its resources is strictly a federal question "upon which neither the statutes nor decisions of either state can be conclusive." Both cases, thus, share the same fundamental ruling as *The Paquete Habana*, namely, that in cases where written statutes and treaties are silent, resort must be had to the principles of CIL universally accepted among civilized peoples. To reject these universally accepted standards of humanity out of hand as inapplicable in the war on terror, as Bush administration attorneys have done, is utterly unconscionable.

(*e*) Allowing customary international law "to rise to the level of federal law" could not possibly create distortions in the Constitution, since customary law is only to be applied to cases where written laws do not extend. In addition, the structure of the Constitution authorizes the recognition of customary international law in its reference to the "law of nations" in Article 1, §8, ¶10 which empowers Congress to construct tribunals whose task would be to assess and interpret the applicability of customary international law norms to criminal activity on the high seas and outside the territory of the United States.

(*f*) In addition, the validity and force of universal humanitarian restrictions implicit in customary international law principles was further reinforced in 1980 by Second Circuit Court of Appeals Judge Irving R. Kaufman, who reminds us, in an opinion delivered in *Filartiga v. Peña-Irala*, 630 F.2d 876, 878, that by passing the Judiciary Act of 1789 the First Congress established original federal jurisdiction over cases where an alien sues for tort committed in violation of the law of nations.[45] Judge Kaufman reversed the judgment of the district court that originally dismissed the complaint of Dolly and Joel Filartiga as not falling within federal jurisdiction. Kaufman held that, regardless of the nationalities of the parties involved, deliberate torture perpetrated "under color of official authority" violates universally accepted norms and principles of international human rights law

(*Id.*, 878). *Filartiga* supports the position that customary norms are admissible as legally binding standards of conduct for officials of foreign governments due to the fact that positive federal legislation enacted by the First Congress of the United States already provides that such norms carry force and weight in federal district courts for aliens seeking a remedy for tort committed in volation of the law of nations.

Position 15.—Having freed the President from the burden of recognizing customary international law norms, Deputy Assistant Yoo proceeds to undermine the binding force of ratified United States treaties.

> Even the inclusion of treaties in the Supremacy Clause does not render treaties automatically self-executing in federal court, not to mention self-executing against the executive branch. If even treaties that have undergone presidential signature and senatorial advice and consent can have no binding legal effect in the United States, then it certainly must be the case that a source of rules that never undergoes any process established by our Constitution cannot be law. (*TTP*, Memo 4, Part IV, §A, ¶3, p. 72)

On the Contrary, (*a*) Yoo's position that customary international norms "cannot be law" relies upon a fallacy of ambiguity in his use of the term "law." For his assertion to be correct, "law" must be solely confined to *statutes* to the exclusion of internationally accepted standards of behavior. While it certainly is the case, as Yoo correctly points out, that CIL is not *positive* law, this does not mean that CIL lacks legally binding force over the behavior of United States government officials, since

1. CIL applies only where positive laws do not extend, and, as previously mentioned,
2. CIL principles are often incorporated directly into the text of *positive* ratified treaties (e.g., GPW, Art. 142, ¶4) as well as non-ratified international desiderata—for instance, the Preamble to the Rome Statute of the International Criminal Court, which recognizes the fragile "common bonds" that link the world's cultures "together in a shared heritage" by claiming that customary international law norms are a kind of "delicate mosaic [that] may be shattered at any time."[46]

According to (1), customary international law does not trump positive statutory law, but merely fills in the cracks where statutes fail to extend. Under

(2), CIL principles have binding force because they lie embedded in the text of positive treaties, and are enjoined upon Congress as a body of rules to be applied in cases of international crimes tried before tribunals constituted by Congress (*Const.*, Art. 1, §8, ¶9).

(*b*) Yoo's assertion that treaties are *not* self-executing in federal court against the executive branch is entirely irrelevant because it misses the fact that there already exists a host of federal criminal statutes which give teeth to key provisions of ratified United States treaties, without excluding executive branch officials from prosecution for statutory violations.[47] For instance, Congress enacted 18 U.S.C. §2340-2340A to define and punish acts of torture in fulfillment of a provisional promise to carry out Part 2, Article 2 of the Convention Against Torture which requires each State Party to enact appropriate legislation "to give effect to the rights recognized in the present Covenant."

In addition, the War Crimes Act of 1996, 18 U.S.C. §2441(a) criminalizes with fines, imprisonment, or death, if death results to the victim, the commission of any war crime, defined under Subsection (c) as any conduct constituting a grave breach in the Geneva Conventions (as defined by GPW, Art. 130), or a violation of Geneva common Article 3, or conduct prohibited by Articles 23, 25, 27, or 28 of the Annex to the Hague Convention IV, respecting the laws and customs of war on land.

(*c*) The non-self-executing aspect of ratified U.S. treaties appears to be a smoke-screen concept, given that treaties become supreme law of the land merely by Senate ratification, *and* not all treaties (for instance, the Geneva Conventions) require additional domestic criminal legislation to have legally binding effect on the behavior of United States personnel. Yoo is correct to assert that treaties acquire their binding force *in U.S. courts* only once they are given teeth by accompanying federal criminal legislation; but even so, we have already amply demonstrated that there exist at least two federal statutes (see *Appendix H* and *I*) by which Congress has explicitly criminalized acts of torture and wanton cruelty committed in violation of Geneva, the CAT, and the Annex to the Hague Convention IV. The mere existence of these statutes renders superfluous Yoo's importation of the non-self-executing aspect of U.S. treaties.

Position 16.—Yoo quotes the opinion of Chief Justice John Marshall grossly out of context when he confidently claims, in *Brown v. United States*, 12 U.S. (8 Cranch) 110 (1814), that

> Justice Marshall . . . stated that customary international law "is a guide which the sovereign follows or abandons at his will. The rule, like other precepts of morality, of humanity, and even of wisdom, is addressed to the judgment of the sovereign; and although it cannot be disregarded by him without obloquy, yet it may be disregarded." [12 U.S., at 128.] In twenty-first century words, overriding customary international law may prove to be a bad idea, or be subject to criticism, but there is no doubt that the government has the power to do it. (*TTP*, Memo 4, Part IV, §A, ¶4, p. 73)

On the Contrary, (*a*) the full context of Justice Marshall's words as quoted from *Brown v. United States* clearly demonstrates that he is arguing only for executive discretion over questions of individual property confiscation in time of war, not executive discretion over whether or not to apply customary international law norms. The case concerns the President's right to confiscate British property on U.S. territory at the outset of the War of 1812. Since no federal provision stipulates what these rights might be, the *Brown* court applied customary international law norms to resolve the issue, and this involves investigating the opinions of jurists, statesmen, and historians.

Yoo quotes John Marshall as if he were saying that customary international law represents a standard of right that the sovereign of a nation follows or abandons at will. But this is grossly mistaken *and* out of context. The grammatical subject of Justice Marshall's half-sentence "is a guide which the sovereign follows or abandons at his will" is not, as Yoo suggests by his lead-in to the quotation, "customary international law," but rather "this usage," i.e., the particular usage of customary international law whereby the President would be allowed to confiscate enemy (British) property at will *so long as it is discovered within United States territory at the declaration or outset of war*.

On the same page of the *Brown* decision from which Yoo draws his quotation, Chief Justice Marshall unambiguously asserts that the President's wartime task as Commander-in-Chief is to *execute* the laws of war, and he may, if necessary, confiscate any property which according to the modern law of nations is subject to confiscation (*Brown v. United States*, 12 U.S., at 128). But if the law of nations does not permit some piece of property to be confiscated by executive order, Justice Marshall contends that a legislative act may be required "to justify the condemnation of . . . property which, *according to modern usage*, ought not to be confiscated" (Id., at 128, emphasis added). It is clear that Marshall intended for customary international law norms to be applied in cases where positive statutes do not extend; and that

Congress should intervene with legislative action to govern cases of property confiscation not normally allowed under the modern law of nations.

In a case decided a year later, *The Nereide*, 13 U.S. 388 (1815), Chief Justice Marshall reiterated his then long-held position that customary international law norms have the binding force of federal law in cases where there exists no contravening legislative act, executive order, or judicial precedent. In *The Nereide* the court recognized a long-standing rule of customary international law that the goods of an enemy found in the vessel of a friend may be held as prize of war while those of a friend found in the vessel of an enemy may be restored. The court held that this rule of customary law has been "fully and unequivocally recognized by the United States" (13 U.S., at 418, 419) and that, if Congress wants Spain to recognize reciprocal rules governing captures at sea, it must then pass an act for that purpose, so that, minus such an act, "the Court is bound by the law of nations *which is part of the law of the land*" (13 U.S., at 423, emphasis added). There is little doubt that the *Nereide* court recognized customary international law as part of federal common law.

In a case decided at the end of the nineteenth century, *The Paquete Habana*, 175 U.S. 677 (1900), the Court upheld customary international law as part of United States federal law. In writing the opinion of the court Justice Gray appears to have actually foreseen the future possible danger that the very words of Justice Marshall's opinion in *Brown v. United States* could easily be quoted out of context:

> In *Brown v. United States*, 8 Cranch 110, there are expressions of Chief Justice Marshall which, taken by themselves, might seem inconsistent with the position above maintained, of the duty of a prize court to take judicial notice of a rule of international law, established by the general usage of civilized nations, as to the kind of property subject to capture. But the actual decision in that case, and the leading reasons on which it was based, appear to us rather to confirm our position.[48]

Justice Gray is saying that Marshall's reasoning on the applicability of customary international law in *Brown v. United States* is not at all inconsistent with the position he wishes to establish in *The Paquete Habana*; namely, that precepts of customary international law ought to be construed as applicable United States law in just those cases where no legislative act, executive order, or judicial decision claims otherwise. All along the debate has been, not whether customary international law is to supplant existing federal law but whether it shall be recognized by United States government officials as binding in cases where positive statutes fail to reach.

(*b*) It was, in point of fact, terribly ill-advised for President Bush to abandon the precepts of humanity by disregarding the limits of customary international law over the capture and detention of enemy combatants in the war on terror for the sake of achieving a series of fleeting short-term foreign policy objectives in Afghanistan and Iraq. It simply serves no strategic purpose to coerce or torment captives of war taken from the field of combat and held as terrorists on suspicion. In fact, detaining these suspects incommunicado for years without charging them with any crime, while denying them access to legal counsel, not only proved to be a bad idea subject to international criticism, but it has eroded America's reputation in the international community as a steadfast defender of human rights, while compromising her ability to coordinate ongoing investigations with other nations around the world concerning the movements and plans of international terrorist groups.

As of November, 2009 there remain some 250 prisoners at the Guantánamo Bay prison facility, eighty of which are slated for release, with others waiting to have their cases litigated. President Obama is now beginning to consider fundamental changes to the military tribunal system established by his predecessor, including civilian trials in federal district courts. And while tens-of-thousands of American and coalition troops remain deployed in Iraq and Afghanistan, equally serious and immediate international terrorist threats are clustering in other parts of the world. Tens of thousands of al-Shabaab (the youth) Islamist militants, committed to an ideology of global jihadism, have arisen from relative political obscurity in less than two years to occupy much of Somalia. The domestic struggle for control of Somalia is part of al-Shabaab's broader global committment to exporting terrorism abroad with the ideological and material support of foreign fighters from Arab Gulf states who are recruiting and indoctrinating Somali youth on Somali soil.[49]

Position 17.—Deputy Assistant Yoo argues that constricting the President's decision-making power in the war on terror by importing customary international law norms into determinations of foreign policy would merely infringe upon his constitutional power as Chief Executive to ignore those norms at will, if he should deem it necessary to do so in prosecuting the global war on terror. Yoo claims that under the Constitution

> the President . . . is given plenary authority over the conduct of the Nation's foreign relations and over the use of the military. Importing customary international law notions concerning armed conflict would represent a direct infringement on the President's discretion as the Commander-in-Chief and Chief Executive to determine how best to conduct the Nation's military affairs. Presidents and courts have agreed that the President enjoys the fullest discretion permitted by the Constitution in commanding troops in the field. It is difficult to see what legal authority under our constitutional system would permit customary international law to restrict the exercise of the President's plenary power in this area. . . . [R]eading customary international law to be federal law would improperly inhibit the President's role as the representative of the Nation in its foreign relations. (*TTP*, Memo 4, Part IV, §A, ¶8, pp. 74-75)

On the Contrary, (*a*) Yoo's position on Presidential war power is logically self-refuting, since, as Hamilton once noted,

> the Executive is charged with the execution of all laws, the laws of Nations as well as the Municipal law, which recognises and adopts those laws. It is consequently bound, by faithfully executing the laws of neutrality, when that is the state of the Nation, to avoid giving a cause of war to foreign Powers.[50] (*Pacificus* No. 1, ¶34)

Hamilton is saying that customary laws are recognized and adopted in the text of positive municipal statutes. This means the *existence* of customary international law is no longer metaphysically problematic, when the text of positive treaties contains explicit reference to the customs and practices of nations. The recent neo-conservative mistrust of customary humanitarian law over the past three decades can no longer take as its basis the statutory non-existence of customary international law norms, since these norms are often incorporated directly into key provisions of U.S. treaties.

Second, Hamilton argues that President George Washington is bound not merely to execute extant federal law, but the customary laws of neutrality in the nation's foreign relations with Britain and France. Hamilton was genuinely concerned that rogue elements from the United States might accidentally ignite the spark of international conflict on the high seas, and was adamant in defending President Washington's executive power to unilaterally proclaim United States neutrality in June of 1793, even though deliberation over questions of war and peace rests with Congress, and so too, the power to officially declare the nation's neutrality or belligerency. Hamilton is clearly reading the Take Care clause of the Constitution (Art. 2, §3) as applying to positive statutes *and* customary international norms. If this reading is correct, then it becomes transparently self-contradictory for Yoo to argue for executive privilege in breaking the law, since the executive is the chief officer primarily charged with preserving and upholding the law.

(*b*) In addition to ratified U.S. treaties and accompanying federal criminal legislation another source of limitation on the President's decision-making power over the fate of detainees awaiting trial in the war on terror comes from the Inter-American Commission on Human Rights (IACHR), which issued, on March 12, 2002, a *Decision on Request for Precautionary Measures* regarding detainees held in U.S. custody at Guantánamo Bay, Cuba. The Inter-American Commission invoked the Martens clause (common to a number of long-standing humanitarian treaties including the Hague Conventions of 1899 and 1907 respecting the laws and customs of war on land) in order to assert that persons who happen to fall outside the protection of the treaty remain under the protection of the principles of the law of nations, "as they result from the usages established among civilized peoples, from the laws of humanity, and the dictates of the public conscience."[51]

Now, let us contrast the Inter-American Commission's plea for precautionary humanitarian restraint with Yoo's invocation of a previous OLC opinion from the Bush administration in 1989 which asserts that

> if the United States is to participate in the evolution of international law, the Executive must have the power to act inconsistently with international law where necessary. (13 Op. O.L.C., at 170)

On the contrary, the OLC's conditional statement here is false, because it is quite possible for the United States to participate in the evolution and growth of international law without necessarily breaking customary international norms of behavior to do so. Recorded standards of civilized human behavior have evolved for over five millennia. Construing violations of these standards as the moral equivalent of growing-pains is an unfortunate analogy that misses the fact that evolving civilized norms do not require law-breakers. Although some traditional institutions such as slavery have evolved, as human rights abuses, into unacceptable modes of behavior, it nevertheless remains true that breaking with customary international law almost always creates the precedent that breaking with international norms is increasingly acceptable in the civilized world.

Position 18.—In a somewhat bizarre conclusion Yoo maintains that

> although the President is not constitutionally bound by the customary laws of war, he can still choose to require the U.S. Armed Forces to obey them through the Uniform Code of Military Justice (UCMJ). Thus, our view that the customary international laws of armed conflict do not bind the President does not, in any way, compel the conclusion that members of the U.S. Armed Forces who commit acts that might be considered war crimes would be free from military justice. (*TTP*, Memo 4, Part IV, §C, ¶s 3 & 4, pp. 78-79)

On the Contrary, (*a*) while Yoo believes the President and his principals are immune from criminal prosecution for violations of federal law and free of the pesky encumbrances of customary international law, the military itself, the very instrument of counterterrorism policy, shall, in stark contrast to their civilian masters, be fully liable for any infractions of the Uniform Code of Military Justice in carrying out executive orders which themselves display no regard for the rule of law.

Arguments which attempt to establish executive privilege to break the law are terribly misplaced when juxtaposed with arguments that call for the prosecution of lower-ranking military personnel, who may have had little choice but to follow the misguided directives of Bush administration superiors.[52]

In fact §1004 of the Detainee Treatment Act (DTA) of 2005[53] protects United States government personnel engaged in authorized interrogations from criminal prosecution by recognizing that many of these officials may not have known in good faith that they were violating federal law in carrying out orders to implement the enhanced interrogation techniques approved by the Working Group Report on Detainee Interrogations in April of 2003.[54]

Subsection 1004(a) of the DTA provides that

> it shall be a defense that such officer, employee, member of the Armed Forces, or other agent did not know that the practices were unlawful and a person of ordinary sense and understanding would not know the practices were unlawful.[55]

Since the enhanced interrogation techniques approved for use in the Working Group Report of 2003 were kept classified until well after the Presidential election of 2004 with their publication in *The Torture Papers* in 2005, there may not have been adequate opportunity for government officials or academicians outside the administration to clarify the legality of the administration's orders for military and intelligence personnel charged with implementing them.

The OLC effectively places all legal liability for actions taken in the field on the shoulders of field commanders, and none at all on high officials charged with actualizing the administration's policy directives. This maldistribution of responsibility from the bottom up reveals the true leadership philosophy of the administration, which for a space of two presidential terms in office successfully created a superexecutive freed from all encumbrances of law, both customary and positive, in the prosecution of the war on terror, with the common soldier wholly liable for any criminal actions taken in the field.

(*b*) No President is immune from federal criminal prosecution for war crimes committed under the aegis of executive military orders. Under Section 2340A of the federal anti-torture statute,[56] for instance, no criminal immunity from prosecution exists for either the President, his immediate subordinates, or regular members of the U.S. Armed Forces for acts of torture committed pursuant to definitions stated in Subsection 2340(1). In addition, Subsection 2340A(c) establishes legal liability for *any person* who conspires to commit an act of torture as defined in Subsection 2340(1), the act itself being the object of the conspiracy.

Position 19.—Yoo's final words to General Counsel Haynes II are these:

> We conclude [1] that neither the federal War Crimes Act nor the Geneva Conventions would apply to the detention conditions in Guantánamo Bay, Cuba, or to trial by military commission of al-Qaeda or Taliban prisoners . . . [2] that customary international law has no binding legal effect on either the President or the military because it is not federal law, as recognized by the Constitution . . . [3] that the President, as Commander-in-Chief, has the constitutional authority to impose the customary laws of war on both the al-Qaeda and Taliban groups and the U.S. Armed Forces. (*TTP*, Memo 4, Conclusion, p. 79)

On the Contrary, (*a*) the federal War Crimes Act does not contain any clause allowing for executive immunity from prosecution for actions carried out by high United States government officials pursuant to executive orders. Nor is there any provision of Geneva that allows a High Contracting Party to temporarily suspend the humanitarian requirements regarding detention, trial, and punishment of detainees taken from the field in Afghanistan. In fact just the opposite is the case. The binding force of both instruments becomes stronger precisely in a time of war when political actors are most likely to find it in their immediate interest to stray from confining humanitarian legal requirements in order to conduct interrogations in pursuit of actionable intelligence.

The administration's presumptive determination of suspect Taliban and al-Qaeda fighters as "unlawful enemy combatants" in absence of any Article 5 hearing in no way impairs the applicability of Geneva or the War Crimes Act to the detention and trial before a military commission of persons held at Guantánamo Bay or at any other detention facility elsewhere in the world.

(*b*) It is both misleading and inaccurate to assert that customary international law has no binding legal effect on U.S. government officials due to the fact that it is not standing federal law, since the Constitution and the courts have for over two hundred and twenty years consistently recognized customary international law as federal common law. Common law is determined, not by this or that legislative enactment and statute, but by judicial precedent. United States federal courts have long recognized and applied rules of customary international law in dozens upon dozens of cases involving nation-to-nation transfers of property, prize of war cases, and expropriations of corporate assets by foreign governments in which the opinions of the great jurists such as Grotius, Pufendorf, and Vattel[57] are quoted at length by the Justices of the Court, not in order to ascertain what the law ought to be, but in order to discover what the law actually is.

(*c*) Strictly speaking, the President of the United States does not even have constitutional authority to "impose" customary laws of war on enemy combatants and U.S. Armed Forces, since, by *Const.*, Art. 1, §8, ¶s 9 & 10, it is Congress, and not the President, that is empowered to constitute tribunals inferior to the Supreme Court (including military tribunals), and to define and punish offences against the law of nations.

There also exists strong judicial precedent in *Madsen v. Kinsela*, 343 U.S. 341 (1952) establishing that

> *in the absence of attempts by Congress to limit the President's power,* it appears that, as Commander-in-Chief of the Army and Navy of the United States,

> he may, in time of war, establish and prescribe the jurisdiction and procedure of military commissions, and of tribunals in the nature of such commissions, in territory occupied by Armed Forces of the United States. (343 U.S., at 348, Justice Burton delivering the opinion of the Court, emphasis added)

Note that while this position allows the executive to craft wartime rules of procedure for trials conducted by military commissions in absence of congressional action, it does not allow him to abrogate the principles of law and rules of evidence normally in play in United States criminal courts.

Congress failed the American people after 9/11 by not asserting, from the beginning, its constitutionally mandated war power to establish military commissions in time of war and their rules of procedure; for, had it done so, there would have existed ample congressional oversight to ensure that both the customary laws of war and international protocol were adhered to by the President and his officials. As it turns out, the neo-conservative legal philosophy that established a detached Chief Executive of state operating in splendid isolation from Congress, the courts, and the people, armored with enhanced presidential war-making powers reaching well beyond constitutional bounds, actually exposed military and intelligence personnel to wrongdoing that might have easily been avoided had the President simply been willing to work constructively in concert with the very powers of state and international institutions he sought so ardently to subvert.

QUESTION FOUR

CAN THE PRESIDENT UNILATERALLY SUSPEND PROVISIONS OF GENEVA AGAINST THOSE SUSPECTED OF AL-QAEDA OR TALIBAN AFFILIATION, EVEN THOUGH NO ARTICLE 5 TRIBUNAL HAS EVER DETERMINED SUCH AFFILIATION?

The February 7 Executive Order

On February 7, 2002, President Bush issued an Executive Order regarding the humane treatment of al-Qaeda and Taliban detainees captured by United States and allied forces in South Central Asia in the war on terrorism. Far from applying the humanitarian provisions of the Geneva Conventions to the conflict in Afghanistan, as common Article 2 demands in *all* cases of partial or total occupation of the territory of a High Contracting Party, President Bush instead concluded that both

> (*a*) Taliban detainees are *not* protected by the humanitarian provisions of Geneva, as they are unlawful combatants who do not qualify as prisoners of war under GPW, Art. 4,[1] and
> (*b*) Al-Qaeda detainees do *not* qualify as prisoners of war, as al-Qaeda is not a High Contracting Party to Geneva.[2]

The fallacies transparent in these assertions stifle the imagination.

In (*a*) the President applies an article of Geneva to the conflict against the Taliban in order to demonstrate that none of the articles of Geneva apply to the conflict against the Taliban. It is not at all clear how anyone can apply an article of an instrument of law to a conflict where all of the articles of that instrument are presumed *not* to apply.

In (*b*) the President confuses part for whole by failing to distinguish a regime from the *state* in which it operates. A regime is part of a state. Two or more regimes may exist within a state at any given moment, but not vice versa. States abide changes in regime, even if such changes occur by violence, social discord, or total revolution. Furthermore, only states are High Contracting Parties to Geneva, yet it is regimes and their people, but not states, that are protected under the instrument.

The President's February 7, 2002, Executive Order is based, in part, on a series of false assurances given him by then-Attorney General John Ashcroft in a Department of Justice memorandum opinion dated February 1, 2002, in which Ashcroft claims that, in order to minimize "various legal risks of liability, litigation, and criminal prosecution" under the federal War Crimes Act of 1996 for military and intelligence personnel charged with the task of carrying out executive military orders, the President must choose between two competing theories in order to provide an official legal rationale for the administration's original premise that al-Qaeda and Taliban detainees do *not* count as prisoners of war.

According to Ashcroft, the President must officially conclude either (1) that Afghanistan was a "failed-state," so that Geneva's protections do not apply to the ongoing conflict in Afghanistan, or (2) that Afghanistan was a Party to Geneva, but that Taliban combatants are not entitled to GPW, Article 4 prisoner of war status because they acted as unlawful combatants.[3]

Ashcroft, however, should have known, and thus reflected in his legal advice to the President, that Prisoner of War status is not a matter to be decided once and for all by blanket executive decree, but (according to GPW, Art. 5, ¶2) on a strict case-by-case basis by means of competent tribunals steadfastly dedicated to implementing the principles of law and rules of evidence normally applicable in criminal cases.

Allow me to briefly set forth the following six objections to the February 7, 2002, Executive Order of President Bush regarding the humane treatment of al-Qaeda and Taliban detainees captured in the war on terror.

Objection 1.—The President boldly proclaims that the war against terrorism "ushers in a new paradigm" which "requires new thinking in the law of war."[4] But the plain truth is that no new paradigm was ever really introduced to the world as a result of al-Qaeda style terrorism, since radical paramilitary Islamist movements have for decades made use of unconventional and asymmetric means of warfare (e.g., car-bombs, hijackings, improvised mortar fire) to target innocent non-belligerents with random deadly violence in order to achieve some stated (or unstated) political, religious, or military objective. In addition, the practices of brigandage, piracy, and terrorism have been outlawed and roundly condemned as contrary to customary laws of war and to the very juridical traditions that President Bush claims need rethinking in this *new* era of counterterrorism.

Objection 2.—President Bush asserts by Executive Order that he has authority under the Constitution to suspend Geneva as between the United States and Afghanistan, but that he declines to exercise that authority at the present time.[5]

First, we have already seen that no President has constitutional authority to unilaterally suspend undesirable portions of ratified U.S. treaties, since ratification unequivocally makes a treaty supreme law of the land. The President has no more authority to suspend treaty requirements under Geneva than he does to suspend or abrogate other federal laws.

Second, if it really was the case that President Bush simply declined to exercise his constitutional authority to suspend Geneva during the conflict in Afghanistan, then why did he feel the need to emphasize his blanket determination of legal status for all captured Taliban suspects as "unlawful combatants" who "do not qualify as Prisoners of War under Article 4 of Geneva"?

The administration's reasoning ran something like this: The President decides to apply Geneva to the Taliban, but since all Taliban are predetermined by executive decree to be "unlawful combatants" in violation of the laws of war, they can not claim Prisoner of War status pursuant to the Conventions, and are therefore barred from reaping the rewards and benefits of humanitarian protection. But this reasoning is seriously flawed. Even criminals convicted of war crimes under competent tribunals receive full humanitarian treatment and protection, though they are housed in prisons after conviction, and may, in some contexts, face penalty of death according to a U.S. reservation to GCP Art. 68, ¶2 (1949).

In addition, even if President Bush had *constitutional* authority as Commander-in-Chief of the Armed Forces to suspend application of Geneva during the conflict in Afghanistan, he does not possess this authority by the words of the instrument. For, by GPW, Art. 142, ¶3 the United States can only denounce, i.e., withdraw entirely from, the Conventions.

Objection 3.—Although the President declines to suspend Geneva vis-à-vis the Taliban, after claiming he could do so if he wished, he then accepts the legal findings of attorneys at the OLC by claiming that he has now

> determine[d] that common Article 3 of Geneva does not apply to either al-Qaeda or Taliban detainees, because, among other reasons, the relevant conflicts are international in scope and common Article 3 applies only to "armed conflict not of an international character."[6]

But even if this assessment is correct and common Article 3 really does not apply to the conflict in Afghanistan (and, on some level at least, it arguably does not), common Articles 1 and 2 most assuredly do.

It is possible, as we have mentioned, that Geneva common Article 3 envisioned civil wars, interethnic conflicts, and internecine urban violence endemic to a particular region, e.g., Israeli-Palestinian border regions, Bosnia, Northern Ireland, the Sudan, etc., none of these regions of conflict originally involving *international* actors. But again, even if common Article 3 were magically removed from the picture, Article 3's prohibition against violence to life and person, the taking of hostages, outrages upon personal dignity, and the passing of sentences without a regularly constituted court would each still apply by means of other articles operative in the body of the instrument, since common Articles 1 and 2 effectively apply the same humanitarian protections to captives taken in the Afghanistan conflict.

By common Article 1 all High Contracting Parties to Geneva undertake to ensure respect for the Conventions in all circumstances. I read the phrase "in all circumstances" to include the unexpected circumstance of a post-9/11 counterterrorist war. If bin Laden were ever captured, Geneva allows the United States to give him an Article 5 hearing to determine his Prisoner of War status. The tribunal, having determined bin Laden to be a non-Prisoner of War, could then remand him to a criminal tribunal that could then find him guilty of war crimes. Upon a verdict of guilty, bin Laden could be sentenced to life in prison or to summary execution. And this entire process is perfectly legal for the United States under Geneva.

By common Article 2 Geneva applies to all cases of total or partial occupation of the territory of a High Contracting Party. Under this provision, since Afghanistan and Pakistan are both High Contracting Parties, the Conventions unambiguously apply to all United States activities and persons active in both countries for as long as they remain Parties to Geneva.

Objection 4.—In Subsection 2(d) of the February 7 Exective Order, President Bush asserts that neither the Taliban nor al-Qaeda qualify as Prisoners of War, but he lays down distinctly different reasons as to why this is so:

1. Members of the *Taliban* fail to qualify as POWs, because the President has already made the unilateral determination that they are all unlawful combatants.
2. Members of *al-Qaeda* fail to qualify as POWs, because Geneva does not apply to the conflict between the United States and al-Qaeda; al-Qaeda being a non-state actor, with Geneva only applicable between states.

Contrary to the President's reasoning in (1), the only authority any President has outside an Article 5 tribunal to determine that individual members of the Taliban are unlawful combatants is by appeal to customary international law norms contained in the opinions of jurists, who provide irrefragable evidence that brigands, pirates, and terrorists are criminals, but not *hostes*[7] in the traditional sense, since the tactics of all three fail to observe the laws and customs of war. But again, this rule of customary international law is only a legal concept that a military prosecutor might have used at trial in a regularly constituted court, and the Bush administration unhesitatingly declined to establish such proceedings for terror suspects.

The legal reasoning presented in (2) is flawed because Geneva actually does apply to the United States conflict with al-Qaeda, even though al-Qaeda is a non-state actor, an international terrorist organization, and not a High Contracting Party to Geneva. Suspected al-Qaeda members are protected by Geneva, since they operate in Afghanistan and Pakistan, and both states are High Contracting Parties to Geneva. Secondly, even if Geneva did not apply to members of al-Qaeda for the reasons outlined by the Bush administration, that fact alone would not preclude members of al-Qaeda from qualifying as POWs, since, by Geneva, all captives of war are to be presumed POWs until an Article 5 tribunal determines otherwise.

Article 5 tribunals establish a burden of proof on the detaining power to show criminal behavior in the accused. It must be proved in a criminal court that a captive of war violated, in some way, the laws and customs of war. And the mere fact of an individual's participation in a transnational terrorist training camp would qualify as illegal conduct according to such customs, and would serve as a basis for criminal conviction of the participant. Laying aside customary international law norms as outmoded in a presumably new age of global terrorism makes even less sense, when one realizes that from these customs derive the very legal concepts that military prosecutors will need to distinguish agents of terror in an unconventional war from lawful enemies.

Objection 5.—In Section 3 of the Order, President Bush acknowledges that the United States shares a set of "values" in common with the many nations of the world which call for humane treatment of all detainees in United States custody including those who the President claims "are not legally entitled to such treatment." Not realizing he lacks proper legal authority to render POW-status determinations, President Bush then hedges away from the all-inclusiveness of this statement, and qualifies it by adding that U.S. Armed Forces shall continue to treat detainees humanely and in a manner consistent with the principles of Geneva, but only "to the extent appropriate and consistent with military necessity."

First, the President lacks both constitutional and statutory authority to unilaterally render POW-status determinations. Consequently there exists no Presidential prerogative by which the executive may determine which captives would or would not be entitled to humane treatment.

Second, the text of GPW, Art. 17, ¶4, the International Covenant on Civil and Political Rights, Art. 7, and the Convention Against Torture, Art. 2, ¶2 are clear: No captive of war, regardless of his identity or the gravity of his offence, even amid a state of national emergency, is ever legally subject to cruel and inhumane treatment for any reason, even while serving out a criminal sentence handed down by a regularly constituted military tribunal. This means no torture, even if you believe your captive has information that could foil a live terrorist plot. If we torture, we abandon our foundational moral principles in a state of war by giving away to the enemy the very ground upon which we originally claimed to stand in self-defense. The President, therefore, lacks the *moral* authority to determine that any person be subjected to dehumanizing treatment, even for national security reasons.

(*a*) There is an ancient juridical term for that set of values shared in common by the many nations of the world which President Bush refers to in section 3 of his Order—namely, the *jus gentium*, the "right of nations," otherwise known as the "customary international law." But far from respecting these common norms of civility, the Bush administration Office of Legal Counsel, as we have seen, placed in suspension any CIL notions that should happen to directly infringe upon the President's discretion as Commander-in-Chief to determine how best to conduct the nation's military affairs in the war on terror.[8] But, by sidestepping these universal standards, the Office of Legal Counsel has utterly neutralized the moral force of the values we share in common with the civilized world at large.

(*b*) The President apparently never harbored any intention of guaranteeing al-Qaeda and Taliban suspects humane treatment in strict accordance with ratified United States treaties. President Bush simply brushed aside GPW, Art. 17, ¶4 standards that prohibit the use of physical or mental torture, or any other form of coercion in order to secure information. Stories of detainee mistreatment in the war on terror at the hands of United States officials abound in numerous print media reports. President Bush heedlessly ignored the humanitarian requirements contained in Article 7 of the International Covenant on Civil and Political Rights prohibiting cruel, inhuman, and degrading treatment of captives of war, and in Article 2, ¶2 of the Convention Against Torture which ensures that no exceptional circumstances whatsoever, "whether a state of war . . . or any other public emergency," may be invoked as a justification of torture.

Unfortunately, the Obama administration appears to be backpedalling from campaign promises of openness and transparency regarding America's detention policies. The administration appears content to continue the policy of dismissing or supressing claims of torture victimization made by those who suffered extraordinary rendition and detention during the Bush administration on the pretext of protecting sensitive intelligence pertaining to vital national security interests. A British court recently released secret intelligence concerning the capture and detention of one Binyam Mohamed, an Ethiopian-born British resident who was, during the Bush administration, according to a *New York Times* editorial dated February 15, 2010, subjected to physical and psychological abuse in Pakistan, Morocco, and a CIA-run prison outside of Kabul, before being sent to Guantánamo. He was released a year ago. And the Ninth Circuit Court of Appeals is currently weighing the Justice Department's recent attempt under President Obama to shut down a civil lawsuit filed by Mr. Mohamed and four others.

Objection 6.—The Bush administration's willingness to compromise Geneva by permitting the use of coercive interrogation techniques in order to gain potentially valuable intelligence information makes it all the more strange that President Bush would then demand (in Section 4 of his Order) that any future possible enemies who gain control of United States personnel be held "responsible for treating such personnel humanely and consistent with applicable law." How can one reasonably expect one's enemies to acknowledge the right to be treated humanely in captivity, if one refuses to guarantee this same basic right in return?

QUESTION FIVE

DO SPECIFIC INTENT AND NECESSITY DEFENSE ARGUMENTS JUSTIFY THE USE OF INTERROGATIONAL COERCION AND TORTURE IN THE WAR ON TERROR?

The Bybee-Gonzales Memo

On August 1, 2002, Assistant Attorney General Jay S. Bybee authored a memorandum opinion for then-White House Counsel Alberto R. Gonzales, exploring the legal dimensions of torture and coercive interrogation techniques for possible use on captives of war detained by United States forces in the global war on terror. The memo has drawn public scorn for Bybee's disturbingly cold conclusion that "under the current circumstances, necessity or self-defense may justify interrogation methods that might violate Section 2340A [of the federal anti-torture statute]."[1]

The Bybee-Gonzales "Torture" memo was quietly withdrawn by Bush administration officials in the run-up to the presidential election of November 2004 and replaced with a more guarded and carefully worded opinion authored by then-Acting Assistant Attorney General Daniel Levin on December 30, 2004, just one week before Judge Gonzales was set to testify before the Senate Judiciary Committee over his recent nomination for Attorney General to replace John Ashcroft.

The Levin-Comey Memo begins by robustly declaring that "torture is abhorrent both to American law and values and to international norms." Levin says this universal repudiation of torture is reflected in United States criminal law by 18 U.S.C. §§2340-2340A, the very sections of code Bybee attempted to jettison just two and a half years earlier as an unnecessary encumbrance on the President that might hamper his ability to prosecute the war on terror.

Levin-Comey displays a far more guarded and restrained legal strategy of backing away from Bybee's original attempt to define the precise meaning of "specific intent" under Section 2340(1) so as to ascertain some theoretical point where interrogation of a detainee becomes "torture" in the strict sense. "In light of the President's directive that the United States not engage in torture," argues Levin, "it would not be appropriate to rely on parsing the specific intent element of the [anti-torture] statute to approve as lawful conduct that might otherwise amount to torture."[2]

It would appear under Levin-Comey that the Bush administration no longer needs to narrowly define the concept of torture or hairsplit the meaning of "specific intent" under the anti-torture statute, since torture is no longer utilized in the war on terror as a matter of official policy. But appearances can be deceiving.

If we read the fine print of Levin-Comey at footnote 8, we find Daniel Levin carefully changing the tenor and mood of his language with the claim that his new memorandum opinion on torture is not really any different from "this Office's prior opinions addressing issues involving treatment of detainees."[3] In other words, the Levin-Comey Memo is *not* to be read as a bellwether change in administration policy on the use of coercive interrogation techniques and torture, because (by footnote 8) previous Bush II OLC memoranda continue to define administration policy on the subject.

Thus Levin-Comey never really altered, nor intended to alter, the administration's status quo ante position of approving and legitimizing the use of coercive interrogation methods in the "New Paradigm" context when dealing with captives suspected of involvement with international terrorism, who might hold potentially valuable information relating to future possible terrorist plots to kill civilians, a policy both brash and bold, but foolhardy and heedless of the law, given that torture is not a reliable method for extracting sensitive intelligence information, and that the United Nations Convention Against Torture (CAT) contains specific language in Article 2, ¶2 to the effect that *no exceptional circumstances whatsoever* shall be invoked by any State Party as justification for torture.

In addition, Congress enacted the anti-torture statute, 18 U.S.C. §§2340-2340A, so as to carry out United States treaty obligations pursuant to the CAT, Art. 2, ¶1 requirement that each State Party take effective legislative, administrative, or judicial measures to prevent acts of torture "in any territory under its jurisdiction." Section 2340(1) defines "torture" as

> an act committed by a person acting under the color of law specifically intended to inflict severe physical or mental pain or suffering (other than pain or suffering incidental to lawful sanctions) upon another person within his custody or physical control.

The statute envisions the grim possibility that officials at some point in the future might administer torture while acting "under the color of law" by providing themselves legal cover or justification for breaking the statute. In his original memorandum opinion to Judge Gonzales, Jay Bybee undertakes to water down the legal definitions of "specific intent" and "severe physical or mental pain" in such a way as to bestow Department of Justice legitimacy to virtually any list of interrogational methods the Defense Department might devise for use on terror suspects. Just such a list was published on April 4, 2003, in the Pentagon's Working Group Report on Detainee Interrogations.

Subsection VIII, ¶1 of the Working Group Report recommends and approves for use enhanced interrogation techniques (numbered 27 to 34: isolation, the use of prolonged interrogations, forced grooming, prolonged standing [in stress positions], sleep deprivation, physical training, face or stomach slap, removal of clothing, increase anxiety by use of aversions), but only on condition that

> 1. There exists a good basis to believe the detainee possesses critical intelligence,
> 2. The detainee has been medically and operationally evaluated as a suitable candidate for interrogation, considering all techniques to be used in combination,
> 3. Interrogators have been specifically trained for the techniques they use,
> 4. A specific interrogation plan is developed, which must include reasonable safeguards, limits on duration, intervals between applications, termination criteria and the presence or availability of qualified medical personnel,
> 5. Immediate supervision is provided, and
> 6. Specified senior level approval has been given for the use of specific interrogation techniques to be used on specific detainees on a case-by-case basis. (*TTP*, Memo 26, p. 347)

Guarded and professional as these Pentagon restrictions may sound, they do not change the fact that the methods they justify inflict gratuitous physical and emotional pain and suffering upon persons detained in United States custody, a clear violation of GPW, Art. 17, ¶4.

The list of interrogation methods approved for use in the Working Group Report presupposes the interrogators involved are generally well-trained in psychology, know the limits of human physiology, and take all the necessary medical precautions, while getting senior level clearance on a case-by-case basis, in order to administer a specific menu of interrogation techniques designed to achieve a specific set of results.

What the report does not say, however, is that these methods are straightforwardly designed to "break" the detainee both physically and psychologically, by deliberately robbing him of his will to resist, and of his sense of place and dignity.

It is misleadingly euphemistic for the report to label these treatment options "interrogation techniques," since prolonged isolation, sleep deprivation, forced grooming, removal of clothing, and the use of aversions to increase anxiety in the detainee are techniques to be used *outside* the interrogation chamber. These techniques appear to be aimed more toward gratuitous cruelty than toward gleaning useful intelligence information.

Now, since acts of terrorism are criminal acts, it only makes sense to pursue an international law enforcement investigation in order to nab future possible terrorists. No one who understands international law would disagree with this, yet neo-conservative politicians and pundits in America style terrorist attacks unexceptionally as "acts of war" following President Bush, but fail to understand that war (*bellum*, πόλεμος) defines a *symmetric* relation between two or more states or regimes, while acts of piracy, terrorism, and brigandage, insofar as they are committed by bands of roaming banditti, are nothing short of criminal acts. Acts of war may be legal and justifiable (as in the case of national self-defense), but nothing justifies terrorism. And while traditional law enforcement interrogations are conducted *after* an offence has occurred, the enhanced interrogation techniques proposed by the Working Group Report and defended as legal in Bybee-Gonzales are ones to be administered *before* and *in anticipation of* a merely possible offence.

Police interrogation of a murder suspect, for instance, is warranted by the collection of physical evidence pointing to a possible culprit along with the fact that an offence has been committed. But the coercive interrogations approved by White House and Pentagon officials in early 2003 are warranted by a merely possible offence, and possible offences (however grave) are not ones for which coercive interrogation is justified on any level by United States officials. If we allow creeping suspicions to justify coercive interrogations, why restrict ourselves to preventing sporadic acts of international terrorism, when we can, by application of the same techniques, presumably also prevent equally horrific acts of grizzly murder, rape, rapine, plunder, and mutilation before they are set to occur?

Proponents of harsh interrogations use the ticking-bomb scenario to justify the distribution of pain upon suspected terrorists in order to gather vital pieces of intelligence information held in secret. Authorities believe a large bomb, for instance, has been planted somewhere in a highly populous metropolitan nerve center, and the only way to locate it and disarm it is to use coercive interrogation techniques (including torture) on the one suspect whom we have reason to believe is secreting some vital piece of information that, if made known, would allow authorities to prevent the bomb from imminent detonation. The problem with the ticking-bomb analysis, however, is that the terrorist who supposedly planted the device has not yet actually committed any crime, but is merely suspected of being about to allow a crime to unfold. Coercive interrogation and torture of a suspect in this scenario is never warranted under principles of law, because the *mens rea* and *actus reus* do not yet exist, even though the time-sensitive nature of our moral dilemma imports urgency to the case. It is not a crime to be *suspected* of knowing too much about a crime that has not materialized.

The ticking-bomb scenario is extremely rare. The question over whether or not to use torture is more likely to arise in cases where a long-time high-value international terrorist kingpin is captured and detained in some undisclosed location. Proponents here must demonstrate that torture and coercion are both a necessary and a more effective means for extracting truth than other methods of interrogation. And, even if torture could be demonstrated to be a more effective means to the truth in some one particular case, there is always the chance our suspect could turn out to be relatively useless as a source of real-time logistical knowledge of future possible terrorist plots, and that torturing him was, therefore, not really necessary, even though he may have revealed information that was marginally useful to investigators.

It would have been more consistent with Geneva for the Pentagon to have borrowed the interrogation strategies developed by police and law enforcement experts such as Detective Jerry Giorgio, the legendary New York City Police Department interrogator. Giorgio's strategy has always been to become cooperatively familiar with the interrogee, using no physical or mental coercion, but rather outguessing and anticipating the interrogee's next move under questioning, in order to make him admit something he did not originally want to admit.[4] The menu of interrogation techniques approved for use in the Working Group Report, however, establishes antipathy by exploiting the interrogee's phobias and weaknesses against him.

The Working Group Report unfortunately neither defines what is specifically required in order for an interrogator to have a "good basis to believe" that a detainee possesses critical intelligence information, nor accounts for the paradox that intelligence information extracted by coercion is actually *less* likely to lead to the capture and trial of international terrorists than information gleaned by non-coercive law enforcement methods.

Information gleaned from a suspect by coercion is just as likely to produce false leads and misdirection as it is to reveal the truth, because coerced information only increases the interrogator's *basis to believe* that the interrogee and/or other detainees hold valuable intelligence, but does not reliably lead to the capture of terrorists. The rapid accumulation of unreliable intelligence only makes it more difficult for investigators to focus their limited resources. And Bybee-Gonzales never raises the possibility that a program of coercive interrogation might actually run the risk of clogging investigative channels with false and misleading information.

Objections to Positions Held in Bybee-Gonzales

Position 1.—Assistant Attorney General Bybee states the overall purpose of his memorandum opinion for Judge Gonzales by asserting that

> we [at the Office of Legal Counsel] conclude . . . that Section 2340A proscribes acts inflicting, and that are specifically intended to inflict, severe pain or suffering, whether mental or physical. [But] those acts must be of an extreme nature to rise to the level of torture within the meaning of Section 2340A and the Convention [Against Torture]. We further conclude that certain acts may be cruel, inhuman, or degrading, but still not produce pain and suffering of the requisite intensity to fall within 2340A's proscription against torture. We conclude by examining possible defenses that would negate any claim that certain interrogation methods violate the statute. . . . We conclude that for an act to constitute torture as defined in Section 2340, it must inflict pain that is difficult to endure. (*TTP*, Memo 14, Introd., ¶1, p. 172)

On the Contrary, (*a*) it is not the case, as Bybee asserts, that acts inflicting severe pain and suffering must also possess the additional quality of being "of an extreme nature" in order to rise to the level of torture within the meaning of Section 2340A, since it is transparently obvious from the definition of "torture" contained in Subsection 2340(1) that nothing in addition to the infliction of severe physical or mental pain is required for an act to constitute torture. By raising the level of physical and psychological pain required before an interrogation process becomes statutory torture under 2340(1), Bybee opens the way for the use of more aggressive techniques that allow interrogators unprecedented access into the mental and physical space of the detainee.

The use of more aggressive interrogation techniques was indeed requested in a memo to General James T. Hill, Commander, Joint Task Force 170 by Staff Judge Advocate, Lt. Col. Diane Beaver in October of 2002 to combat intransigent detainees held at the base whom Beaver described as tenaciously resisting the interrogation methods then in use by interrogation officials at the base. Lt. Col. Beaver grounded her request upon a failed piece of legal reasoning borrowed directly from the Yoo-Haynes II and Bybee-Gonzales opinions that detainees held in United States custody do not have legal standing as Enemy Prisoners of War (EPW), and that the Geneva Conventions limitations that would ordinarily govern the interrogation process of captured enemy personnel are not binding on United States officials conducting interrogations of detainees held at the base.

The Pentagon's Working Group Report of April 2003 eventually approved a specific list of enhanced interrogation techniques. This list was borrowed directly from the list of techniques commonly deployed by the Israeli General Security Services (GSS) prior to a watershed Israeli Supreme Court ruling in 1999 prohibiting the use of torture and other cruel, inhuman, or degrading treatment during the interrogation process.[5]

In *The Public Committee Against Torture in Israel v. The State of Israel*, 53(4) *PD* 817 (1999), the Israeli Supreme Court held that GSS agents did not have authority to employ certain methods of interrogation challenged by petitioners claiming interrogational victimization. But the court also held that the "necessity defense" found in Israeli Penal Law could serve to allow GSS to employ these same interrogation practices *ex ante* (that is, based upon unpredictable dangers that might lie ahead).[6] The court did not rule out the possibility that the "necessity defense" would also be available *post factum* to GSS in the event that criminal charges were brought against them.

In 1987, twelve years prior to the ruling, and in direct response to an upsurge in acts of terrorism throughout Israel, the West Bank, and Gaza sparked by a massive Palestinian Arab uprising known as the *intifada*, a commission, headed by Israeli Supreme Court justice Moshe Landau, issued a report effectively allowing GSS to use "moderate physical pressure" and "nonviolent psychological pressure" in interrogating prisoners suspected of having information that could prevent a terrorist attack.

The findings of the Landau Commission opened a Pandora's box for GSS interrogators to use the so-called "ticking-bomb" scenario as a catch-all category to excuse cruel and degrading treatment of detainees. It even became routine practice, not long after the Landau Commission issued its report in 1987, for GSS to apply harsh and coercive interrogation techniques well in excess of GPW, Article 17, ¶4 prohibitions. GSS relied so heavily upon the use of coercive methods that more than two-thirds of Palestinians taken into custody (during the First Intifada) were subject to highly coercive methods of interrogation.[7]

(*b*) Bybee's contention that acts of interrogational coercion must be of an "extreme nature" to rise to the level of torture within the meaning of Section 2340A sets a dangerous precedent at the Department of Justice because it ignores the highly infectious nature of cruelty in man. In 1971, for instance, researchers in the Department of Psychology at Stanford University conducted a two-week experiment where they randomly assigned 24 students to serve as either prison guards or inmates in the basement cells of the campus psychology building. Within days, reports John Schwartz,

> the "guards" had grown swaggering and sadistic, to the point of placing bags over the prisoners' heads, forcing them to strip naked and encouraging them to perform sexual acts."[8]

Things grew so out of control in the basement chambers of the psychology building at Stanford that Professor Philip Zimbardo had to shut down the experiment more than a week earlier than planned. The Stanford University prison experiment was extraordinary: It proved that giving guards total power over the physical and mental space of inmates only awakened inward and deeply repressed impulses to sadism and cruelty against the helpless in subjects not normally prone to violent or destructive behavior.

Situations of group domination over the helpless can bring out the worst in people, who, operating within their own social mores, would not normally be inclined to engage in sadistic or extreme behavior. A groupthink mentality empowers the individual to do things he would never dream of doing by removing his sense of shame while re-aligning his core values with those of the group.

The group elevates the individual beyond himself, instilling in him a sense of personal superiority and supremacy over others outside the group nexus, freeing him of awkward and limiting social barriers, rendering him unaccountable to any higher authority.

According to a study published in the fall of 2000 by Law Professor Mordechai Kremnitzer and Researcher Re'em Segev of Hebrew University of Jerusalem, the principal interrogation methods used by the GSS on Palestinians suspected of involvement with terrorism included

> arrest and detention of the interrogee in isolation from the outside world for prolonged periods—the length of which was unknown to the interrogee—in harsh conditions; sleep deprivation, sometimes almost total deprivation, for days; shackling the interrogee in painful positions for long periods, usually with his head covered with a filthy, opaque sack which makes breathing difficult, and with loud music playing non-stop over loudspeakers; beating, including shaking the interrogee back and forth; and making threats relating to the interrogee and his family.[9]

Each of these interrogation methods may appear innocuous at first sight. Who, after all, has not been subjected at some point in life to a neighbor's loud music well into the night? or suffered some loss of sleep? or stood in a painful position once or twice for an hour or two in line? But, when used as an instrument to break the will and spirit of an interrogee, they become cruel, unusual, inhuman, and degrading. Prolonged indefinitely these simple methods may easily become torture, since *by means of them* the interrogee becomes completely divorced from any sense of self, place, time, and context, helpless at the mercy of his interrogators, quivering at the uncertainty of his fate, incapable of discerning truth from falsehood, hope from fear, salvation from imminent pain and possible death.

(*c*) Jay Bybee ought to have at least acknowledged the Israeli Supreme Court's bold assertion in *Public Committee* (1999) that "a reasonable interrogation is necessarily one free of torture, cruel or inhuman treatment of the subject and free of any degrading handling whatsoever" (HCJ 5100/94, at §23, ¶2). The people of Israel have suffered repeated terrorist attacks over the past decades, and no nation-state is more aware of the strategic need to gather vital intelligence information. Yet Bybee neglectes the Court's central contention:

> Human dignity includes the dignity of the suspect being interrogated. . . . This conclusion is in accord with international law treaties—to which Israel is a signatory—which prohibit the use of torture, cruel, inhuman treatment and degrading treatment. . . . These prohibitions are "absolute." There are no exceptions to them and there is no room for balancing. (HCJ 5100/94, at §23, ¶2)

Let us contrast the Court's prohibition of torture with its endorsement for the use of so-called "sophisticated techniques" which it says are "accepted in the most progressive of societies" and its final claim that "the legality of an investigation [into possible terrorist acts] is deduced from the propriety of its purpose and from its methods" (HCJ 5100/94, at §23, ¶3). According to this reasoning, the Court concludes that the method of sleep deprivation (i.e., deliberately keeping the interrogee awake and alert) for a "prolonged period" is allowed, but "at night when [sleep deprivation] is not necessary to the investigation time-wise, [it] may be deemed disproportionate" (HCJ 5100/94, at §23, ¶3).

(*d*) Even if we accept Bybee's interpretation that cruel and inhuman acts causative of severe physical or mental pain in a detainee during an interrogation process do not constitute torture under Section 2340A, unless these acts be also of an extreme nature, it misses the fact that Article 16 of the CAT already reserves the same menu of rights (spelled out in Articles 10, 11, 12, and 13) for victims of cruel and inhuman treatment, as it does for victims of torture. For instance, Article 13 of the CAT guarantees victims of torture "a prompt and impartial investigation" by competent state authorities, but, by Article 16, this same right holds also for any victim of cruel, inhuman or degrading treatment or punishment. Bybee, therefore, interprets Section 2340A as allowing for extensive levels of cruelty manifestly forbidden under Article 16 of the CAT.

(*e*) Interpreting federal statute §2340(1) in such a way as to place military and intelligence officials in jeopardy of violating several key provisions of ratified United States treaties represents especially unwise counsel on the part of Bybee-Gonzales, since it places these same officials in additional violation of customary international law norms. According to Hugo Grotius, honor demands that every Sovereign strive to preserve his treaties, even after suffering grievous injury at the hands of his treaty partners:

> It is the part of a generous soul to stand firm to his treaties made, even after injuries received, for which reason a wise Indian by the name of Jarchas once praised the king, who, having suffered injury at the hands of his neighboring treaty partner, "would not break faith given under oath, saying that he had sworn quite solemnly that he would not inflict injury upon his neighbor, even after receiving an injury from him."[10] (*De Jure Belli ac Pacis Libri Tres*, book 3, ch. 19, §19.4)

(*f*) Even if Bybee were correct in his assessment that so long as cruel and inhuman methods of interrogation fall short of being extreme in nature they do not constitute torture under Section 2340A, nevertheless, customary international law already openly forbids cruel, inhuman, and degrading treatment of any kind whatsoever (whether extreme or not) on captives of war. Grotius, for instance, quotes several authorities on this score.

> May the opinion of Augustine be added here: "In a fight one ought to kill an enemy only out of necessity, and unwillingly. For just as violence may be returned against armed resistance, so clemency is due the captive and the vanquished, especially where there is no fear of disturbing the peace." Xenophon says of Agesilaus that "he ordered his soldiers not to punish captives of war as criminals, but to watch over them as human beings." In the work of Diodorus Siculus there is this line: "All Greeks fought off the belligerent, but spared the vanquished." The same author tells of the Macedonians, who, under Alexander "conducted themselves more harshly toward the Thebans than the law of war allows."[11] (*De Jure Belli ac Pacis Libri Tres*, book 3, ch. 11, §13.1)

It is plain to see that minimal standards of decency are traditionally expected from civilized nations at war. There simply was no political advantage to Bybee's redefining the anti-torture statute in such a way as to allow cruel, inhuman, and degrading treatment of captives of war in U.S. custody.

It must also be borne in mind—and this is paramount—that Bybee's revised legal definition of "torture" became *the* official Bush administration definition, so that, when administration officials, including the President, publicly denied ever using torture on captives, they meant "torture" as Bybee specifically defines it, not as defined by Article 1, ¶1 of the Convention Against Torture.

There are two problems plaguing necessity defense arguments justificatory of torture and other coercive interrogation techniques.

First, if the necessity defense were ever written into federal legislation permitting the use of interrogational coercion and torture against suspected terrorists inside or outside the United States, then similar necessity defense arguments could easily be advanced to justify the coercion of suspected child rapists, serial murderers, mutilators, repeat sex-offenders, heroin dealers, pornographers, and newspaper editors who advance highly controversial political opinions that might jeopardize the President's ability to defend the United States against foreign dangers, since each of these enumerated types of behavior present society with a host of dangers arguably both imminent and deadly, and which, on the Bush II OLC philosophy, *must* be prevented straightaway in order to save lives.

Although no specific necessity defense statute exists in United States federal law, it does exist in Section 34(1) of the Israeli Penal Law (1977), according to which

> a person will not bear criminal liability for committing any act immediately necessary for the purpose of saving the life, liberty, body or property, of either himself or his fellow person, from substantial danger of serious harm, in response to particular circumstances during a specific time, and absent alternative means for avoiding the harm.

This provision of the Penal Law was used by the state of Israel in defense of GSS interrogators against charges of criminal behavior brought by petitioners represented by The Public Committee Against Torture in Israel in 1999. The necessity defense argument underlying the Israeli statute is only as strong as the certainty GSS investigators have at any given moment that their target suspect (as opposed to others) has the precise information needed to forestall an imminent deadly danger. But this certainty itself may have arisen from information extracted by coercive maltreatment.

The second problem facing the necessity defense argument is this: Torture is generally not a reliable method for acquiring actionable intelligence. Even assuming that interrogators could somehow arrive at a reasonable certainty that a ticking-bomb is set to explode in a populous area but for the interrogee's valuable last-minute input; even assuming that such a device will explode, if no interrogation is conducted, there is no guarantee at all that *coercive* interrogation so harsh as to involve torture would even work in extracting the correct information in time. The bomb is ticking away in the original scenario, so time is scarce. Do we have a week? a day? an hour? a few minutes? If you inflict severe pain now, there is no guarantee that the interrogee will tell you anything valuable. His instinctual animal reaction, in point of fact, will be to thwart your every attempt to get at the needed information. It is far more likely that he will tell you anything he believes will make the torturing stop.

Necessity defense arguments require us to postulate far too many background assumptions about the mental state of our interrogee, the complexity of his suppressed information, and the inevitability of the danger at issue for us to justify this illegal free-fall into torture.

In every hypothetical necessity defense scenario it seems we must presuppose as indubitably true that 1. the danger at issue is imminent and deadly; 2. the danger will materialize, if interrogators do not acquire the information needed to forestall it; 3. we have in custody just such a person, who has precise information that would, if made know, allow us to prevent the danger from materializing; and 4. this individual is secreting the information as we speak; but 5. refuses to divulge it to us, so that; 6. acquiring this information is now necessary in order to save innocent lives from a ticking bomb that is 7. set to detonate at any moment, and that, therefore, 8. methods of torture and other coercive interrogation techniques may be used in order to glean the needed information from the interrogee in time to make use of it, because, after all, 9. the use of mental and/or physical torture will most certainly work on this particular man of this particular build and physiology. Why, indeed, we have a team of trained medical professionals ready on hand to assist us should the interrogee suddenly leap into cardiac arrest during interrogation. Should we proceed with coercive interrogation at this point? If yes, then what moral or legal reasoning would stop us from expanding these same techniques of cruelty to persons suspected of heinous crimes other than international terrorism?

***Position** 2.*—Borrowing sporadically from statutes defining an emergency medical condition[12] for purposes of distinguishing between various levels of mental and physical pain, Bybee contends that

> physical pain amounting to torture must be equivalent in intensity to the pain accompanying serious physical injury, such as organ failure, impairment of bodily function, or even death. For purely mental pain or suffering to amount to torture under Section 2340, it must result in significant psychological harm of significant duration, e.g., lasting for months or even years. We conclude that the mental harm also must result from one of the predicate acts listed in the statute, namely: threats of imminent death;

> threats of infliction of the kind of pain that would amount to physical torture; infliction of such physical pain as a means of psychological torture; use of drugs or other procedures designed to deeply disrupt the senses, or fundamentally alter an individual's personality. . . . We conclude that the statute, taken as a whole, makes plain that it prohibits only extreme acts. . . . We conclude that the . . . text [of the CAT] prohibits only the most extreme acts by reserving criminal penalties solely for torture and declining to require such penalties for "cruel, inhuman, or degrading treatment or punishment." This confirms our view that the criminal statute penalizes only the most egregious conduct. (*TTP*, Memo 14, Introd., ¶s 2-3, p. 172)

On the Contrary, (*a*) although it is true, as Bybee points out, that Article 4, ¶1 of the CAT requires States Parties to criminalize acts of torture, but not acts of a cruel, inhuman, or degrading nature, this does not imply that the CAT fails to prohibit acts of a merely cruel or inhuman nature; for Article 16 seeks to ban both torture as well as acts of cruel and inhuman treatment. Reading Article 16 into the structure of Article 12, for instance, means that States Parties must conduct an impartial criminal investigation whenever there is reasonable ground to believe that acts of a cruel, inhuman, or degrading nature have been committed in any territory under its jurisdiction. Article 16 exists precisely because there is a legal gray area between cruelty and acts of torture *per se,* and States Parties wanted to ensure that a technical difference between the two would not be used as legal cover for those who may have committed acts of cruelty arguably less severe than torture.

(*b*) By defining mental torture as psychological harm of significant duration "lasting for months or even years" Bybee makes it virtually impossible for courts of law to *verify* actual cases of psychological torture at trial. If cases of abuse cannot be tried because it takes several years to document the negative side effects of psychological torture, interrogators are placed beyond the law. It is well known that American pilots shot down over North Korea during the Korean War (1950-1953) faced capture, imprisonment, humiliation, and torture for alleged war crimes. These pilots were exposed to prolonged psychological trauma and physical stress lasting for months, sometimes years, with negative side effects lasting a lifetime. The psychological damage caused by torture is invisible, inward, and hidden, so that requiring a victim of torture to undergo years of debilitating loss before charges can be filed in a court of law against some distant perpetrator makes little sense, unless Bybee sought to immunize U.S. officials from prosecution for federal crimes under Section 2340A.

(*c*) By defining physical torture as involving only the most extreme pain and suffering, equivalent in intensity to the pain accompanying serious physical injury such as organ failure, impairment of bodily function, or even death, Bybee legitimizes the implementation of interrogational techniques of exquisite cruelty. An interrogee must now be so harshly treated as to arrive at the threshold of death or complete organ failure during an interrogation process before the treatment doled out to him rises to the level of "torture" on Bybee's reading of Section 2340(1).

Using statutes defining an emergency medical condition for the purpose of defining health benefits for ailing patients, Bybee defines "severe pain" so narrowly that the interrogee must essentially die in United States custody, or go into cardiac arrest or seizure during interrogation, for any coercive methods used against him to count as torture under 2340(1). If the interrogee should happen to survive his brush with death free of any permanent impairment of bodily function, he cannot be said to have been tortured under Bybee's narrowed interpretation of "torture" under 2340(1).

Position 3.—Expanding upon his bold and new definition of torture, Bybee argues that for an interrogator to stand in violation of Section 2340A

> the statute requires that severe pain and suffering must be inflicted [on the interrogee] with specific intent. See *United States v. Carter*, 530 U.S. 255, 269 (2000); Black's Law Dictionary at 814 (7th ed. 1999) (defining specific intent as "[t]he intent to accomplish the precise criminal act that one is later charged with"). . . . [B]ecause Section 2340A requires that a defendant act with the specific intent to inflict severe pain, the infliciton of such pain must be the defendants precise objective. . . . If the statute had required only general intent, it would be sufficient to establish guilt by showing that the defendant "possessed knowledge with respect to the actus reus of the crime" *Carter*, 530 U.S. at 268. If the defendant acted knowing that severe pain or suffering was reasonably likely to result from his actions, but no more, he would have acted only with general intent. . . . As a theoretical matter, therefore, knowledge alone that a particular result is certain to occur does not constitute specific intent. . . . Thus, even if the defendant knows that severe pain will result from his actions, if causing such harm is not his objective, he lacks the requisite specific intent even though the defendant did not act in good faith. Instead, a defendant is guilty of torture only if he acts with the express purpose of inflicting severe pain or suffering on a person within his custody or physical control. (*TTP*, Memo 14, Part I, §A, ¶s 1-3, pp. 174-75)

On the Contrary, (*a*) Bybee's model interrogator uses coercive interrogation in a knightly fashion, only reluctantly, and always as the lesser of alternative evils, with an immediate purpose beyond that of merely causing gratuitous pain and suffering in the helpless. But this idealized model of the self-policing action-hero interrogator is grossly out of touch with basic human psychology; it simply does not mesh with the patterns of behavior witnessed in GSS interrogators during the First Intifada, nor with the behavior of United States personnel operating at GTMO and Abu Ghraib.

The Fay-Jones Report of August 2004, for instance, notes that at Abu Ghraib prison in Iraq the CIA would routinely interrogate so-called "ghost detainees" who would suddenly appear at the facility then disappear without a trace. The report notes that CIA interrogators did not follow the established procedures for detainee in-processing, such as fully identifying detainees by name, biometric data, and Internee Serial Number.[13]

In one instance the CIA interned three Saudi nationals, who were medical personnel working for coalition forces in Iraq. The report notes that the Saudi general in charge of these men requested U.S. authorities to check their records in search of them. But an examination of all databases yielded nothing. The U.S. Embassy in Riyadh also requested a search; but again nothing turned up. Even Secretary of State Colin Powell requested a search be done, but again, the three men were nowhere to be found.

It was only when a Joint Interrogation and Detention Center official recalled seeing CIA officers whisk three men together into the facility, and a quick discussion with detainees disclosed the names of these men, that a match was finally found for the Saudi general's original name-search request.[14]

(*b*) If self-defense, the defense of others, or the prevention of a supposedly imminent terrorist attack is the interrogator's specific intent during interrogation, he may act toward the interrogee "knowing that severe pain or suffering was reasonably likely to result from his actions" and, according to Bybee, his acts would not violate Section 2340A of the torture statute, even though he failed to act in good faith,[15] because he inflicted pain upon the interrogee with general intent only—that is, the infliction of pain was secondary to his original purpose of forestalling an imminent terrorist attack. Had alternative means for avoiding the harm been available to Bybee's hypothetical interrogator, he most certainly would have used those means to achieve his precise objective of saving the life, liberty, and property of defenseless civilians.

According to David Luban, professor of philosophy and law at Georgetown University,

> an interrogator who intends to inflict pain, but does not specifically intend it to be as severe as the pain accompanying organ failure, death, or serious bodily injury—even if the pain actually turns out to be severe under this definition—has not specifically intended to commit severe pain, and therefore has not tortured.[16]

In other words, Bybee requires that, in addition to inflicting severe pain (of an extreme nature) during an interrogation process, the interrogator must also possess a specific mind-set or be in a certain mental state during his interrogation, in order for his actions to count as criminal under Section 2340A of the torture statute.

Just as committing assault with (specific) intent to forcibly steal another's property is more benign from a legal perspective than committing the same assault with (specific) intent to rape, so (Bybee wants us to believe that) coercively interrogating a suspect with intent to extract actionable intelligence is more benign than coercively interrogating him with specific intent to cause extreme pain or suffering.

Bybee's hypothetical interrogator takes no inward joy whatsoever at the suffering of others, indeed he reviles it himself, applying force only when and where needed on detainees at just the precise moment in time, always retrieving useful intelligence, and always using caution, moderation, and forethought during interrogation sessions, diligently recording relevant data to learn as much as possible about the psyche and inner workings of each detainee.

(*c*) On Bybee's construction of "specific intent" the job of the interrogator is comparable to that of the family dentist. The family dentist knows you well. He removes decaying teeth from your mouth, not with the specific intent of causing you to suffer, but with the precise objective of extracting unhealthy teeth, preventing gum disease, gingivitis, and tooth decay, his general intent, like that of any good medical practitioner, being to foster a condition of health in his patients. For the dentist and his patient there is simply no way around the pain and discomfort of the visit; but both go away from the experience better off than before the procedure began.

Likewise, Bybee wants us to envision his interrogator as a man reluctantly choosing to inflict agonizing pain on others as a "lesser evil" than the pain of a future possible mass-casualty terrorist attack upon the United

States. Bybee's interrogator extracts much needed intelligence information from suspects, not with the specific intent of causing them pain and suffering (for these are simply the unavoidable side-effects of invasive interrogation), but with the precise objective of extracting information that promotes his broader general intent of preventing another terrorist attack. The problem with Bybee's interrogator is that he is pure fiction from a planet unlike our own, not of this world, and not a creature with a conscience—his ability to restrict himself in the chamber from taking an interrogation too far simply does not match the realities of interrogational torture, nor their long-term ill-effects on *both* interrogator and interrogee.

(*d*) In *Public Committee* (1999) the Israeli High Court unambiguously banned any further use of what had become, for GSS interrogators, common preinterrogational warmup methods such as placing suspects to be interrogated in the Shabach position or the Frog Crouch for hours.[17] The court ruled that the Frog Crouch position "does not serve any purpose inherent to an investigation. It is degrading and infringes an individual's human dignity."[18] The position of the court is that the Shabach and Frog Crouch are specifically designed, and therefore specifically intended, to "break" the suspect's will to resist his interrogator's persistent demands.

To reduce an interrogee's excruciating pain to a mere side-effect of coercive methods like the Shabach, or other more invasive in-session techniques is to miss the point that these methods are specifically designed to destroy the interrogee's dignity; they are deployed with the specific intent of causing various levels of excruciating physical and mental pain in the interrogee. The traditional *mens rea* requirement of specific intent is satisfied in all cases where interrogators are reasonably well aware that the use of their methods is causative of pain.

If interrogators were somehow *unaware* that their use of a specific menu of techniques on an interrogee caused him significant pain, that menu would be utterly useless to the overall strategy of using coercion to force confessions as a method of acquiring information. Thus, Bybee's blurring of the line between specific and general intent appears to be the legal cover of choice to supply U.S. interrogators operating overseas with just the color of law needed to legalize torture, as envisioned by the language of the anti-torture statute §2340(1). If an interrogator deploys enhanced techniques that he *knows* have a reasonable likelihood of causing severe pain and suffering in the interrogee, as long as the infliction of pain is not his *specific* intent, he is not culpable of torture under 18 U.S.C. §2340A, according to Bybee.

Position 4.—In defining the scope of the anti-torture statute at Section 2340(2)(B) concerning the administration of mind-altering substances or other procedures calculated to disrupt profoundly the senses and personality, Bybee again deliberately raises the level of severe pain and suffering required of an interrogee before his suffering may rise to the level of torture under Subsection 2340(2)(B).

> By requiring that the procedures and the drugs create a *profound* disruption, the statute requires more than that the acts "forcibly separate" or "rend" the senses or personality. Those acts must penetrate to the core of an individual's ability to perceive the world around him, substantially interfering with his cognitive abilities, or fundamentally alter his personality. (*TTP*, Memo 14, Part I, §C(2), ¶5, p. 181, Bybee's emphasis)

On the Contrary, under Bybee's reading of the law, but contrary to the letter and spirit of Subsection 2340(2)(B), an interrogator may legally administer mind-altering substances to a detainee during an interrogation process, so long as the drugs do not permanently alter the detainee's personality or permanently interfere with his basic cognitive functioning. In other words, so long as interrogators stop somewhere short of inducing a permanent or semi-permanent vegetative psychological state in an otherwise healthy interrogee, rendering him mentally dissociated from himself and his surroundings in the manner of a drug addict, caught forever on the fringes of conscious awareness, they are free of culpability under Subsection 2340(2)(B).

Bybee's interpretation of federal statute 2340A gave the President and his principals, and the United States military and intelligence personnel charged with carrying out their orders the false assurance that virtually anything goes inside the interrogation chamber. Under Bybee's reading of the statute, if allegations of torture against a U.S. official ever came to rest upon his or her administration of mind-altering substances to an interrogee during an interrogation process, those substances would have to "penetrate to the core of the [interrogee's] ability to perceive the world around him" before allegations of torture would be legally substantiative.

Position 5.—Bybee then attempts to retrofit his overly narrowed reading of the "specific intent" requirement of Section 2340(1) onto the text of the CAT from which it arises. But this move only places the cart before the horse, since §2340(1) exists in federal law only because Article 4, ¶1 of the CAT originally required the United States to ensure that all acts of torture count as offences under its criminal law. According to Bybee,

> the text of the [CAT, Article 1, ¶1] requires that an individual act "intentionally." This language might be read to require only general intent for violations of the Torture Convention. We believe, however, that the better interpretation is that the use of the phrase "intentionally" also created a specific intent-type standard. In that event, the Bush administration's understanding represents only an explanation of how the United States intended to implement the vague language of the Torture Convention. If, however, the Convention established a general intent standard, then the Bush understanding represents a modification of the obligation undertaken by the United States. (*TTP*, Memo 14, Part II, Introd., ¶1, n. 7, p. 184)

On the Contrary, (*a*) the language of the Torture Convention is not vague, as Bybee imagines, but clear and simple in demanding that all States Parties take whatever legislative and judicial measures may be necessary to prevent acts of torture. CAT Article 1, ¶1 defines torture as

> severe pain or suffering, whether physical or mental, [that] is intentionally inflicted on a person for such purposes as obtaining from him or a third person information or a confession, punishing him for an act he or a third person has committed or is suspected of having committed, or inimidating or coercing him or a third person, or for any reason based on discrimination of any kind, when . . . inflicted by or at the instigation of a public official or other person acting in an official capacity.

Since Article 2, ¶2 of the CAT envisions cases of "public emergency" that might be invoked by politicians of States Parties as legal justification for a policy of torture, the language of the CAT could hardly be more clear and explicit than it already is. The Convention unambiguously bans torture, no exceptions. If interrogators become stymied in their search for actionable intelligence for want of alligator clips, electrodes, cattle prods, and an automobile battery, they aren't conducting a criminal investigation in any proper sense of the term, they are improvising a cruel and unusual inquisition. Investigatory cooperation is more likely to be secured from terrorism suspects by using incentives and rewards rather than cruelty and torture.

Bybee informs us that his reading of the specific intent requirement of Section 2340(1) may very well represent a "modification of" legal obligations undertaken by the United States in ratifying the CAT. He fails to tell us, however, that to be in violation of the treaty is to be in violation of United States federal law. From the very beginning it has been the policy of the Bush administration to exempt from prosecution for alleged violations of federal law any and all government officials explicitly ordered to carry out executive torture commands in the war on terror; this especially includes application of enhanced interrogation techniques on detainees held in CIA custody at so-called "black sites" across the world.

Jane Mayer reports in *The New Yorker*, November 2005, for instance, that "the Abu Ghraib scandal seems not to have chastened [Vice-President Dick] Cheney or any other administration officials; in fact, they are for the first time arguing openly and explicitly that CIA personnel should be exempt from [legal and ethical] standards that apply to every other American."[19]

From Bybee's perspective at the OLC, if Bush administration operatives, CIA field agents, or other investigatory personnel were suddenly forced to account before United States courts for alleged violations of federal law in carrying out administration torture directives, this practice would hinder America's efforts in the war on terrorism because it would represent a direct infringement on the President's discretion as Commander-in-Chief and Chief Executive to determine how best to manage the nation's military affairs. And no one can deny that the President is the sole organ of state in the field of foreign relations, as well as the only Commander-in-Chief designated to lead United States armed forces in a time of war, according to the Constitution.

(*b*) Bybee continues to ignore the obvious point that the requirement of specific intent contained in the anti-torture statute at §2340(1) imports into federal law a far narrower construction of intentionality than is originally contained in the CAT requirement that severe pain and suffering be "intentionally inflicted" to count as torture. An interrogator might well intentionally inflict severe pain and suffering on an interrogee, breaking treaty law under Article 1, ¶1 of the CAT, even though his *specific intent* might have been to prevent another mass-casualty terrorist attack against the United States, in which case his inflicting of pain and suffering would *not* violate Section 2340A of the anti-torture statute as Bybee reads "specific intent" in Section 2340(1).

Contrary to what the administration wants us to believe, it ultimately makes no difference to international law how interrogators assess the complexity of their world, or what they think of the relative dangerousness or usefulness of the interrogees they handle, or how they personally rank the nation's national security objectives. Nothing justifies torture under federal law, pure and simple. Torture is a vile and disgusting enterprise, the moral equivalent of terrorism itself—that is, the use of unconventional and asymmetric means of warfare to target helpless individuals in no position to defend themselves or their dignity from the random (and often deadly) infliction of severe pain and suffering meted out to them in order to achieve some officially stated (or unstated) political, religious, or military objective.

President Bush believed America's struggle against terrorism was nothing short of a global crusade against the primary forces of evil in the world. He believed that God uniquely appointed him (above all others) to be President of the United States at a crucial juncture in history. His stated objective in this self-empowering but indeterminately long war against global terrorism was to achieve total victory over an indeterminately scattered enemy that perpetually metastasizes across hemispheres and time zones. But total victory is decisive, it has a definite beginning, middle, and end, it represents what is final, terminal, and concluded once and for all. If victory involves the prevention of future possible acts of random deadly violence, how can this prevention ever be fully "total" by the use of conventional military means alone? The President sought total victory over an "Axis of Evil" (i.e., Iran, Iraq, and North Korea). But victory, even against an ill-defined enemy, is not possible if we become the moral equivalent of the evil we seek to defeat. The best defense is not to become like one's enemy.

Position 6.—Bybee informs White House Counsel Gonzales that

> Article 16 of [the] CAT requires State[s] Parties to "undertake to prevent . . . other acts of cruel, inhuman or degrading treatment or punishment *which do not amount to torture* as defined in Article 1." CAT thus establishes a category of acts that are not to be committed and that states must endeavor to prevent, but that states need not criminalize, leaving those acts without the stigma of penalties for torture alone. CAT reserves criminal penalties and the stigma attached to those penalties for torture alone. In so doing, CAT makes clear that torture is at the farthest end of impermissible actions, and that it is distinct and separate from the lower level of "cruel, inhuman, or degrading treatment or punishment." (*TTP*, Memo 14, Part II, Introd., ¶2, p. 185, Bybee's emphasis)

On the Contrary, although it is true that torture far eclipses more moderate forms of cruel, inhuman, and degrading treatment in intensity, scope, and duration, belonging as it does to the extreme fringes of pain, it is simply bad lawyering for Bybee not to inform the President that federal laws (other than the anti-torture statute) attach explicit criminal penalties (including fines, imprisonment, or even death) for maltreatment of captives of war falling well short of the severity of statutory torture.

Bybee should have noticed that the War Crimes Act specifically bans "outrages upon personal dignity" and "humiliating and degrading treatment" of captives falling well short of torture *per se.*[20] Section 2441(c)(1) of the act bans any behavior constituting a grave breach under GPW, Article 130, including what the CAT refers to as "inhuman treatment" and "wilfully causing great suffering or serious injury to body or health" in a detainee, as well as "depriving a POW of the rights of fair and regular trial"—each of which fall well short of torture.

Position 7.—According to Bybee, the President is constitutionally empowered to interpret the scope and language of international treaties and to unilaterally abrogate, suspend, or alter them, in part or in whole, at will and for however long he feels it necessary.

> The President is responsible for the day-to-day interpretation of a treaty and retains the power to unilaterally terminate a treaty. *See Goldwater v. Carter*, 617 F.2nd 697, 707-08 (D.C. Cir.) (en banc) *vacated and remanded with instructions to dismiss on other grounds*, 444 U.S. 996 (1979). The Executive's interpretation is to be accorded the greatest weight in ascertaining a treaty's intent and meaning. *See, e.g., United States v. Stuart*, 489 U.S. 353, 369 (1989) ("the meaning attributed to treaty provisions by the Government agencies charged with their negotiation and enforcement is entitled to great weight") (quoting *Sumitomo Shoji America, Inc. v. Avagliano*, 457 U.S. 176, 184-85 (1982)); *Kolovrat v. Oregon*, 366 U.S. 187, 194 (1961) ("While courts interpret treaties for themselves, the meaning given them by the department of government particularly charged with their negotiation and enforcement is given great weight."); *Charlton v. Kelly*, 229 U.S. 447, 468 (1913) ("A construction of a treaty by the political departments of the government, while not conclusive upon a court . . . is nevertheless of much weight"). [T]he Execuitve branch's interpretation and understanding of CAT reveals that Congress codified the view that torture included only the most extreme forms of physical and mental harm. When it submitted the Convention to the Senate, the Reagan administration took the position that CAT reached only the most heinous acts . . . S. Treaty Doc. No. 100-20, 4-5. (*TTP*, Memo 14, Part II, §A, ¶1, pp. 185-86)

On the Contrary, (*a*) the President does not retain the constitutional power to unilaterally terminate a treaty. On December 22, 1978, a week after President Jimmy Carter announced that he had decided to terminate a 1954 Mutual Defense Treaty with Taiwan, Senator Barry Goldwater along with seven other senators filed suit in federal district court seeking injunctive relief from the President's termination of the treaty.[21] Bybee cites the district court case from the D.C. circuit, but does not discuss *Goldwater v. Carter*, 444 U.S. 996 (1979), wherein the Supreme Court remanded the case back to the district court with directions to dismiss Senator Goldwater's original complaint.

The reason the case was held not ripe for judicial review by the Supreme Court is simple: President Carter was formally terminating the 1954 Treaty *in accordance with its provisions*, and on December 15, 1978, he duly informed the American people that he was giving formal notice to Taiwan to this effect. Carter was simply letting the clock run out on a treaty he inherited as President. He broke no laws. And, as Chief Executor of all federal laws including treaties, Carter was constitutionally free as President to either follow out the expiration provisions of the treaty or seek to renew it.

Had President Carter sought instead to unilaterally withdraw the United States from the N.A.T.O. alliance at the height of the cold war, or had he sought to wriggle out of the U.S.-U.S.S.R. Anti-Ballistic Missile Treaty of 1972 that the Nixon administration had worked tirelessly to perfect, he would have been excoriated in the courts, burned in the media, and most likely humiliated by a one-sided Senate vote on a resolution demanding that full advice and consent be sought before any treaty denouncement could become law.

Of course President Carter never assumed unilateral executive power to terminate treaties. In fact, at the time the Supreme Court decided to dismiss the Goldwater complaint, the Senate had considered a resolution declaring that its formal approval be necessary for the termination of any mutual defense treaty (125 Cong. Rec. S7015, S7038-S7039, June 6, 1979). But, as Justice Powell points out in his concurrence, no final Senate vote had ever been taken on the resolution (*Goldwater v. Carter*, 444 U.S., at 998).

In his concurrence with the court decision to dismiss the complaint, Justice Rehnquist writes that

> no constitutional provision explicitly confers upon the President the power to terminate treaties. Further, Art. 2, §2 of the Constitution authorizes the

> President to make treaties with the advice and consent of the Senate. Article VI provides that treaties shall be a part of the supreme law of the land. These provisions add support to the view that the text of the Constitution does not unquestionably commit the power to terminate treaties to the President alone. (444 U.S., at 999)

(*b*) Bybee misses the fact that the *Goldwater* court reserved for itself the exclusive power of final arbitration over federal questions arising from conflicting interpretations of law between the executive and legislative departments. Justice Rehnquist claims, for instance, that

> If the President and the Congress had reached irreconcilable positions [over the termination of a treaty], final disposition of the question presented by this case would eliminate, rather than create, multiple constitutional interpretations. The specter of the Federal Government brought to a halt because of the mutual intransigence of the President and the Congress would require this Court to provide a resolution pursuant to our duty "to say what the law is." (*United States v. Nixon,* 418 U.S. 683, 703 (1974), quoting *Marbury v. Madison,* 1 Cranch 137, 5 U.S. 177 (1803)). (444 U.S., at 1001)

Justice Rehnquist is arguing that the court's power to say what the law is implies the additional power of resolving legal disputes that may arise from time to time over conflicting claims to power made by the executive and legislative departments in the interpretation of treaties. The court's right of interpreting the scope, intent, and constitutionality of United States treaties is implicit in *Marbury v. Madison,* 5 U.S. 137, at 177, 178 (1803) and explicit in the text of the Constitution, Art. 3, §2, ¶1.

(*c*) Bybee not only ignores the concurrence of Justices Powell and Rehnquist in *Goldwater,* he also misses a key piece of analysis provided of the case by David Gray Adler, a constitutional historian of note quoted in a previous Bush II OLC opinion (*TTP*, p. 65, n. 78). According to Adler, since there has been no predominant method of treaty termination in United States history, some treaty terminations occurring by unilateral presidential directive, some by congressional resolution, others by Senate command,

> there is no support for President Carter's contention that "history, practice, and precedent . . . for the last 60 years . . . suggests an acknowledgment that the President has the constitutional authority to act on his own initiative" in treaty termination.[22]

Adler's caution applies equally to Bybee's contention that executive interpretation of treaties is to be afforded the *greatest* weight in ascertaining a treaty's meaning and intent—that is, a weight greater than that of any other department of state.

(*d*) The President's interpretation of the language and intent of a treaty is not to be accorded the *greatest* weight in the land, however, because this would imply that the President is the final arbiter in the interpreting of existing federal laws, which power of final review is reserved for the federal judiciary by *Const.*, Art. 3, §2, ¶1:

> The judicial power shall extend to all cases in law and equity, arising under this constitution, the laws of the United States, and treaties made, or which shall be made, under their authority.

Bybee even quotes a passage from *Sumitomo Shoji America, Inc. v. Avagliano*, 457 U.S. 176, 184, 185 (1982) grossly out of context in attempting to establish unilateral executive power to interpret and/or suspend treaties by directive. In quoting the words of Chief Justice Burger that "the meaning attributed to treaty provisions by the Government agencies charged with their negotiation and enforcement is entitled to great weight" Bybee conveniently fails to tell us that Burger's sentence begins with the clause "although not conclusive [on any federal court]." In other words, Justice Burger is claiming that what the President and the Senate say about the meaning of the provisions of a treaty is extremely important from a political point of view, but not determinative of what the federal courts should decide in the matter. The judiciary is not, in *Sumitomo*, abdicating its inherent constitutional right to agree or disagree with the interpretation of a treaty offered by other departments of state, nor is it ceding its right of final arbitration in such questions.

(*e*) Bybee then quotes another Court dictum from *Charlton v. Kelly*, 229 U.S. 447 (1913) that actually proves the opposite of his own stated position that the executive's interpretation is to be accorded the greatest weight in ascertaining a treaty's intent and meaning. Quoted in full, Justice Lurton maintains that

> a construction of a treaty by the political departments of the government, while not conclusive upon a court called upon to construe such a treaty in a matter involving personal rights, is nevertheless of much weight. (229 U.S., at 468)

The executive's interpretation of a treaty cannot possibly be of the *greatest* weight, if it is not conclusive upon the courts. Lurton's opinion implies that federal courts have jurisdiction to overturn and reject interpretations of treaty provisions offered by the President and Congress in defense of policy objectives, if those interpretations violate constitutional principles on some fundamental level, regardless of the desirability of the policy objectives.

Simply because the President and Congress create, implement, and apply treaties in the political realm does not mean that the courts must remain silent and ignore their constitutionally assigned duty to try all cases in law and equity arising under existing United States treaties. The Constitution allows the court to determine as unlawful any piece of legislation enacted by Congress to implement provisions of a Presidential directive, as was the case recently in *Boumediene v. Bush*, 553 U.S. ___ (2008), where Justice Kennedy found not only that the Military Commissions Act of 2006, §7, 28 U.S.C.A. §2241(e)(Supp. 2007) was unconstitutional, but that the combatant status review tribunal procedures (originating from the executive and imposed upon detainees by Congress in the Detainee Treatment Act) are "an inadequate substitute for habeas corpus."[23]

Position 8.—Bybee advances an unusual argument that not only opens another legal loophole for the use of so-called "truth drugs" on persons captured in the global war on terrorism, but explicitly contravenes his own previously stated OLC position that acts of cruelty must cause *permanent* harm in the interrogee "lasting for months or even years" to rise to the level of torture. Bybee contends that

> CAT's negotiating history offers more than just support for the view that pain or suffering must be extreme to amount to torture. First, the negotiating history suggests that the harm sustained from the acts of torture need not be permanent. In fact, "the United States considered that it might be useful to develop the negotiating history which indicates that although conduct resulting in permanent impairment of physical or mental faculties is indicative of torture, it is not an essential element of the offence." *CAT Handbook*, at 44. Second, the State[s] Parties to CAT rejected a proposal to include in CAT's definition of torture the use of truth drugs, where no physical harm or mental suffering was apparent. This rejection at least suggests that drugs were not viewed as amounting to torture per se. *See id.* at 42. (*TTP*, Memo 14, Part II, §B, ¶4, p. 191)

On the Contrary, (*a*) from the beginning of his memorandum opinion for Judge Gonzales (*vide* Position 2), Bybee defined torture as pain equivalent to serious physical injury such as organ failure, impairment of bodily function, or even death, conditions that are unambiguously *permanent* in nature. He also defined mental torture as psychological harm "of significant duration . . . lasting for months or even years."[24] But now Bybee suggests that the harm caused by cruelty need not be permanent at all to count as torture. We know from the definition of "torture" provided in Article 1, ¶1 of the CAT that a detainee need not suffer permanent injury or impairment as a result of his detention experience in order to claim he was tortured. It appears that Bybee now agrees, and has modified his earlier position[25] that the mental pain and suffering required to constitute torture must be permanent, resulting in "significant psychological harm of significant duration" to the detainee.

(*b*) Bybee then backpedals on this concession by intimating that the use of so-called "truth-drugs" on interrogees is legally allowable under the CAT, but only so long as no physical or mental suffering is "apparent." On the contrary, allowing truth-drugs into the interrogation process opens a Pandora's Box to the use of other mentally invasive methods of breaking a detainee for questioning, such as the use of prolonged isolation, sleep deprivation, the use of phobias, and psychological experimentation, all of which happen to be in plain violation of GPW, Article 13's ban on inhumane treatment and medical experimentation, even though they remain central to the menu of counter-resistance techniques taught to military personnel today in the Survival Evasion Resistance Escape (SERE) program pioneered by the United States Air Force immediately after the Korean War, in the wake of dozens of American POWs (mostly Air Force pilots downed over Korea) who claimed to have been psychologically tortured, malnourished, and medically mishandled or neglected in North Korean Prisoner of War camps. Since the North Koreans predetermined all U.S. pilots to be unlawful enemy combatants independently of any judicial process, they were denied Geneva Conventions humanitarian protections guaranteed to all civilians and soldiers captured in a zone of combat.

The SERE program is designed to harden United States military personnel against the very real dangers of being captured by enemy forces in the line of duty. Soldiers are taught how to survive, evade, and resist an enemy's harsh interrogation and confinement conditions. But shortly after 9/11 there surfaced strong evidence, from FBI, military, and intelligence leaks, that these SERE methods were being turned on detainees. In an effort to stem this alarming trend, one senior army psychologist involved with the SERE program, Col. Louie (Morgan) Banks, began to require all graduates of SERE to sign a statement vowing not to apply the program's counter-resistance techniques to detainees held in U.S. custody. "We did this," said Banks, "when we learned people were flipping it."[26]

(*c*) If dosing detainees with so-called "truth drugs" is permissible during an interrogation process, so long as such drugs cause no *apparent* physical or mental suffering, as Bybee suggests, then it must be the case that psychological experimentation (which is also a form of detainee mind control), along with prolonged isolation, sleep deprivation, and abject neglect of the detainee's person and hygiene are also permissible over long periods of confinement so long as they cause no *apparent* suffering in the victim. But Bybee ought to have noticed that military physicians were puzzled at the mental condition of many of the American POWs who returned home from the Korean War, because they bore no outward visible scars from their confinement, yet remained deeply withdrawn and emotionally scarred from their experience in captivity.[27]

By the time solid investigative reports began to surface in the American media of prison abuse at Abu Ghraib and GTMO, Jay Bybee had already accepted a new job beyond the administration as a federal appellate court judge. But the loopholes opened by his memorandum opinion for Judge Gonzales paved the way for the following incidents of detainee abuse.

Abdul Aziz al-Swidi, client of Scott Sullivan, attorney at Allen & Overy, claimed to have been interrogated by a psychiatrist at GTMO that kept showing him pictures of commonly identifiable household items and asking him to name each. When Swidi would correctly identify the object in the picture, the psychiatrist would angrily correct him by deliberately misidentifying the item for something that it clearly was not. Sullivan believes this technique was used repeatedly on Swidi in an effort to make him think he was going crazy.[28]

"In one case," reports Jane Mayer, "interrogators [at GTMO] were told a detainee had a profound fear of the dark, and ways were suggested to exploit this phobia, in order to break down the detainee's resistance to questioning."[29] A military policy statement had even instructed caregivers at GTMO base to offer clinical information about the personal history of any detainee to interrogation teams upon request. This type of information sharing is arguably unethical, since it constitutes a breach of doctor-patient confidentiality, and illegal, when used to perform medical or psychological experimentation on a detainee in search of his breaking point. Medical treatment and testing are to be administered under GPW, Art. 13, ¶1 only when it is *in the interest* of the prisoner. Any purpose of medical treatment other than the prisoner's own health and well-being violates both Geneva and the Hippocratic oath.

Position 9.—Seeking again to establish his thesis that only the most severe cruelties count as torture during interrogation, but not lesser forms of coercion, Bybee argues that

> the European Court of Human Rights concluded [in *Ireland v. United Kingdom*, 23 Eur. Ct. H.R. (ser. B) at 3 (1976)] that . . . [interrogation] techniques [such as prolonged wall standing, hooding, subjection to loud noise, sleep deprivation, and deprivation of food and drink, when] used in combination, and applied for hours at a time, were inhuman and degrading but did not amount to torture. (*TTP*, Memo 14, Part IV, §A, ¶4, p. 197)

On the Contrary, (*a*) Bybee conveniently fails to mention that the Israeli Supreme Court decision in *The Public Committee Against Torture in Israel v. The State of Israel*, 53(4)*PD* 817 (1999), from which he originally drew his reference to *Ireland v. United Kingdom*, established that prolonged wall standing, hooding, subjection to intensely loud noise, sleep deprivation, and deprivation of food and drink did not count as methods of torture per se, but yet concluded that "since [these methods] subjected the suspect to 'inhuman and degrading' treatment, they were nonetheless prohibited [by the European Court of Human Rights]."[30] Bybee omits this last important component of the Israeli court's analysis of the European court's decision in *Ireland v. United Kingdom*, and simply uses the case to butress his own irrelevant point that there is a palpable legal difference between torture versus mere cruelty. But even if we acknowledge a legal difference between the two it does not erase the fact that Articles 12 and 16 of the CAT essentially dissolve this difference entirely by requiring States Parties to conduct a prompt and impartial law enforcement investigation whenever there arise reasonable grounds to believe that acts involving cruel and inhuman treatment have been committed against persons detained in its custody, even if no torture was used. The Israeli Supreme Court decision in *Public Committee* does *not* decriminalize acts of cruelty and inhumanity that are committed by GSS during the interrogation process of suspected terrorists. Instead, it recognizes that the European Court of Human Rights prohibited such cruelty and inhumanity outright, even though it also recognizes that these categories of treatment are not as severe as torture.

(*b*) Since the Eighth Amendment bans cruel and unusual punishment that may cause pain of significantly less intensity than torture, and since constitutional principles ought to be applied to anyone detained anywhere for some reason by authority of the United States, Bybee ought to have seen that distinguishing cruelty from torture makes no legal difference. The original proponents of the Eighth Amendment did *not* recognize a gradational difference in pain intensity between interrogational cruelty versus torture that would have permitted the former but barred the latter. Therefore, neither cruelty nor torture are to be applied to suspects detained in United States custody in an ongoing criminal investigation conducted according to constitutional principles of fairness and equity.

But again, the Bush administration balked at applying constitutional principles to the investigation of terror suspects from the beginning of the war. By late 2005 revelations of widespread detainee abuse from Abu Ghraib prison in Iraq, Guantánamo Bay, Cuba, and hidden facilities located in Afghanistan and Eastern Europe were not only brushed aside by the Bush II White House, they prompted Vice President Dick Cheney and CIA Director Porter J. Goss to request from Congress that CIA employees be exempt from legislation (then endorsed by ninety Senators) that would have prohibited cruel, inhuman or degrading treatment of any prisoner held in United States custody.[31]

Within three years of 9/11 the CIA had established a hidden global internment network of secret prisons to whisk key suspects in the war on terror out of the purview of U.S. courts and media, and off the books forever. Working in secret with foreign intelligence agencies, the CIA had not only captured an estimated 3,000 people whose legal status and whereabouts remain completely unknown, it had conducted scores of illegal renditions of terrorist suspects out of its custody to countries such as Egypt, Syria, Jordan, Thailand, and Eastern Europe.[32]

According to a 2005 *Washington Post* review of military tribunal testimony at GTMO base and other records, the CIA was discovered to have transferred about a dozen persons to GTMO who had been mistakenly suspected of terrorist collusion and rendered out of United States custody abroad for purposes of interrogation. GTMO Base had effectively become a dumping ground for CIA mistakes. There is even a case of an innocent man named Mohamedou Oulad Slahi from Mauritania, a former resident of Canada, who was illegally rendered to Jordan for eight months of intense interrogation even after he freely and peaceably turned himself in to the Mauritanian authorities just 18 days after the 9/11 attacks because he heard the Americans were looking for him.[33]

Position 10.—In *Public Committee* (HCJ 5100/94, 1999) the Israeli Supreme Court effectively placed a watershed ban on the use of torture and other (less severe) forms of interrogational coercion that had been deployed by GSS against terrorist suspects in the occupied territories since the beginning of the first Palestinian intifada in 1987. We have already seen how the five physical methods at issue in this case came to be used by GSS on as many as two-thirds of their Palestinian captives. Yet Bybee stubbornly insists upon reading *Public Committee* as banning torture, while allowing lesser (physical) forms of interrogational coercion to be used during an investigatory process.

> While the Israeli Supreme Court concluded that . . . [the five] acts [in question—namely, 1. vigorously shaking the interrogee's upper torso, 2. the Shabach, 3. the Frog Crouch, 4. excessive tightening of handcuffs, and 5. sleep deprivation] amounted to cruel, and inhuman treatment, the court did not expressly find that they amounted to torture. To be sure, such a conclusion was unnecessary because even if the acts amounted only to cruel and inhuman treatment the GSS lacked authority to use the five methods. Nonetheless, the decision is still best read as indicating that the acts at issue did not constitute torture. (*TTP*, Memo 14, Part IV, §B, ¶3, p. 199)

On the Contrary, the decision of the Israeli Supreme Court in *Public Committee* is *not* best read as indicating that the Frog Crouch, the Shabach, or prolonged wall-standing are legal because they lack the severity of pain associated with torture. Bybee even admits point blank that any gradational distinction in severity of pain meted out to an interrogee is irrelevant since under Israeli law GSS "lacked authority to use the five methods at issue."

Yet, as if in denial of a painful truth, Bybee ignores the policy implications of the High Court's decision. The Court held that authority to establish directives regarding the implementation of physical means during the course of a GSS interrogation cannot be implied from the "necessity defense."[34] Section 34(1) of the Israeli Penal Law contains a defense against criminal liability that may be used by an interrogator accused of going too far.

The interrogator can avoid criminal liability if he can successfully prove that he had to rough up his suspect in order to extract valuable information in circumstances of necessity "for the purpose of saving the life, liberty, body or property" of himself or others. But the necessity defense would only apply in U.S. courts, if at all, retroactively and after the fact; it is not available as legal warrant for future possible torture in quest of actionable intelligence, nor for a policy instituting a menu of enhanced techniques.

Position 11.—Bybee goes on to contend that

> even if an interrogation method arguably were to violate Section 2340A [of the federal anti-torture statute], the statute would be unconstitutional if it impermissibly encroached on the President's constitutional power to conduct a military campaign. As Commander-in-Chief, the President has the constitutional authority to order interrogations of enemy combatants to gain intelligence information concerning the military plans of the enemy. The demands of the Commander-in-Chief power are especially pronounced in the middle of a war in which the nation has already suffered a direct attack. In such a case, the information gained from interrogations may prevent future attacks by foreign enemies. Any effort to apply Section 2340A in a manner that interferes with the President's direction of such core war matters as the detention and interrogation of enemy combatants thus would be unconstitutional. (*TTP*, Memo 14, Part V, Introd., p. 200)

On the Contrary, (*a*) the President's constitutional power to conduct and lead a military campaign does not place him beyond the rule of law. Military and intelligence officials are not, therefore, magically freed from criminal liability under Section 2340A simply because they acted pursuant to a Presidential directive in applying enhanced interrogation techniques in wartime, especially as war and international conflict represent the paradigm occasions for applying the statute in the first place. Nor do federal laws become unconstitutional in proportion as they limit the President's range of acceptable policy options.

(*b*) The President does not enjoy constitutional latitude to approve the use of interrogational methods that place United States personnel in direct violation of ratified treaties. In fact, in order for the United States government to legally implement the Working Group Report's menu of enhanced interrogation techniques, Congress (following the lead of the President) would have to:

1. Formally withdraw from or denounce all relevant humanitarian treaties through appropriate Senate resolutions, and in exact conformity with the terms of each, which could take years and would remove the United States from membership participation in the Geneva Conventions, the Convention Against Torture, and the International Covenant on Civil and Political Rights;
2. Formally revoke or abrogate both the federal anti-torture statute and the War Crimes Act;
3. Formally enact legislation authorizing United States military and intelligence personnel to apply enhanced interrogation techniques amounting to cruel, inhuman, or degrading treatment, if circumstances appear to require the use these techniques as self-defense.

Although no senator has yet stepped forward to propose that the United States withdraw from its humanitarian treaty commitments, there have been successfully disturbing backdoor legislative efforts to strip detainees of humanitarian protections under Geneva. For instance, Section 948a(1) of the Military Commissions Act of 2006 recognizes, as valid and binding, all status determinations made under the CSRT system then in use at GTMO (in place of GPW, Article 5 competent tribunals). Section 948b(g) of the Act brazenly adds that "no alien unlawful enemy combatant subject to trial by military commission . . . may invoke the Geneva Conventions as a source of rights."[35]

The scope of executive power to authorize enhanced interrogation techniques is also an issue of central importance in the Israeli Supreme Court's decision in *Public Committee* (1999), where the court opined that if the state wishes to enable GSS to utilize physically and mentally invasive methods of interrogation on suspected terrorists in circumstances of perceived imminent danger in which no alternatives but coercion appear available in order to forestall the danger (and are, for this reason, necessary for the defense of self or others), then the state must explicitly enact appropriate legislation to this effect.[36] In other words, the decision-making power to allow physically coercive means to be used during interrogation does not rest with the chief executive of state in Israel, but with the Knesset, as a matter to be deliberated and determined by popular will.

The Israeli Supreme Court was clear: "The fact that the GSS forms part of the executive branch is not, in itself, sufficient to invest it with the authority to interrogate."[37] No chief executive of state in any freely elected democratic government operates above the law. And so, neither the Israeli GSS nor the American CIA are exempt from criminal liability for violations of their respective state laws, since these officials operate as an expression of executive will.

As an indication of how stubbornly the Bush administration remained committed to the use of interrogational coercion and torture, consider that when bipartisan political opposition began to mount in Washington in mid-2005 in favor of legislation that would bar the U.S. military from engaging in "cruel, inhuman or degrading treatment" of detainees, and the CIA from secreting prisoners out of the purview of the Red Cross, and from using interrogation techniques not authorized in the Army Field Manual, administration officials actually lobbied fiercely to block such legislation.[38]

By October of 2005 an amendment to the 2006 defense appropriations bill sponsored by Sen. John McCain (R-Arizona) banning cruel, inhuman, and degrading treatment of captives in U.S. military custody passed the Senate by an overwhelming margin of 90 to 9, but Vice President Dick Cheney sought to persuade members of the House-Senate conference committee to adopt new language that would nullify the McCain amendment.[39] Cheney continues on to the present day vigorously defending the Bush administration's institutionalization of torture as a tactical necessity in a new age of couterterrorism.

Position 12.—According to Bybee,

> as the Supreme Court has recognized, and as we will explain further below, the President enjoys complete discretion in the exercise of his Commander-in-Chief authority and in conducting operations against hostile forces. Because both "[t]he executive power and the command of the military and naval forces is vested in the President," the Supreme Court has unanimously stated that it is "*the President alone* who is constitutionally invested with the *entire charge of hostile operations*." *Hamilton v. Dillin*, 88 U.S. (21 Wall.) 73, 87 (1874). That authority is at its height in the middle of a war. In light of the President's complete authority over the conduct of war, without a clear statement otherwise, we will not read a criminal statute as infringing on the President's ultimate authority in these areas. (*TTP*, Memo 14, Part V, §B, ¶s 1-2, p. 202, Bybee's emphasis)

On the Contrary, (*a*) Bybee is using the constitutional power of the President as Commander-in-Chief of the Army and Navy in wartime as a wedge to advance and defend a host of absolute and unenumerated executive powers which (presumably) include the freedom to ignore any criminal statutes which threaten to limit the President's horizon of policy options. So long as the President deems it necessary for national security reasons, he has the power, says Bybee, to order an operative to conduct an illegal interrogation (torture included), and neither he (the President) nor the operative is subject to prosecution under federal criminal law.

(*b*) While it is certainly refreshing to see Bybee correctly reading the court decision in *Hamilton v. Dillin* as asserting the President's sole command authority in charge of hostile operations in time of war, he nevertheless seems to confuse the President's *de facto* authority as Commander-in-Chief to order (operative) *A* to do (action) *x*, with the President's *de jure* authority to order the same. The President has *de facto* authority to order almost any action his operatives are willing to carry out in the field and to proclaim as lawful virtually anything he desires, but the scope of his *de jure* authority to command and to proclaim is limited by moral conceptions of obligation to others, of personal dignity, and of inherent natural value in all life, and by numerous constitutional and statutory restrictions.

Bybee's blurring of the distinction between *de facto* and *de jure* types of authority is no mere accident, but a deliberate sleight of hand. He is attempting to argue in a manner reminiscent of Plato's Thrasymachus (cf. *Republic* 338c) that "justice is the advantage of the stronger": that which is lawful being whatever the stronger element in society says it is, or whatever the stronger branch of government interprets it to be. But this angry political ethos of Might Makes Right, the brainchild of Vice President Dick Cheney and his protégé, Chief of Staff David Addington,[40] is dangerously inconsistent with the principles of an open society in a constitutional democracy where no department of state is allowed to operate in secret isolation beyond the rule of law. Just because the President enjoys *de facto* command authority to order *A* to do *x*, it does not follow, if the value of *x* turns out be a piece of interrogational torture committed at the hands of *A* for reasons of perceived necessity, that the President and his principals are exempt from federal prosecution under criminal conspiracy charges pursuant to Subsection 2340A(c) of the anti-torture statute.

Nowhere in his opinion for Judge Gonzales does Bybee appear to acknowledge that the anti-torture statute was originally intended to apply to the behavior of United States government officials, including elected representatives of state *regardless of rank or position,* and that it was originally passed into law as the correlative counterpart to the Torture Victims Protection Act (TVPA) of 1991 (28 U.S.C. §1350), which establishes a civil remedy in United States courts for individuals victimized by torture under the color of law of any foreign nation.

Position 13.—According to Bybee

> in order to respect the President's inherent constitutional authority to manage a military campaign against al-Qaeda and its allies, Section 2340A must be constructed as not applying to interrogations undertaken pursuant to his Commander-in-Chief authority. [C]ongress lacks authority under [*Const.*] Article I to set the terms and conditions under which the President may exercies his authority as Commander-in-Chief to control the conduct of operations during a war. . . . [T]he President's power to detain and interrogate enemy combatants arises out of his constitutional authority as Commander-in-Chief. A construction of Section 2340A that applied the provision to regulate the President's authority as Commander-in-Chief to determine the interrogation and treatment of enemy combatants would raise serious constitutional questions. Congress may no more regulate the President's ability to detain and interrogate enemy combatants than it may regulate his ability to direct troop movements on the battlefield. Accordingly, we would construe Section 2340A to avoid this constitutional difficulty, and conclude that it does not apply to the President's detention and interrogation of enemy combatants pursuant to his Commander-in-Chief authority. This approach is consistent with previous decisions of our Office involving the application of federal criminal law. (*TTP*, Memo 14, Part V, §B, ¶4, p. 203)

On the Contrary, (*a*) Bybee speaks of presidential command powers "inherent" in the Constitution, but he ought to have recalled Justice Robert Jackson's famous warning, in *Youngstown Sheet & Tube Co. v. Sawyer*, 343 U.S. at 646, 647 (1952), against excessive claims to inherent constitutional power made by the Solicitor General on behalf of President Truman's assertion of unilateral executive authority to stop an imminent nationwide strike of steel workers by seizing the nation's steel mills. Jackson writes that

> Loose and irresponsible use of adjectives colors all nonlegal and much legal discussion of presidential powers. "Inherent" powers, "implied" pow-

> ers, "incidental" powers, "plenary" powers, "war" powers and "emergency" powers are used, often interchangeably and without fixed or ascertainable meanings. . . . [The forefathers] knew what emergencies were, knew the pressures they engender for authoritative action, knew, too, how they afford a ready pretext for usurpation. We may also suspect that they suspected that emergency powers would tend to kindle emergencies. Aside from suspension of the privilege of the writ of habeas corpus in time of rebellion or invasion, when the public safety may require it, they made no express provision for exercise of extraordinary authority because of a crisis. I do not think we rightfully may so amend their work, and, if we could, I am not convinced it would be wise to do so.[41]

Since Bybee argues that the President's power to detain and interrogate suspects in wartime arises from his *inherent* constitutional authority as Commander-in-Chief, it is important to pin down just what Bybee means by this type of authority. We know that inherent authority is authority not expressly stated or allocated to any branch anywhere in the Constitution. Thus, in utilizing unexpressed executive powers implicit in the text of the Constitution, Bybee avoids the inconvenience of having to explain why the text of the instrument allocates to Congress, but not to the President, various war powers, such as the power to call forth the military to execute federal laws, suppress insurrection, or repel invasion.

(*b*) There is no clause in the Constitution providing for executive immunity from prosecution for criminal violations of federal law. In fact, the Constitution contains an explicit network of legislative and judicial checks on the executive department designed to ensnare any President who might assert his command authority beyond the law during a time of national crisis. Article 3, Section 4 of the Constitution, for instance, provides for the removal from office of the President, Vice President, and any civil officers on impeachment for and conviction of treason, bribery, or other high crimes and misdemeanors. Openly flouting provisions of Geneva, the CAT, and the ICCPR counts as a "high crimes" under Art. 3, §4 of the Constitution; that is, a crime which only the highest officials of state, the President and his principals, can commit due to their unique position. When a President faces impeachment charges, the Senate has sole power to conduct the trial, the Chief Justice of the Supreme Court presides, and a two-thirds vote of all senators present are required for conviction. (Art. 1, §3, ¶6). Although impeachment only removes an official from his post while disqualifying him or her from seeking any further office of trust, honor, or profit within the

United States, the party convicted nevertheless remains "liable and subject to indictment, trial, judgment, and punishment, according to law" (Art. 1, §3, ¶7). This means the President remains fully liable for breaking federal laws even *after* formal impeachment. The plain language of Art. 1, §3, ¶7 establishes executive criminal liability for policy decisions while in office, and this trumps any OLC assertions of executive immunity from prosecution for crimes that may have been committed by executive officials as a result of policy directives issued by the President or members of his administration.

As we shall see in Bybee's next move, an OLC opinion from the Reagan era is resurrected to argue that executive branch officials who are called upon to testify before Congress in relation to alleged violations of federal law are immune from application of the contempt of Congress statute. This means that if a Bush administration official (such as the President's former Chief of Staff, Carl Rove) is called upon by, but refuses to testify before Congress, he faces no legal repercussions as a result of his refusal, and is free to ignore the demands of Congress *ad infinitum*. This move is not good for the health of our democracy because it removes the President and his principals from any direct accountability before the American People over allegations of criminal wrongdoing. Such assertions of executive privilege pave the way to claims of naked dictatorial absolutism.

Position 14.—Bybee contends that

> we [in the Office of Legal Counsel, U.S. Department of Justice] have previously construed the congressional contempt statute [2 U.S.C. §§192, 194] not to apply to executive branch officials who refuse to comply with congressional subpoenas because of an assertion of executive privilege. In a published 1984 opinion, we concluded that "if the executive officials were subject to prosecution for criminal contempt whenever they carried out the President's claim of executive privilege, it would significantly burden and immeasurably impair the President's ability to fulfill his constitutional duties. Therefore, the separation of powers principles that underlie the doctrine of executive privilege also would preclude an application of the contempt of Congress statute to punish officials for aiding the President in asserting his constitutional privilege." *Prosecution for Contempt of Congress of an Executive Branch Official Who Has Asserted a Claim of Executive Privilege*, 8 Op. O.L.C. 101, 134 (May 30, 1984). Likewise, we believe that, if executive officials were subject to prosecution for conducting interrogations when they were carrying out the President's Commander-in-Chief powers, "it would significantly burden and immeasurably impair the Pres-

ident's ability to fulfill his constitutional duties." These constitutional principles preclude an application of Section 2340A to punish officials for aiding the President in exercising his exclusive constitutional authorities. (*TTP*, Memo 14, Part V, §B, ¶5, pp. 203-04)

On the Contrary, (*a*) Bybee attempts to defend, under a concept of executive privilege not contained anywhere in the Constitution, the right of *any* executive branch official (including himself) to freely choose *not* to comply with a congressional subpoena to appear as a witness before an investigatory committee of either house of Congress, in spite of the fact that wilful failure to appear as a witness, or refusal to answer any question put, or to produce papers, records, and other documents as required is a misdemeanor under Title 2 of the United States Code, §194. In other words, Bybee is stripping Congress (and the American people) of its authority to call into account members of the Bush administration for possible illegal activity related to the President's conduct of foreign affairs.

Even if Bybee happens to be giving his President legal advice that ends up implicating himself along with other executive officials in future wrongdoing, it doesn't really matter from *his* perspective, because executive privilege allows high officials to ignore congressional subpoenas with impunity. And so it is that, in the opinion of Bybee, the highest officers of state responsible for the conduct of foreign affairs may excuse themselves from accountability before the American people. The challenge for Bybee is to find a loophole around Section 194 of Title 2, which provides that

> Whenever a witness summoned as mentioned in section 192 of this title fails to appear to testify or fails to produce any books, papers, records, or documents, as required . . . a statement of fact constituting such failure is reported to and filed with the President of the Senate or the Speaker of the House, it shall be the duty of the said President of the Senate or Speaker of the House, as the case may be, to certify, and he shall so certify, the statement of facts aforesaid . . . to the appropriate United States attorney, whose duty it shall be to bring the matter before the grand jury for its action.

Section 194 applies to *every person* regardless of rank in society or position in government, who might be called upon to testify before a select investigatory committee of either house of Congress. But because Section 194 requires congressional authorities to certify a witness's failure to comply "to the appropriate United States attorney" inside the Department of Justice operating under the Executive aegis, and because this attorney must "bring the matter before the grand jury for its action," a conflict of interest appears to arise in just those cases where the witness called upon to testify happens to be an executive branch official.

In effect, Section 194 empowers Congress to require executive branch officials in the Department of Justice to initiate prosecutorial proceedings against any executive branch official who fails to comply with a congressional subpoena by bringing each instance of non-compliance before a grand jury.

The language of Section 194 makes abundantly clear that the United States Attorney is required to refer *every* case of non-compliance to a grand jury. No exceptional circumstances to grand jury notification are countenanced in Section 194. But according to the Reagan administration era Office of Legal Counsel opinion upon which Bybee draws in defense of his own position, Section 194

> does not on its face actually purport to require the United States Attorney to proceed with the *prosecution* of a person cited by a house of Congress for contempt . . . [so that] even if a grand jury were to return a true bill, the United States Attorney could refuse to sign the indictment and thereby prevent the case from going forward. (8 Op. O.L.C. 101, at 118, 1984)

What Olson is saying here is that even if the grand jury were to determine that an accusation of criminal misconduct against an executive branch official, if proved, were sufficient to bring about conviction of the accused, the United States Attorney could simply refuse to sign the grand jury's indictment, thus aborting the very legal process he is obligated to originate from his office under Section 194. This type of meandering executive noncompliance that would have a United States Attorney subvert legal process over technicalities in the wording of a statute smacks of obstruction of justice at the highest level.

(*b*) It is not at all inconsistent with our constitutional system of checks and balances for one branch of government to force or pressure another branch into compliance with federal law. Congress, for instance, may conduct ethics investigations into the activities of its own members whenever it chooses. The President may veto, and thus nullify, any piece of congressional legislation he happens not to like. The judiciary may pronounce as unconstitutional any legislative or executive action it sees fit. The United

States military conducts criminal investigations into the alleged abuses and misdeeds of its own personnel under the UCMJ. But no one on the American political scene has questioned any of these procedures. Yet Bybee wants to claim, following 8 Op. O.L.C. 101, 113 (1984), that congressional subpoenas of executive branch witnesses, records, or documents represent an undue interdepartmental *encroachment* of power onto executive domain.

But was it interdepartmental encroachment for Justice Marshall to assert appellate jurisdiction to issue writs of mandamus against executive branch officials in *Marbury v. Madison*, 5 U.S. 137, at 175 (1803)? Was it an undue encroachment of power when the *Youngstown* court dramatically stopped Truman from seizing and operating the nation's steel mills in 1952? Was it encroachment for Justice Anthony Kennedy to opine, in *Boumediene v. Bush*, 553 U.S. ___, at Introd., ¶2 (2008), that the Combatant Status Review Tribunal procedures established by Deputy Secretary of Defense Paul Wolfowitz in July of 2004 (for detainees at GTMO) were "not an effective or adequate substitute for habeas corpus"?

Bybee is not arguing that Section 194 ought to be jettisoned from the books. He is saying rather that Section 194 simply does not (and should not) apply to executive branch officials claiming executive privilege. As Bybee sees it, executive privilege avoids the inherent conflict of interest brought on by Section 194's demand that United States attorneys (working under executive aegis in the Department of Justice) be used to prosecute other executive branch officials who ignore congressional subpoenas.

The Reagan era OLC opinion cited by Bybee in defense of executive privilege was authored by then-Assistant Attorney General Theodore B. Olson. Olson, a gifted attorney and sagacious scholar of the law, originates his concept of executive privilege, not from the Constitution, but from an ingenious confluence of two separate and distinct ideas which, by themselves in isolation from one another are completely innocuous, but when combined create a Chief Executive vested with infinite and irresponsible powers to sidestep the law.

The first idea comprising Olson's concept of executive privilege is that the President's unique constitutional role as Chief Executive places him in charge of taking care that the laws be faithfully executed (*Const.*, Art. 2, §3). This duty to *execute* the law yields what Olson calls the "doctrine of prosecutorial discretion"—namely, the idea that only the executive branch, to the exclusion of other departments, has the right to choose both whether and whom to prosecute.

Olson's doctrine of prosecutorial discretion is based upon the false inference that, since the President's *primary* constitutional duty is to execute federal law, he thereby has *exclusive* authority to prosecute executive branch violations of it. But primacy of function does not imply exclusivity of the same. The President's authority to execute the law, while foremost among the branches, and universal in scope, since it applies to *all* federal laws, is by no means exclusive. In fact, no exclusivity of prosecutorial discretion follows from the bare fact that the President is constitutionally vested with the power to execute and enforce the law. Other branches of government can, and often do, participate in and conduct formal hearings to determine whether or not crimes have been committed by high government officials. The executive's prosecutorial discretion over executive branch infractions of law is therefore neither exclusive nor inviolate.

But, from the (untrue) opinion that the executive maintains exclusive authority to prosecute violations of federal law, Olson draws the corollary that "neither the Judicial nor Legislative Branches may directly interfere with the prosecutorial discretion of the Executive by directing the Executive Branch to prosecute particular individuals" (8 Op. O.L.C. 101, at 115, 1984). In other words, Section 194 is an unconstitutional legislative encroachment upon the executive under Olson's interpretation of the Take Care clause (*Const.*, Art. 2, §3). And this interpretation effectively invalidates Section 194 of Title 2 of the U.S. Code requiring executive branch compliance with congressional subpoenas.

The self-contradictory flavor of Olson's logic is transparent: If confidentiality (or national security) is claimed by an executive branch official under the banner of executive privilege as a pretext for ignoring a congressional subpoena, then this piece of executive non-compliance with an ongoing congressional investigation into possible illegal activity would, by itself, represent a salient deviation from the executive branch duty to execute and enforce the laws which the President was sworn into office to protect! In other words, we ought to reject out of hand Olson's interpretation of the Constitution as handing the Chief Executive of state the singular prerogative to break with his duty of enforcing the laws on just those occasions where he deems it necessary to do so.

The second idea comprising Olson's concept of executive privilege derives from the doctrine of separation of powers, which Olson finds stated, not in the Constitution, but in a dictum from a Supreme Court decision in 1976 highlighting the central intent of the Framers that "the powers of the three great branches of the National Government be largely separate from one another" (*Buckley v. Valeo*, 424 U.S. 1, 119-20, 1976).[42] Note the important qualifier "largely" which means "to a great extent; in great part; generally; chiefly" (*Random House Webster's Unabridged Dictionary*, 2nd edition, p. 1084, 1998). The court in *Buckley* is saying that separation of powers between the branches of the federal government exists for the most part and in general, but not *absolutely*. Olson appears to ignore this subtle nuance of language in the *Buckley* dictum.

Olson's synthesis-concept of executive privilege is reached by fusing together the doctrine of (absolute) executive prosecutorial discretion with the doctrine of (absolute) separation of powers. But this bastard patchwork of absolute and exclusive powers and privileges, once vested in any President, creates a Frankenstein executive, who not only has the constitutional duty to execute the laws, but the exclusive extraconstitutional *privilege* of doing so whenever he chooses. The word "privilege" derives from the Latin *privilegium* signifying a "law" (cf. *lex*) applying "uniquely" or "individually" (cf. *privus*) to just one person, and to no one else. If the President has total discretion over which criminal indictments be pursued or abandoned at the Department of Justice, he then has total prosecutorial discretion to abort any federal indictments of his principals and members of staff, their surrogates, or anyone acting pursuant to his orders.

Olson's concept of executive privilege requires that we interpret the Constitution as prescribing an *absolute* separation of powers between the branches, which would then allow for *no* mixing or sharing of power in government; strange for a federalist system of checks and balances where each branch is deliberately empowered to amend or make void the actions of any other. Olson also admits that his doctrine of separation of powers is not explicitly contained anywhere in the Constitution.[43]

(*c*) It is logically absurd to maintain a hard and fast separation of powers between the branches of our federal government. If the judiciary, for instance, had absolute and separate power to interpret law, then no President would ever have authority at any time to issue any proclamation for any reason, even if it reflected a correct interpretation of existing law, and was required to preserve the peace and security of the nation. If the legislature had absolute authority to initiate war, then the President would have no authority to respond militarily to a foreign invasion or enemy attack, even if that enemy were operating on United States soil. If the President's veto power over proposed legislation were absolute, then the Senate would not have been given the power to reject treaties proposed to them by the President. If the President had absolute prosecutorial discretion to enforce the laws of the United States, then the Senate would never have been given the power to conduct trials of impeachment of the President, vice president, and other civil officers for treason, bribery, or other high crimes and misdemeanors. In fact, since executive branch failure to comply with a congressional subpoena represents a misdemeanor offence under the provisions of Section 194 of Title 2 of the U.S. Code, the Senate is constitutionally empowered to construe this matter as an impeachable offence under Article 2, Section 4 of the Constitution.

(*d*) The doctrine of executive privilege is founded on the idea that the President, in order to effectively carry out his constitutionally assigned responsibility to execute and enforce law, must be able, when he so chooses, to protect the confidentiality of documents, communications, and witnesses within the executive branch (see *United States v. Nixon*, 418 U.S. 683, 708, 1974). Bybee accentuates this element by emphasizing the Presidential prerogative to protect classified information vital to preserving United States national security interests abroad. The problem here, however, is that international terrorist organizations do not generally spy on American personnel, assets, and projects *in order to mimic them* or *build more effective defenses*. Terrorists may be in the planning stages of an attack, but the complexities of this planning are not at all comparable to the sophistication of cold-war era counterintelligence operations undertaken by the Soviet KGB. Bybee appears to be relying upon cold-war era strategic reasoning that simply no longer justifies the administration's presumptive need to protect the content of sensitive intelligence brought to light by congressional investigation.

According to Olson, executive branch confidentiality may be required in order for the President to carry out his constitutionally designated responsibilities, including the responsibility to execute the laws. If disclosure of information from the executive branch were to impair the President's ability to fulfill these duties, he must be able to claim some form of privilege in order to preserve his constitutional powers. But the danger of inventing *exclusive* prosecutorial discretion at Justice, in order to protect executive branch officials, is that it leads one to infer that *any* attempt by Congress or the courts to coax executive officials into compliance with the law would represent an undue infringement of power onto executive domain. But shielding executive officials from accountability to the American people befits more an imperial monarch than a President of the United States.

Position 15.—Having defended the Nixon doctrine of executive privilege as redefined in the 1984 opinion of Theodore B. Olson in the Reagan administration OLC, Bybee goes on to infer the following.

> It could be argued that Congress enacted [the anti-torture statute] 18 U.S.C. §2340A with full knowledge and consideration of the President's Commander-in-Chief power, and that Congress intended to restrict his discretion in the interrogation of enemy combatants. Even were we to accept this argument, however, we conclude that the Department of Justice could not enforce Section 2340A against federal officials acting pursuant to the President's constitutional authority to wage a military campaign. Indeed, in a different context, we have concluded that both courts and prosecutors should reject prosecutions that apply federal criminal laws to activity that is authorized pursuant to one of the President's constitutional powers. . . . [W]e concluded that the Department of Justice could not bring a criminal prosecution against a defendant who had acted pursuant to an exercise of the President's constitutional power. . . . Although Congress may define federal crimes that the President, through the Take Care Clause, should prosecute, Congress cannot compel the President to prosecute outcomes taken pursuant to the President's own constitutional authority. If Congress could do so, it could control the President's authority through the manipulation of federal criminal law. (*TTP*, Memo 14, Part V, §C, ¶s 1-2, p. 204)

On the Contrary, (*a*) the criminal implications of Bybee's counsel are astounding. Since the President may knowingly break the law, and after the fact claim executive privilege (in withholding subpoenaed documents and witnesses from Congress), he need not worry over authorizing his officials to break the law in applying coercive interrogation techniques to suspected terrorists. If the President authorizes and orders *A* to apply enhanced interrogation technique *x* to detainee *B* pursuant to his Commander-in-Chief authority to direct strategy in a war authorized by Congress, and if *A*, in applying *x* to *B*, oversteps the limits of humane treatment during an interrogation process that violates Section 2340A of the anti-torture statute, and even if there exists ample evidence of this violation, both courts and prosecutors, says Bybee, will *most likely* reject prosecutions that apply federal criminal laws to activity authorized pursuant to one of the President's constitutional powers.

In 1974 several key members of the Nixon White House staff along with other political supporters of the President's re-election campaign came to be indicted for alleged violations of federal law. In order to block the prosecutorial process, Nixon claimed executive privilege of presidential communications and filed a motion to quash the special prosecutor's subpoena that would have forced him to produce specific tapes and documents pertaining to particular meetings and conversations with key staff members. The District Court, however, issued an order for an *in camera* examination of the subpoenaed materials, having rejected Nixon's argument that 1. the dispute between himself and the special prosecutor was non-justiciable on the grounds that it constituted an intraexecutive conflict of interest, and 2. the judiciary lacked constitutional authority to review the President's assertion of executive privilege.

In *United States v. Nixon*, 418 U.S. 683 (1974) Chief Justice Warren Burger, delivering the opinion of the court, acknowledged President Nixon's presumptive privilege to confidentiality of executive communications on the idea that the President and his staff "must be free to explore alternatives in the process of shaping policies and making decisions, and to do so in a way many would be unwilling to express except in private" (*Id.*, at 708). But Burger also recognized that while the President certainly does have a presumptive claim to confidentiality of communications (the way judges may claim confidentiality in their deliberations), this presumption of privilege begins to vanish whenever asserting that privilege would hinder the administration of justice or impede the rule of law. Justice Burger opines:

> We have elected to employ an adversary system of criminal justice in which the parties contest all issues before a court of law. The need to develop all relevant facts in the adversary system is both fundamental and comprehensive. The ends of criminal justice would be defeated if judgments were to be founded on partial or speculative presentation of the facts. The very integrity of the judicial system and public confidence in the system depend on full disclosure of all the facts, within the framework of the rules of evidence. To ensure that justice is done, it is imperative to the function of the courts that compulsory process be available for the production of evidence needed either by the prosecution or by the defense. (418 U.S., at 709, citations omitted)

Bybee ought to have informed then-White House counsel Gonzales and President Bush that attempts to suppress evidence or to ignore or avoid a congressional subpoena might prove hazardous, since Chief Justice Burger clearly and powerfully asserted in *Nixon* the right of the courts to employ "compulsory process" to force a reluctant President or members of his staff to testify or to hand over key documents and other communications in an ongoing investigation into alleged wrongdoing. He should have told the President that both Congress and the courts are most likely to demand full disclosure of all relevant evidence and that justice cannot be served in United States courts on a partial presentation of the facts.

(*b*) Bybee ostensibly seeks to avoid the phantom of a bully Congress that would somehow "manipulate" the President's foreign policy decision-making process by actively enforcing federal criminal laws against indicted administration officials. Bybee incorrectly advises his client that "Congress cannot compel the President to prosecute outcomes taken pursuant to the President's own constitutional authority" (*TTP*, p. 204). But he fails to provide even a cursory defense against anyone who, in applying the word of 2 U.S.C. §194, would point out that it is a misdemeanor offence for any administration official, regardless of rank or position, to ignore a congressional subpoena. Bybee simply adopts Olson's obstructionist perspective that even if the foreman of a grand jury were to indorse an indictment as a true bill,[44] the United States Attorney could simply refuse to sign the indictment and prevent the case from going forward (8 Op. O.L.C. 101, 118). Such bold pretensions of prosecutorial discretion for the executive ignore the power of federal courts to issue writs of mandamus, and effectively place the President and his principals beyond the pale of accountability.

Position 16.—It is abundantly clear that the Bush II OLC envisioned its "new paradigm" policy of preemptive counterterrorism as necessitating a program of systematic interrogational coercion (featuring both CIA "black site" as well as renditional torture[45]) of suspected terrorists and others suspected of concealing valuable intelligence. Bybee even portends a brave new world where the United States and its allies stand to be victimized repeatedly by a series of ticking-bomb emergency scenarios where vital intelligence must be harvested hurriedly from key terrorist operatives, who, as chance would have it, are conveniently held in United States custody:

> It may be the case that only successful interrogations can provide the information necessary to prevent the success of covert terrorist attacks upon the United States and its citizens. Congress can no more interfere with the President's conduct of the interrogation of enemy combatants than it can dictate strategic or tactical decisions on the battlefield. Just as statutes that order the President to conduct warfare in a certain manner or for specific

> goals would be unconstitutional, so too are laws that seek to prevent the President from gaining the intelligence he believes necessary to prevent attacks upon the United States. (*TTP*, Memo 14, Part V, §C, ¶7, p. 207)

On the Contrary, (*a*) Bybee failed to countenance the possiblity that cooperation with suspects might be a more effective path to useable intelligence than brutal interrogations which jeopardize traditional investigatory avenues of information access, and that a policy of systematized coercion might place our friends and sympathizers in the Islamic world on edge, making them significantly less likely to cooperate with U.S. led investigatory efforts to hunt down and capture international criminal conspirators, and more likely to desire to stymie such efforts in the future.

(*b*) According to Bybee, the anti-torture statute becomes unconstitutional in proportion as it hinders or prevents President Bush from acquiring the foreign intelligence information he believes necessary to prevent future terrorist attacks upon the United States. But this position is inaccurate given the following facts:

1. There is no provision in the Constitution that allows the President to violate federal law with impunity, and
2. It is not the laws themselves, but rather the legislative and judicial branches of government that, strictly speaking, impinge upon the President's horizon of policy options in the exercise of his executive war powers.

For instance, the anti-torture statute does not govern the *direction of strategy* in the President's campaign against terrorism, but it does govern the *interrogational process* in accordance with humanitarian restrictions contained in the Geneva Conventions, the International Covenant on Civil and Political Rights, and the Convention Against Torture. Since Bybee sees coercive interrogation as a powerful and necessary tool in the President's arsenal of weapons in the struggle against terrorism, he feels the President should be endowed with absolute discretion over all interrogational processes, regardless of any limitations of international law and the potential for negative political repercussions.

Even if an administration-approved interrogation method arguably crosses the line drawn in Section 2340 prohibiting torture, and application of this statute in litigation against executive branch officials was not held in the courts to be an unconstitutional infringement of Presidential power,

Bybee still believes that "under current [post-9/11] circumstances certain justification defenses might be available that would potentially eliminate criminal liability." But the problem with this type of justification, often called the "choice-of-evils" or "necessity" defense, is that, even if such a defense were admissible in federal court, it could not be used retroactively as an excuse for justifying the programmatic torturing of suspects.

In other words, however elaborate one's choice-of-evils defense may be, it could only be wielded in a federal court (if at all) *when an interrogator has actually succeeded in preventing more evil than the evil he deployed against his captive in the interrogation chamber*. According to the American Law Institute's Model Penal Code, §3.02, "Conduct which the actor believes to be necessary to avoid a harm or evil to himself or to another is justifiable, provided that the harm or evil sought to be avoided by such conduct is greater than that sought to be prevented by the law defining the offence charged." According to Professor Michael S. Moore "[this] defense is only available when the actor did what was on balance the right thing to do (that is, he prevented more harm or evil than he caused by his action)."[46] Bybee nowhere accounts for the thicket of legal difficulties involved in proving that more harm was prevented than the harm of interrogational torture.

The burden of proof that greater evils were actually forestalled by torturing suspects rests by law on the shoulders of the interrogator, not his victims. Such a proof in court requires physical evidence that could only be acquired from the use of traditional non-coercive criminal investigation methods, and the avoidance of sloppy interrogation sessions. In other words, the more careless interrogators happen to be in the tank, the less likely they are to acquire the hard evidence they will later need in court to show that the people they were dehumanizing were actual dangers to society.

Even if Section 22 of the Israeli Penal Law (1977), which provides for a criminal defense of necessity, were engrafted upon the fabric of United States federal law, it would provide no sanctuary for torturers, because the burden of proof it contains is too rigid to justify torture undertaken as part of a broader program of systematic coercion. Section 22 provides that

> a person may be exempted from criminal responsibility for an act or omission if he can show that it was done or made in order to avoid consequences which could not otherwise be avoided and which would have inflicted grievous harm or injury on his person, honour, or property or on the person or honour of others whom he was bound to protect or on prop-

> erty placed in his charge: provided that he did no more than was reasonably necessary for that purpose and that the harm caused by him was not disproportionate to the harm avoided.[47]

Successful application of this criminal defense requires that the defendant present evidence that: 1. the evil he sought to avoid "could not otherwise be avoided" but for the doing of the act or omission for which he is being charged, and 2. he refrained from doing more than was "reasonably necessary" for the purpose of preventing the evil, and 3. the harm he caused was not "disproportionate" to the harm avoided.

These three requirements are stringent because they do not provide legal cover for interrogators who got their information about an imminent danger they sought to prevent by coercing suspect *A* from a previous suspect *B*, who was tortured in some other context to extract circumstantial information that initially led investigators to suspect that *A* had valuable information in the first place. Sloppy interrogations are the mother of unreliable intelligence. When intelligence information of dubious authenticity points its finger at a ticking-bomb suspect, the relevance of the sources of that originative intelligence takes on central importance in applying the defense of necessity at trial.

As it exists under Israeli Penal Law the availability of the defense in court is inversely proportional to the severity of the injuries sustained by the interrogee. Gratuitously violent or sadistic interrogations are likely to weigh against application of the necessity defense at trial, because the interrogator is bound to refrain from causing harm *disproportionate* to the harm to be avoided, and must do no more than was necessary to acquire the needed intelligence—even if it could be shown by defense counsel that application of invasive interrogation techniques forced the interrogee to divulge vital information.

There is no United States federal statute establishing a defense of necessity. And, the anti-torture statute, as encoded in Section 2340A, does not countenance exceptional cases where torture might be allowed to prevent the occurrence of an exponentially greater evil than the evil of torture, e.g., the suffering of hunderds of civilians trapped under the rubble of a building gutted by a terrorist car-bomb versus the interrogational suffering of one or two suspects whose information could foil the attack before it occurs. But even when faced with such looming terrorist threats, the morality of interrogational coercion is *not* reducible to some choice-of-evils scenario where you (and only you) happen to be standing right next to a trolley track where there is mounted a manually operated Thomson-switch stationed a half mile ahead of a runaway trolley that is currently barrelling out of control and set to pass by your point in a few seconds. If you flip the switch up, the trolley forks left, mowing down eight track workers. If you flip the switch down, the trolley forks right, crushing three visiting Japanese school children. Should you then, in facing this horrible choice of evils, turn the switch onto the innocent school children, all souls being equally precious to God? Or should you wait it out and do nothing as you watch eight members of your community fall under the merciless steel wheels of the trolley?

From a purely consequentialist point-of-view the choice appears clear-cut. We go to our moral calculators to discover that the net pain and loss involved in the horrific bodily injury of eight individuals outweighs that of merely three. We choose to divert the trolley onto the children, and the case appears closed. Our choice eventuates the lesser of two evils. But in making this choice we have neglected a host of moral considerations that have more to do with acknowledging the inherent value of other people's lives, one's duty to others, and the maintenance of one's own set of action-guiding principles, than with the empty fallout of consequences. The meaning of life is tied in great measure to the very principles we ignore as consequentialists.

Such clear choices as the one we just made to save eight lives while sacrificing three does not generally reflect how the world works. The question of whether or not one ought to coerce and/or torture another human being (to acquire information) is not at all comparable to flipping a switch. Flip the Thomson-switch in our trolley problem, and consequences fall out with the regularity of clockwork. Torture a suspected terrorist, and you may get handed a pile of useless lies fabricated to make the pain go away. The trolley problem funnels an agent's universe of choices down to a manually operated lever, whereas there exist multiple options to torture that could prove more effective in the short run at getting information needed to prevent an imminent attack. The person at the Thomson-switch could argue that her choices were obvious, the trolley came roaring down the hill, the track forked at a certain point, and two options with apparent and manifest consequences presented themselves.

An interrogator standing at a torture-switch that, when flipped, forces an electric charge to course through the twitching body of an interrogee shackled to a metal table in a stuffy interrogation cell, cannot possibly argue that her choices were clear-cut, since there is no real cause-and-effect relationship between torture and actionable intelligence, since the existence of such intelligence depends upon factors *not* controlled by the choices the interrogator makes inside the cell. An interrogee who is being subjected to severe pain by torture-switch may not really be who he is suspected of being, he may know nothing of the plot he is suspected of hatching, and, if he does, he will be significantly less likely to cooperate with authorities who have no regard for his person.

Position 17.—Bybee sets up a complex three-part argument to establish a formal defense of necessity that he hopes will help executive branch officials (and others acting pursuant to executive orders) to avoid criminal liability for future possible violations of the anti-torture statute. The first part of his argument reads thusly:

> We believe that a defense of necessity could be raised, under the current circumstances to an allegation of a Section 2340A violation. Often referred to as the "choice-of-evils" defense, necessity has been defined as follows: Conduct that the actor believes to be necessary to avoid a harm or evil to himself or to another is justifiable, provided that: [1] the harm or evil sought to be avoided by such conduct is greater than that sought to be prevented by the law defining the offense charged; and [2] neither the Code nor other law defining the offense provides exceptions or defenses dealing with the specific situation involved; and [3] a legislative purpose to exclude the justification claimed does not otherwise plainly appear. Model Penal Code §3.02. *See also* Wayne R. LaFave & Austin W. Scott, 1 Substantive Criminal Law §5.4 at 627 (1986 & 2002 supp.). Although there is no federal statute that generally establishes necessity or other justifications as defenses to federal criminal laws, the Supreme Court has recognized the defense. See *United States v. Bailey*, 444 U.S. 394, 410 (1980). . . . According to LaFave and Scott, "[t]he law ought to promote the achievement of higher values at the expense of lesser values, and sometimes the greater good for society will be accomplished by violating the literal language of the criminal law," at 629. (*TTP*, Memo 14, Part VI, §A, ¶s 1-2, pp. 207-08)

On the Contrary, (*a*) violating the literal language of criminal statutes by committing interrogational torture for the "greater good" is as legally risky and morally depraved, for Bybee's interrogator, as it would be for a medical doctor under Hippocratic oath to justify injurious medical experimentation on uninformed patients where an infectious disease of some sort is implanted in each subject in order to produce physiological effects that are then tabulated empirically, for the reason that on rare occasions this manipulation of a patient's equilibrium state of health may yield highly useful scientific information about human physiology that would, if discovered, greatly benefit society.

Does Bybee really believe he is promoting the greater good for society by green-lighting the use of programmatic torture for the President? What possible threat to society can possibly be posed by a suspected terrorist held in captivity by U.S. personnel? Torture makes neither tactical nor moral sense. The practice of dehumanizing the helpless dehumanizes us, compromises our collective moral principles, and accounts life as having no inherent natural value. If we accept the harsh realities of torture as necessary for counterterrorist operations in the future, what is there left to fight for in fighting terrorism? Are we not trading away the very moral principles and values upon which we stand united as a nation?

(*b*) If we follow Bybee's summation of the necessity defense at criterion [1] as provided in Section 3.02 of the Model Penal Code, then an interrogator is free to administer cruel and unusual punishment in the coercion of any suspected terrorist, so long as the evil he seeks to avoid is greater than the evil wrought by violating the law through coercion. But if, as we have already argued, terrorism and torture are morally equivalent, as both represent a kind of random (and often deadly) violence perpetrated against helpless individuals incapable of defending themselves at the point of attack, then how can anyone be sure that the evil the interrogator seeks to avoid is any worse than the one committed in administering torture? If we extend Bybee's understanding of LaFave and Scott's principle of the "greater good" to other parts of the criminal law, then a suspected rapist could himself be dehumanized during interrogation, so long as the evil sought to be avoided by the interrogator is greater than the evil forbidden by the law forbidding interrogational coercion and torture. It both appears and *is* unjust to terrorize a suspected terrorist in order to prevent the evil of some future possible act of terrorism, which the suspect cannot possibly commit, consummate, or command once detained incommunicado by authorities.

(*c*) It is not clear why Bybee reasserts the text of LaFave & Scott at 629 which says that "sometimes the greater good for society will be accomplished by violating the literal language of the criminal law" and that "the law ought to promote the achievement of higher values at the expense of lesser values." What precisely are these "higher" values? And why must "lesser" values be jettisoned for their sake? Are we dealing here with Nietzschean values that define the Will of the nobility, values "higher" than the lowly values of the peasantry? Why must these higher values supplant the so-called "lesser" values from time to time? Since Bybee fails to elaborate why these words are relevant to his purpose, it is difficult to know what to make of them.

And what of the text quoted from the Model Penal Code? Is Bybee quoting this text to add a veneer of legitimacy to his justification for torture by showing that somewhere in the code it is permissible for us to jettison our moral principles when emergency situations present themselves? The words he quotes from the code and from the LaFave & Scott Substantive Criminal Law import value judgments about the purpose and tenor of positive law that simply go unevaluated in his memorandum opinion for Judge Gonzales.

Even if the moral reasonings Bybee trots out in justification of torture were arguable before a judge in a United States federal court under a defense of necessity, it seems quite uncertain whether they could be used to justify a defendant's illegal deeds once those deeds are recognized as part of a broader conspiracy to commit torture emanating from the highest levels of the executive.

Position 18.—The second part of Bybee's argument for the defense of necessity consists of five segments:

> First, the defense is not limited to certain types of harms. Therefore, the harm inflicted by necessity may include homicide, so long as the harm avoided is greater (i.e., preventing more deaths). [LaFave & Scott, 1 Substantive Criminal Law], at 634. Second, it must actually be the defendant's intention to avoid the greater harm; intending to commit murder and then learning only later that the death had the fortuitous result of saving other lives will not support a necessity defense. *Id.* at 635. Third, if the defendant reasonably believed that the lesser harm was necessary, even if, unknown to him, it was not, he may still avail himself of the defense. As LaFave and Scott explain, "if A kills B reasonably believing it to be necessary to save C and D, he is not guilty of murder even though, unknown to A, C and D could have been rescued without the necessity of killing B." *Id.* at 635. Fourth, it is for the court, and not the defendant to judge whether the harm avoided outweighed the harm done. *Id.* at 636. Fifth, the defendant cannot rely upon the necessity defense if a third alternative is open and known to him that will cause less harm. *Id.* at 636. (*TTP*, Memo 14, Part VI, §A, ¶3, p. 208)

On the Contrary, (*a*) not content with his unbridled legitimation of institutionalized coercion, Bybee goes on to provide us with a subtle five part justification for interrogational homicide—Yes, a legal justification for murdering an interrogee while trying to secure from him valuable intelligence! Yet LaFave & Scott's strict withdrawal (*Id.*, at 635) of the necessity defense protection from any defendant who, in conducting interrogational coercion, intended to murder his suspect, and carries out the act caring not a whit for the avoidance of harm to others (but learns only later that his homicide "had the fortuitous result of saving other lives") appears to apply to any system of detention and interrogation that places paramount importance on the gathering of intelligence information from suspects at the expense of securing criminal convictions at trial. Legal permission to systematize torture is nowhere contained in any of the texts that Bybee cites from LaFave & Scott in his interpretation of the necessity defense. And he fails to countenance the possibility that cooperation with suspects under interrogation might work *more* effectively in the gathering of intelligence than physical and mental coercion. The Pentagon's recommendation of enhanced interrogation techniques in its Working Group Report of April 2004 (issued just eight months after the legal template drafted in Bybee-Gonzales) appears to regard suspected terrorists, not as rational agents with worldly interests, but as wild beasts that must be caged, secured, and manipulated.[48]

(*b*) The third segment of Bybee's interpretation of the defense of necessity borrows another page from LaFave and Scott, *Id.*, at 636, which defines necessity as based on a defendant's "reasonable belief" at the time he administered interrogational pain in excess of that allowed in Section 2340A. Since an interrogator's *belief* about the relative necessity of the coercion he applies to his interrogee is not qualified (in LaFave and Scott) in any significant way other than that it must be *reasonable,* nothing prevents this reasonable belief from being grounded entirely on hearsay evidence gleaned from unwilling suspects by means of interrogational coercion. Whittling down "reasonable belief" to "belief in hearsay evidence" opens the door to the collection of any and all types of hearsay evidence that can be gleaned, which further encourages the institutionalization of torture. The Defense Department's subsequent establishment of a CSRT system (in July of 2004) seems to fulfill Bybee's original vision because it actually encourages the gathering of hearsay evidence by officially validating it for use in trial as sufficient proof of the continued unlawful enemy combatant status of the detainee.

(*c*) Since Bybee himself cites LaFave and Scott, *Id.* at 636, to show that it is up to a court of law and a judge, and not the defendant, to decide whether the suspected harm the interrogator (successfully) avoided was greater than the harm done by his interrogational killing of the suspect, it makes no sense for Bybee to justify, as legally defensible, acts of coercion that clearly establish Section 2340A violations. Even if the defendant had, in point of fact, halted and prevented a terrorist attack on others by her deployment of coercion leading to torture and then to eventual interrogational homicide, she still must prove that there was not an alternative option available at the time of her violation of Section 2340A. The demands for proof contained in the necessity defense offer little sanctuary for those who may have committed acts of torture.

In order to legally institute a system of interrogational coercion there must exist a real and abiding international terrorist threat from without: No threat, no emergency circumstance. And perhaps this is why Bybee goes to great lengths to ramp up the level of public anxiety and hostility over terrorism by emphasizing the emergence of new and imminent deadly dangers from sleeper cells here in the United States to al-Qaeda plans to develop chemical, biological and radiological weapons. According to Bybee,

> al-Qaeda plans apparently include efforts to develop and deploy chemical, biological and nuclear weapons of mass destruction. Under these circumstances, a detainee may possess information that could enable the United States to prevent attacks that potentially could equal or surpass the September 11 attacks in their magnitude. Clearly, any harm that might occur during an interrogation would pale in insignificance compared to the harm avoided by preventing such an attack, which could take hundreds or thousands of lives.[49]

Future possible mass casualty attacks on civilians by terrorists using asymmetric means of warfare are more akin to criminal deeds than to tactical military maneuvers. It would have therefore behooved the administration to emphasize traditional methods of organized crime investigation rather than the invasive and adversarial interrogation techniques actually deployed. For instance, if detainees were afforded comptetent legal counsel and the presumption of innocence before trial as stipulated in the Geneva Conventions, it is quite possible that investigators would see greater levels of cooperation by detainees willing to reveal useful information, than a situation where the investigation process itself becomes a tool of coercion.

Position 19.—In the third part of his justification for the defense of necessity Bybee articulates what might be called the administration's Torture Doctrine, according to which, under the President's calculus

> two factors will help indicate when the necessity defense could appropriately be invoked. First, the more certain that government officials are that a particular individual has information needed to prevent an attack, the more necessary interrogation will be. Second, the more likely it appears to be that a terrorist attack is likely to occur, and the greater the amount of damage expected from such an attack, the more that an interrogation to get information would become necessary. Of course the strength of the necessity defense depends on the circumstances that prevail, and the knowledge of the government actors involved, when the interrogation is conducted. While every interrogation that might violate Section 2340A does not trigger a necessity defense, we can say that certain circumstances could support such a defense. . . . [I]f Congress explicitly has made clear that violation of a statute cannot be outweighed by the harm avoided, courts cannot recognize the necessity defense. (*TTP*, Memo 14, Part VI, §A, ¶9, p. 209)

On the Contrary, (*a*) the more certainty a government official possesses that a terrorist suspect has valuable information that could forestall an attack, the more necessary interrogation will only be *perceived* to be. Bybee misses the nuance between perception and reality when he implies a cause-and-effect relationship between the interrogation official's subjective mental state of certainty (about the prospect of attack) and the objective necessity of his use of enhanced techniques to make the interrogee talk. It is, of course, questionable whether coercion and hyperaggressive interrogation techniques that might violate Section 2340A are even capable of becoming *necessary* tools in the prevention of terrorism as Bybee suggests. If enhanced techniques create an irreversible antipathy between interrogator and interrogee, and if they clog investigative channels with useless fabrications and lies invented by the interrogee to appease his captors, would it not be necessary to abandon their use entirely?

The ground of my assertion here is that harsh confrontation and relentless dehumanization make useful intelligence generally more difficult for investigators to acquire, not easier. The person under duress is more useful for what he knows, than for what he does not. Forcing humans into evasion and resistance modes of behavior makes them generally uncooperative. If a bomb is really out there ticking, and one day there may very well be, how do you know, how do I know, how do government officials know that the man we suspect of having planted the device really possesses any actionable intelligence to begin with? How did you and I come upon our information? Was torture used at a distant site to extract what we know? Do we even know who it is that acquired the information that prompted our original suspicions about the danger at issue?

(*b*) If it is true, as Philip Zimbardo recently observed in *The Lucifer Effect* that "anger, revenge, and outrage at perceived injustice are the motivational triggers for deciding to die for the cause,"[50] then the use of invasive interrogation techniques that end up engendering these same mental antipathies are more likely to backfire by making interrogees wish for death in preference to revealing the information interrogators seek.[51]

Position 20.—Twisting the legal opinion of law professor Michael S. Moore so far out of context as to make the professor's views on the necessity defense match the administration's own authoritarian vision of legalized interrogational coercion and programmatic torture, Bybee admits that

> an enemy combatant in detention does not himself present a threat of harm. He is not actually carrying out the attack; rather, he has participated in the planning and preparation for the attack, or merely has knowledge of the attack through his membership in the terrorist organization. Nonetheless, leading scholarly commentators believe that interrogation of such individuals using methods that might violate Section 2340A would be justified under the doctrine of self-defense, because the combatant by aiding and promoting the terrorist plot "has culpably caused the situation where someone *might* get hurt. If hurting him is the only means to prevent the death or injury of others put at risk by his actions, such torture should be permissible, and on the same basis that self-defense is permissible" (Michael S. Moore, "Torture and the Balance of Evils," 23 *Israel L. Rev.* 280, 323, 1989). (*TTP*, Memo 14, Part VI, §B, ¶8, pp. 211-12, emphasis added)

On the Contrary, (*a*) Bybee deliberately misquotes the text of Moore to buttress his own legitimation of invasive interrogation techniques by failing to tell us that Moore's words apply only to cases where the interrogee has "culpably caused [a] situation where someone *must* get hurt."[52] Bybee supplies "might" where Moore originally has "must." In other words, an imminent terrorist attack *must* be known to be in the works, and innocent life *must* be on the brink of being lost, and all this without importing distant speculation based on hearsay evidence of dubious authenticity.

Reading Moore's original sentence, the interrogee *must* be directly involved in an imminent and ongoing attack, and he or she *must* culpably cause the situation to unfold wherein one or more persons are *bound* to get hurt or killed, if an interrogator is to justify hurting a suspect out of self-defense. Once the immediate danger has passed, once it is no longer impending or over hanging, hurting the suspect is no longer self-defense but mutilation. And this is precisely the line that Bybee appears to blur by misquoting Moore.

The way Bybee has it, an interogee may be tortured even though the imminent attack in question may or may not happen. But this is tantamount to saying that the attack is no longer imminent. What makes an attack imminent is precisely its *certainty* of occurrence. Once we lose that certainty, we lose whatever moral leverage we might have had to justify our infliction of pain on an interrogee who is suspected of knowing too much, assuming that such pain is ever justifiably inflicted on another person. What we have here is a case where Bush II OLC attorneys have actually manipulated the text of an officially published legal analysis in order to foist their own agenda of mistrust, fear, and suspicion onto the general public. Bybee neglects to tell us that Moore radically limits the range of use for the necessity defense to just those rare cases where "the actor did what was on balance, the right thing to do (that is, he prevented more harm or evil than he caused by his action)."[53] Moore's position here is too morally principled for Bybee to extract from it the position he wants to defend: that acts of torture are defensible in court, regardless of whether the potential danger of attack was imminent or not, because Congress remains silent over whether violations of Section 2340A can be outweighed by the potential harm avoided.

(*b*) Bybee also neglects to inform us of Moore's cautionary warning that "there are some acts so wrong that even good consequences cannot justify them."[54] Even if an interrogator successfully forestalled a terrorist attack by using a quick last-minute waterboarding, or some other piece of coercion on the suspect that allowed him to acquire just the right information at just the right time, the act itself is so morally depraved that it should never have been done to begin with, even though this could spell the death of innocent people that might have otherwise been saved as a side-effect of the application of interrogational pain and torture. How could Bybee have overlooked the importance of Moore's comment that "Israel too seeks a criminal law that reflects its fundamental moral beliefs. One of those beliefs is that the end, no matter how good, does not justify the use of any means to achieve it"?[55]

(*c*) Although Bybee admits that his hypothetical detainee may not have actually carried out any terrorist attack, he goes on to warrantlessly infer that the detainee, qua enemy combatant, "has participated in the planning and preparation" for an attack. But this is to assume a detainee guilty of wrongdoing not only by association and peremptory categorization, but prior to and independent of any Article 5 competent tribunal hearing.

I can only recall the warning contained in the dissenting opinion of Justice Brandeis in *Olmstead v. United States*, 277 U.S. 438 (1928), a valuable case for neo-conservative lawyers because the majority held that the obtaining of evidence by telephone wiretap of United States citizens by officials of the United States government, and its use at trial, does *not* constitute a violation of the Fourth Amendment protecting the right of the American people to be secure in their persons, houses, papers, and effects from unreasonable searches and seizures:

> Decency, security and liberty alike demand that government officials shall be subjected to the same rules of conduct that are commands to the citizen. In a government of laws, existence of the government will be imperiled if it fails to observe the law scrupulously. Our Government is the potent, the omnipresent teacher. For good or for ill, it teaches the whole people by its example. Crime is contagious. If the Government becomes a lawbreaker it breeds contempt for law; it invites every man to become a law unto himself; it invites anarchy. To declare that, in the administration of criminal law, the end justifies the means—to declare that the Government may commit crimes in order to secure the conviction of a private criminal—would bring terrible retribution. (277 U.S., at 485)

The Brandeis dissent in *Olmstead* is visionary for the fact that it illustrates that even during times where the Court afforded unconstitutional latitude to government investigators, it never intended that such expanded authority be used as a pretext for breaking the law in order to enforce it.

APPENDICES

Appendix A
Military Order of November 13, 2001
President George W. Bush

Executive Orders
Federal Register: November 16, 2001 (Volume 66, Number 2)
Presidential Documents, Page 57831-57836

DETENTION, TREATMENT, AND TRIAL OF CERTAIN NON-CITIZENS IN THE WAR AGAINST TERRORISM

By the authority vested in me as President and as Commander-in-Chief of the Armed Forces of the United States by the Constitution and the laws of the United States of America, including the Authorization for Use of Military Force Joint Resolution (Public Law 107-40, 115 Stat. 224) and Sections 821 and 836 of Title 10, United States Code, it is hereby ordered as follows:

I. FINDINGS

(a) International terrorists, including members of al-Qaida, have carried out attacks on United States diplomatic and military personnel and facilities abroad and on citizens and property within the United States on a scale that has created a state of armed conflict that requires the use of United States Armed Forces.

(b) In light of grave acts of terrorism and threats of terrorism, including the terrorist attacks on September 11, 2001, on the headquarters of the United States Department of Defense in the national capital region, on the World Trade Center in New York, and on civilian aircraft such as in Pennsylvania, I proclaimed a national emergency on September 14, 2001 (Proc. 7463, Declaration of National Emergency by Reason of Certain Terrorist Attacks).

(c) Individuals acting alone and in concert involved in international terrorism possess both the capability and the intention to undertake further terrorist attacks against the United States that, if not detected and prevented, will cause mass deaths, mass injuries, and massive destruction of property, and may place at risk the continuity of the operations of the United States Government.

(d) The ability of the United States to protect the United States and its citizens, and to help its allies and other cooperating nations protect their nations and their citizens, from such further terrorist attacks depends in significant part upon using the United States Armed Forces to identify terrorists and those who support them, to disrupt their activities, and to eliminate their ability to conduct or support such attacks.

(e) To protect the United States and its citizens, and for the effective conduct of military operations and prevention of terrorist attacks, it is necessary for individuals subject to this order pursuant to Section 2 hereof to be detained, and, when tried, to be tried for violations of the laws of war and other applicable laws by military tribunals.

(f) Given the danger to the safety of the United States and the nature of international terrorism, and to the extent provided by and under this order, I find consistent with Section 836 of Title 10, United States Code, that it is not practicable to apply in military commissions under this order the principles of law and the rules of evidence generally recognized in the trial of criminal cases in the United States district courts.

(g) Having fully considered the magnitude of the potential deaths, injuries, and property destruction that would result from potential acts of terrorism against the United States, and the probability that such acts will occur, I have determined that an extraordinary emergency exists for national defense purposes, that this emergency constitutes an urgent and compelling government interest, and that issuance of this order is necessary to meet the emergency.

II. DEFINITION AND POLICY

a. The term "individual subject to this order" shall mean any individual who is not a United States citizen with respect to whom I determine from time to time in writing that:

(1) there is reason to believe that such individual, at the relevant times,

i. is or was a member of the organization known as al-Qaida;

ii. has engaged in, aided or abetted, or conspired to commit, acts of international terrorism, or acts in preparation therefor, that have caused, threaten to cause, or have as their aim to cause, injury to or adverse effects on the United States, its citizens, national security, foreign policy, or economy; or

iii. has knowingly harbored one or more individuals described in Subparagraphs (i) or (ii) of Subsection 2(a)(1) of this order; and

(2) it is in the interest of the United States that such individual be subject to this order.

b. It is the policy of the United States that the Secretary of Defense shall take all necessary measures to ensure that any individual subject to this order is detained in accordance with Section 3, and, if the individual is to be tried, that such individual is tried only in accordance with Section 4.

c. It is further the policy of the United States that any individual subject to this order who is not already under the control of the Secretary of Defense but who is under the control of any other officer or agent of the United States or any State shall, upon delivery of a copy of such written determination to such officer of agent, forthwith be placed under the control of the Secretary of Defense.

III. DETENTION AUTHORITY OF THE SECRETARY OF DEFENSE

Any individual subject to this order shall be—

(a) detained at an appropriate location designated by the Secretary of Defense outside or within the United States;

(b) treated humanely, without any adverse distinction based on race, color, religion, gender, birth, wealth, or any similar criteria;

(c) afforded adequate food, drinking water, shelter, clothing, and medical treatment;

(d) allowed the free exercise of religion consistent with the requirements of such detention; and

(e) detained in accordance with such other conditions as the Secretary of Defense may prescribe.

IV. AUTHORITY OF THE SECRETARY OF DEFENSE REGARDING TRIALS OF INDIVIDUALS SUBJECT TO THIS ORDER

a. Any individual subject to this order shall, when tried, be tried by military commission for any and all offenses triable by military commission that such individual is alleged to have committed, and may be punished in accordance with the penalties provided under applicable law, including life imprisonment or death.

b. As a military function and in light of the findings in Section 1, including Subsection (f) thereof, the Secretary of Defense shall issue such orders and regulations, including orders for the appointment of one or more military commissions, as may be necessary to carry out Subsection (a) of this Section.

c. Orders and regulations issued under Subsection (b) of this Section shall include, but not be limited to, rules for the conduct of the proceedings of military commissions, including pretrial, trial, and posttrial procedures, modes of proof, issuance of process, and qualifications of attorneys, which shall at a minimum provide for—

(1) military commissions to sit at any time and any place, consistent with such guidance regarding time and place as the Secretary of Defense may provide;
(2) a full and fair trial, with the military commission sitting as the triers of both fact and law;
(3) admission of such evidence as would, in the opinion of the presiding officer of the military commission (or instead, if any other member of the commission so request at the time the presiding officer renders that opinion, the opinion of the commission rendered at that time by a majority of the commission), have probative value to a reasonable person;
(4) in a manner consistent with the protection of information classified or classifiable under Executive Order 12958 of April 17, 1995, as amended, or any successor Executive Order, protected by statute or rule from unauthorized disclosure, or otherwise protected by law, (A) the handling of, admission into evidence of, and access to materials and information, and (B) the conduct, closure of, and access to proceedings;
(5) conduct of the prosecution by one or more attorneys designated by the Secretary of Defense and conduct of the defense by attorneys for the individual subject to this order;
(6) conviction only upon the concurrence of two-thirds of the members of the commission present at the time of the vote, a majority being present;
(7) sentencing only upon the concurrence of two-thirds of the members of the commission present at the time of the vote, a majority being present; and
(8) submission of the record of the trial, including any conviction or sentence, for review and final decision by me or by the Secretary of Defense if so designated by me for that purpose.

V. OBLIGATIONS OF OTHER AGENCIES TO ASSIST THE SECRETARY OF DEFENSE

Departments, agencies, entities, and officers of the United States shall, to the maximum extent permitted by law, provide to the Secretary of Defense such assistance as he may request to implement this order.

VI. ADDITIONAL AUTHORITIES OF THE SECRETARY OF DEFENSE

(a) As a military function and in light of the findings in Section 1, the Secretary of Defense shall issue such orders and regulations as may be necessary to carry out any of the provisions of this order.
(b) The Secretary of Defense may perform any of his functions or duties, and may exercise any of the powers provided to him under this Order (other than under Section 4(c)(8) hereof) in accordance with Section 113(d) of Title 10, United States Code.

VII. RELATIONSHIP TO OTHER LAW AND FORUMS

a. Nothing in this order shall be considered to—
   (1) authorize the disclosure of state secrets to any person not otherwise authorized to have access to them;
   (2) limit the authority of the President as Commander-in-Chief of the Armed Forces or the power of the President to grant reprieves and pardons; or
   (3) limit the lawful authority of the Secretary of Defense, any military commander, or any other officer or agent of the United States or of any State to detain or try any person who is not an individual subject to this order.

b. With respect to any individual subject to this order—
   (1) military tribunals shall have exclusive jurisdiction with respect to offenses by the individual; and
   (2) the individual shall not be privileged to seek any remedy or maintained any proceeding, directly or indirectly, or to have any such remedy or proceeding sought on the individual's behalf, in (i) any court of the United States, or any State on the individual's behalf, in (ii) any court of any foreign nation, or (iii) any international tribunal.

c. This order is not intended to and does not create any right, benefit, or privilege, substantive or procedural, enforceable at law or equity by any party, against the United States, its departments, agencies, or other entities, its officers or employees, or any other person.

d. For purposes of this order, the term "State" includes any State, district, territory, or possession of the United States.

e. I reserve the authority to direct the Secretary of Defense, at any time hereafter, to transfer to a governmental authority control of any individual subject to this order. Nothing in this order shall be construed to limit the authority of any such governmental authority to prosecute any individual for whom control is transferred.

VIII. PUBLICATION

This order shall be published in the Federal Register.

GEORGE W. BUSH

THE WHITE HOUSE

November 13, 2001.

Appendix B
Executive Order of February 7, 2002
President George W. Bush

Memorandum for the Vice President
The Secretary of State
The Secretary of Defense
The Attorney General
Chief of Staff to the President
Director of Central Intelligence
Assistant to the President for National Security Affairs
Chairman of the Joint Chiefs of Staff

Subject: Humane Treatment of al-Qaeda and Taliban Detainees

1. Our recent extensive discussions regarding the status of al-Qaeda and Taliban detainees confirm that the application of the Geneva Convention Relative to the Treatment of Prisoners of War of August 12, 1949 (Geneva) to the conflict with al-Qaeda and the Taliban involves "High Contracting Parties," which can only be States. Moreover, it assumes the existence of "regular" armed forces fighting on behalf of States. However, the war against terrorism ushers in a new paradigm, one in which groups with broad, international reach commit horrific acts against innocent civilians, sometimes with the direct support of States. Our Nation recognizes that this new paradigm—ushered in not by us, but by terrorists—requires new thinking in the law of war, but thinking that should nevertheless be consistent with the principles of Geneva.
2. Pursuant to my authority as Commander-in-Chief and Chief Executive of the United States, and relying on the opinion of the Department of Justice dated January 22, 2002, and on the legal opinion rendered by the Attorney General in his letter of February 1, 2002, I hereby determine as follows:

a. I accept the legal conclusion of the Department of Justice and determine that none of the provisions of Geneva apply to our conflict with al-Qaeda in Afghanistan or elsewhere throughout the world because, among other reasons, al-Qaeda is not a High Contracting Party to Geneva.

b. I accept the legal conclusion of the Attorney General and the Department of Justice that I have the authority under the Constitution to suspend Geneva as between the United States and Afghanistan, but I decline to exercise that authority at this time. Accordingly, I determine that the provisions of Geneva will apply to our present conflict with the Taliban. I reserve the right to exercise this authority in this or future conflicts.

c. I also accept the legal conclusion of the Department of Justice and determine that common Article 3 of Geneva does not apply to either al-Qaeda or Taliban detainees, because, among other reasons, the relevant conflicts are international in scope and common Article 3 applies only to "armed conflict not of an international character."

d. Based on the facts supplied by the Department of Defense and the recommendation of the Department of Justice, I determine that Taliban detainees are unlawful combatants and, therefore, do not qualify as prisoners of war under Article 4 of Geneva. I note that, because Geneva does not apply to our conflict with al-Qaeda, al-Qaeda detainees also do not qualify as prisoners of war.

3. Of course, our values as a Nation, values that we share with many nations in the world, call for us to treat detainees humanely, including those who are not legally entitled to such treatment. Our nation has been and will continue to be a strong supporter of Geneva and its principles. As a matter of policy, the United States Armed Forces shall continue to treat detainees humanely and, to the extent appropriate and consistent with military necessity, in a manner consistent with the principles of Geneva.

4. The United States will hold states, organizers, and individuals who gain control of United States personnel responsible for treating such personnel humanely and consistent with applicable law.

5. I hereby reaffirm the order previously issued by the Secretary of Defense to the United States Armed Forces requiring that the detainees be treated humanely and, to the extent appropriate and consistent with military necessity, in a manner consistent with the principles of Geneva.

6. I hereby direct the Secretary of State to communicate my determinations in an appropriate manner to our allies, and other countries and international organizations cooperating in the war against terrorism of global reach.

[Signed George Bush]

Appendix C
Order Establishing Combatant Status Review Tribunal July 7, 2004, Deputy Secretary of Defense Paul Wolfowitz

Memorandum for the Secretary of the Navy
Subject: Order Establishing Combatant Status Review Tribunal

This Order applies only to foreign nationals held as enemy combatants in the control of the Department of Defense at the Guantánamo Bay Naval Base, Cuba ("detainees").

a. Enemy Combatant. For purposes of this Order, the term "enemy combatant" shall mean an individual who was part of or supporting Taliban or al-Qaeda forces, or associated forces that are engaged in hostilities against the United States or its coalition partners. This includes any person who has committed a belligerent act or has directly supported hostilities in aid of enemy armed forces. Each detainee subject to this Order has been determined to be an enemy combatant through multiple levels of review by officers of the Department of Defense.

b. Notice. Within ten days after the date of this Order, all detainees shall be notified of the opportunity to contest designation as an enemy combatant in the proceeding described herein, of the opportunity to consult with and be assisted by a personal representative as described in paragraph (c), and of the right to seek a writ of habeas corpus in the courts of the United States.

c. Personal Representative. Each detainee shall be assigned a military officer, with the appropriate security clearance, as a personal representative for the purpose of assisting the detainee in connection with the review process described herein. The personal representative shall be afforded the opportunity to review any reasonably available information in the possession of the Department of Defense that may be relevant to a determination of the detainee's designation as an enemy combatant, including any records, determinations, or reports generated in connection with earlier determinations or reviews, and to consult with the detainee concerning that designation and any challenge thereto. The personal representative may share any information with the detainee, except for classified information, and may participate in the Tribunal proceedings as provided in Paragraph (g)(4).

d. Tribunals. Within 30 days after the detainee's personal representative has been afforded the opportunity to review the reasonably available information in the possession of the Department of Defense and had an opportunity to consult with the detainee, a Tribunal shall be convened to review the detainee's status as an enemy combatant.

e. Composition of Tribunal. A Tribunal shall be composed of three neutral commissioned officers of the U.S. Armed Forces, each of whom possesses the appropriate security clearance and none of whom was involved in the apprehension, detention, interrogation, or previous determination of status of the detainee. One of the members shall be a judge advocate. The senior member (in the grade of 0-5 and above) shall serve as President of the Tribunal. Another non-voting officer, preferably a judge advocate, shall serve as the Recorder and shall not be a member of the Tribunal.

f. Convening Authority. The Convening Authority shall be designated by the Secretary of the Navy. The Convening Authority shall appoint each Tribunal and its members, and a personal representative for each detainee. The Secretary of the Navy, with the concurrence of the General counsel of the Department of Defense, may issue instructions to implement this Order.

g. Procedures.

(1) The Recorder shall provide the detainee in advance of the proceedings with notice of the unclassified factual basis for the detainee's designation as an enemy combatant.

(2) Members of the Tribunal and the Recorder shall be sworn. The Recorder shall be sworn first by the President of the Tribunal. The Recorder will then administer an oath, to faithfully and impartially perform their duties, to all members of the Tribunal to include the President.

(3) The record in each case shall consist of all the documentary evidence presented to the Tribunal, the Recorder's summary of all witness testimony, a written report of the Tribunal's decision, and a recording of the proceedings (except pro-

ceedings involving deliberation and voting by the members), which shall be preserved.

(4) The detainee shall be allowed to attend all proceedings, except for proceedings involving deliberation and voting by the members or testimony and other matters that would compromise national security if held in the presence of the detainee. The detainee's personal representative shall be allowed to attend all proceedings, except for proceedings involving deliberation and voting by the members of the Tribunal.

(5) The detainee shall be provided with an interpreter, if necessary.

(6) The detainee shall be advised at the beginning of the hearing of the nature of the proceedings and of the procedures accorded him in connection with the hearing.

(7) The Tribunal, through its Recorder, shall have access to and consider any reasonably available information generated in connection with the initial determination to hold the detainee as an enemy combatant and in any subsequent reviews of that determination, as well as any reasonably available records, determinations, or reports generated in connection therewith.

(8) The detainee shall be allowed to call witnesses if reasonably available, and to question those witnesses called by the Tribunal. The Tribunal shall determine the reasonable availability of witnesses. If such witnesses are from within the U.S. Armed Forces, they shall not be considered reasonably available if, as determined by their commanders, their presence at a hearing would affect combat or support operations. In the case of witnesses who are not reasonably available, written statements, preferably sworn, may be submitted and considered as evidence.

(9) The Tribunal is not bound by the rules of evidence such as would apply in a court of law. Instead, the Tribunal shall be free to consider any information it deems relevant and helpful to a resolution of the issue before it. At the discretion of the Tribunal, for example, it may consider hearsay evidence, taking into account the reliability of such evidence in the circumstances. The Tribunal does not have the authority to declassify or change the classification of any national security information it reviews.

(10) The detainee shall have a right to testify or otherwise address the Tribunal in oral or written form, and to introduce relevant documentary evidence.

(11) The detainee may not be compelled to testify before the Tribunal.

(12) Following the hearing of testimony and the review of documents and other evidence, the Tribunal shall determine in closed session by majority vote whether the detainee is properly detained as an enemy combatant. Preponderance of evidence shall be the standard used in reaching this determination, but there shall be a rebuttable presumption in favor of the Government's evidence.

(13) The President of the Tribunal shall, without regard to any other provision of this Order, have authority and the duty to ensure that all proceedings of or in relation to the Tribunal under this Order shall comply with Executive Order 12958 regarding national security information.

h. The Record. The Recorder shall, to the maximum extent practicable, prepare the record of the Tribunal within three working days of the announcement of the Tribunal's decision. The record shall include those items described in Paragraph (g)(3) above. The record will then be forwarded to the Staff Judge Advocate for the Convening Authority, who shall review the record for legal sufficiency and make a recommendation to the Convening Authority. The Convening Authority shall review the Tribunal's decision and, in accordance with this Order and any implementing instructions issued by the Secretary of the Navy, may return the record to the Tribunal for further proceedings or approve the decision and take appropriate action.

i. Non-Enemy Combatant Determination. If the Tribunal determines that the detainee shall no longer be classified as an enemy combatant, the written report of its decision shall be forwarded directly to the Secretary of Defense or his designee. The Secretary or his designee shall so advise the Secretary of State, in order to permit the Secretary of State to coordinate the transfer of the detainee for release to the detainee's country of citizenship or other disposition consistent with domestic and international obligations and the foreign policy of the United States.

j. This Order is intended solely to improve management within the Department of Defense concerning its detention of enemy combatants at Guantánamo Bay Naval Base, Cuba, and is not intended to, and does not, create any right or benefit, substantive or procedural, enforceable at law, in equity, or otherwise by any party against the United States, its departments, agencies, instrumentalities or entities, its officers, employees or agents, or any other person.

k. Nothing in this Order shall be construed to limit, impair, or otherwise affect the constitutional authority of the President as Commander-in-Chief or any authority granted by statute to the President or the Secretary of Defense.

This Order is effective immediately. [Signed Paul Wolfowitz]

Appendix D
International Covenant on Civil and Political Rights (Preamble with Articles 1-18 and 26)

G.A. res. 2200A (XXI)
21 United Nations General Assembly Resolution Supp. (No. 16) at 52
U.N. Doc. A/6316 (1966)
United Nations Treaty Series 171, *entered into force* Mar. 23, 1976
United States Senate Resolution of Ratification
138 Cong. Rec. S8068-S8071, 102nd Cong., Apr. 2, 1992

PREAMBLE

The States Parties to the present Covenant,

Considering that, in accordance with the principles proclaimed in the Charter of the United Nations, recognition of the inherent dignity and of the equal and inalienable rights of all members of the human family is the foundation of freedom, justice and peace in the world,

Recognizing that these rights derive from the inherent dignity of the human person, *Recognizing* that, in accordance with the Universal Declaration of Human Rights, the ideal of free human beings enjoying civil and political freedom and freedom from fear and want can only be achieved if conditions are created whereby everyone may enjoy his civil and political rights, as well as his economic, social and cultural rights,

Considering the obligation of States under the Charter of the United Nations to promote universal respect for, and observance of, human rights and freedoms,

Realizing that the individual, having duties to other individuals and to the community to which he belongs, is under a responsibility to strive for the promotion and observance of the rights recognized in the present Covenant,

Agree upon the following articles:

PART I

Article 1.—1. All peoples have the right of self-determination. By virtue of that right they freely determine their political status and freely pursue their economic, social and cultural development.

2. All peoples may, for their own ends, freely dispose of their natural wealth and resources without prejudice to any obligations arising out of international economic co-operation, based upon the principle of mutual benefit, and international law. In no case may a people be deprived of its own means of subsistence.

PART II

Article 2.—1. Each State Party to the present Covenant undertakes to respect and to ensure to all individuals within its territory and subject to its jurisdiction the rights recognized in the present Covenant, without distinction of any kind, such as race, colour, sex, language, religion, political or other opinion, national or social origin, property, birth or other status.

2. Where not already provided for by existing legislative or other measures, each State Party to the present Covenant undertakes to take the necessary steps, in accordance with its constitutional processes and with the provision of the present Covenant, to adopt such legislative or other measures as may be necessary to give effect to the rights recognized in the present Covenant.

3. Each State Party to the present Covenant undertakes:

(a) to ensure that any person whose rights or freedoms as herein recognized are violated shall have an effective remedy, notwithstanding that the violation has been committed by persons acting in an official capacity;

(b) to ensure that any person claiming such a remedy shall have his right thereto determined by competent judicial, administrative or legislative authorities, or by any other competent authority provided for by the legal system of the State, and to develop the possibilities of judicial remedy;

(c) to ensure that the competent authorities shall enforce such remedies when granted.

Article 3. The States Parties to the present Covenant undertake to ensure the equal right of men and women to the enjoyment of all civil and political rights set forth in the present Covenant.

Article 4.—1. In time of public emergency which threatens the life of the nation and the existence of which is officially proclaimed, the States Parties to the present Covenant may take measures derogating from their obligations under the present Covenant to the extent strictly required by the exigencies of the situation, provided that such measures are not inconsistent with their other obligations under international law and do not involve discrimination solely on the ground of race, colour, sex, language, religion or social origin.

2. No derogation from Articles 6, 7, 8 (paragraphs 1 and 2), 11, 15, 16, and 18 may be made under this provision.

3. Any State Party to the present Covenant availing itself of the right of derogation shall immediately inform the other States Parties to the present Covenant, through the intermediary of the Secretary-General of the United Nations, of the provisions from which it has derogated and of the reasons by which it was actuated. A further communication shall be made, through the same intermediary, on the date on which it terminates such derogation.

Article 5.—1. Nothing in the present Covenant may be interpreted as implying for any State, group or person any right to engage in any activity or perform any act aimed at the destruction of any of the rights and freedoms recognized herein or at their limitation to a greater extent than is provided for in the present Covenant.

2. There shall be no restriction upon or derogation from any of the fundamental human rights recognized or existing in any State Party to the present Covenant pursuant to law, conventions, regulations or custom on the pretext that the present Covenant does not recognize such rights or that it recognizes them to a lesser extent.

PART III

Article 6.—1. Every human being has the inherent right to life. This right shall be protected by law. No one shall be arbitrarily deprived of his life.

2. In countries which have not abolished the death penalty, sentence of death may be imposed only for the most serious crimes in accordance with the law in force at the time of the commission of the crime and not contrary to the provisions of the present Covenant and to the Convention on the Prevention and Punishment of the Crime of Genocide. This penalty can only be carried out pursuant to a final judgement rendered by a competent court.

3. When deprivation of life constitutes the crime of genocide, it is understood that nothing in this article shall authorize any State Party to the present Covenant to derogate in any way from any obligation assumed under the provisions of the Convention on the Prevention and Punishment of the Crime of Genocide.

4. Anyone sentenced to death shall have the right to seek pardon or commutation of the sentence. Amnesty, pardon or commutation of the sentence of death may be granted in all cases.

5. Sentence of death shall not be imposed for crimes committed by persons below eighteen years of age and shall not be carried out on pregnant women.

6. Nothing in this article shall be invoked to delay or to prevent the abolition of capital punishment by any State Party to the present Covenant.

Article 7. No one shall be subjected to torture or to cruel, inhuman or degrading treatment or punishment. In particular, no one shall be subjected without his free consent to medical or scientific experimentation.

Article 8.—1. No one shall be held in slavery; slavery and the slave-trade in all their forms shall be prohibited.

2. No one shall be held in servitude.

3. (a) No one shall be required to perform forced or compulsory labour;

(b) Paragraph 3(a) shall not be held to preclude in countries where imprisonment with hard labour may be imposed as a punishment for a crime, the performance of hard labour in pursuance of such punishment by a competent court;

(c) For the purpose of this paragraph the term "forced or compulsory labour" shall not include: i. any work or service, not referred to in Subparagraph (b), normally required of a person who is under detention in consequence of a lawful order of a court, or of a person during conditional release from such detention; ii. any service of a military character and, in countries where conscientious objection is recognized, any national service required by law of conscientious objectors; iii. any service exacted in cases of emergency or calamity threatening the life or well-being of the community; iv. any work or service which forms part of normal civil obligations.

Article 9.—1. Everyone has the right to liberty and security of person. No one shall be subjected to arbitrary arrest or detention. No one shall be deprived of his liberty except on such grounds and in accordance with such procedure as established by law.

2. Anyone who is arrested shall be informed, at the time of arrest, of the reasons for his arrest and shall be promptly informed of any charges against him.

3. Anyone arrested or detained on a criminal charge shall be brought promptly before a judge or other officer authorized by law to exercise judicial power and shall be entitled to trial within a reasonable time or to release. It shall not be the general rule that persons awaiting trial shall be detained in custody, but release may be subject to guarantees to appear for trial, at any other stage of the judicial proceedings, and, should occasion arise, for execution of the judgement.

4. Anyone who is deprived of his liberty by arrest or detention shall be entitled to take proceedings before a court, in order that that court may decide without delay on the lawfulness of his detention and order his release if the detention is not lawful.

5. Anyone who has been the victim of unlawful arrest or detention shall have an enforceable right to compensation.

Article 10.—1. All persons deprived of their liberty shall be treated with humanity and with respect for the inherent dignity of the human person.

2. (a) Accused persons shall, save in exceptional circumstances, be segregated from convicted persons and shall be subject to separate treatment appropriate to their status as unconvicted persons;

(b) Accused juvenile persons shall be separated from adults and brought as speedily as possible for adjudication.

3. The penitentiary system shall comprise treatment of prisoners and essential aim of which shall be their reformation and social rehabilitation. Juvenile offenders shall be segregated from adults and be accorded treatment appropriate to their age and legal status.

Article 11. No one shall be imprisoned merely on the ground of inability to fulfil a contractual obligation.

Article 12.—1. Everyone lawfully within the territory of a State shall, within that territory, have the right to liberty of movement and freedom to choose his residence.

2. Everyone shall be free to leave any country, including his own.

3. The above-mentioned rights shall not be subject to any restrictions except those which are provided by law, are necessary to protect national security, public order, public health or morals or the rights and freedoms of others, and are consistent with the other rights recognized in the present Covenant.

4. No one shall be arbitrarily deprived of the right to enter his own country.

Article 13. An alien lawfully in the territory of a State Party to the present Covenant may be expelled therefrom only in pursuance of a decision reached in accordance with law and shall, except where compelling reasons of national security otherwise require, be allowed to submit the reasons against his expulsion and to have his case reviewed by, and be represented for the purpose before, the competent authority or a person or persons especially designated by the competent authority.

Article 14.—1. All persons shall be equal before the courts and tribunals. In the determination of any criminal charge against him, or of his rights and obligations in a suit at law, everyone shall be entitled to a fair and public hearing by a competent, independent and impartial tribunal established by law. The press and the public may be excluded from all or part of a trial for reasons of morals, public order or national security in a democratic society, or when the interest of the private lives of the parties so requires, or to the extent strictly necessary in the opinion of the court in special circumstances where publicity would prejudice the interests of justice; but any judgement rendered in a criminal case or in a suit at law shall be made public except where the interest of juvenile persons requires or the proceedings concern matrimonial disputes or the guardianship of children.

2. Everyone charged with a criminal offence shall have the right to be presumed innocent until proven guilty according to law.

3. In the determination of any criminal charge against him, everyone shall be entitled to the following minimum guarantees, in full equality:

(a) To be informed promptly and in detail in a language which he understands of the nature and cause of the charge against him;

(b) To have adequate time and faculties for the preparation of his defence and to communicate with counsel of his own choosing;

(c) To be tried without undue delay;

(d) To be tried in his presence, and to defend himself in person or through legal assistance of his own choosing; to be informed, if he does not have legal assistance, of this right; and to have legal assistance assigned to him, in any case where the interests of justice so require, and without payment by him in any such case if he does not have sufficient means to pay for it;

(e) To examine, or have examined, the witnesses against him and to obtain the attendance and examination of witnesses on his behalf under the same conditions as witnesses against him;

(f) To have the free assistance of an interpreter if he cannot understand or speak the language used in court;

(g) Not to be compelled to testify against himself or to confess guilt.

4. In the case of juvenile persons, the procedure shall be such as will take account of their age and desirability of promoting their rehabilitation.

5. Everyone convicted of a crime shall have the right to his conviction and sentence being reviewed by a higher tribunal according to law.

6. When a person has by a final decision been convicted of a criminal offence and when subsequently his conviction has been reversed or he has been pardoned on the ground that a new or newly discovered fact shows conclusively that there has been a miscarriage of justice, the person who has suffered punishment as a result of such conviction shall be compensated according to law, unless it is proved that the non-disclosure of the unknown fact in time is wholly or partly attributable to him.

7. No one shall be liable to be tried or punished again for an offence for which he has already been finally convicted or acquitted in accordance with the law and penal procedure of each county.

Article 15.—1. No one shall be held guilty of any criminal offence on account of any act or omission which did not constitute a criminal offence, under national or international law, at the time when it was committed. Nor shall a heavier penalty be imposed than the one that was applicable at the time when the criminal offence was committed. If, subsequent to the commission of the offence, provision is made by law for the imposition of the lighter penalty, the offender shall benefit thereby.

2. Nothing in this Article shall prejudice the trial and punishment of any person for any act or omission which, at the time it was committed, was criminal according to the general principles of law recognized by the community of nations.

Article 16. Everyone shall have the right to recognition everywhere as a person before the law.

Article 17.—1. No one shall be subjected to arbitrary or unlawful interference with his privacy, family, home or correspondence, nor to unlawful attacks on his honour and reputation.

2. Everyone has the right to the protection of the law against such interference or attacks.

Article 18.—1. Everyone shall have the right to freedom of thought, conscience and religion. This right shall include freedom to have or to adopt a religion or belief of his choice, and freedom, either individually or in community with others and in public or private, to manifest his religion or belief in worship, observance, practice and teaching.

2. No one shall be subject to coercion which would impair his freedom to have or to adopt a religion or belief of his choice.

3. Freedom to manifest one's religion or beliefs may be subject only to such limitations as are prescribed by law and are necessary to protect safety, order, health, or morals or the fundamental rights and freedoms of others.

4. The States Parties to the present Covenant undertake to have respect for the liberty of parents and, when applicable, legal guardians to ensure the religious and moral education of their children in conformity with their own convictions.

Article 26. All persons are equal before the law and are entitled without any discrimination to the equal protection of the law. In this respect, the law shall prohibit any discrimination and guarantee to all persons equal and effective protection against discrimination on any ground such as race, colour, sex, language, religion, political or other opinion, national or social origin, property, birth or other status.

Appendix E
United Nations Convention Against Torture and Other Cruel, Inhuman or Degrading Treatment or Punishment (Articles 1-16 and 31)

Adopted and opened for signature, ratification and accession by
General Assembly Resolution 39/46 of 10 December 1984
entered into force 26 June 1987, in accordance with article 27(1)
United States Senate Resolution of Ratification
136 Cong. Rec. S36192-S36199, 101st Cong., Oct. 27, 1990

The States Parties to this Convention,

Considering that, in accordance with the principles proclaimed in the Charter of the United Nations, recognition of the equal and inalienable rights of all members of the human family is the foundation of freedom, justice and peace in the world,

Recognizing that those rights derive from the inherent dignity of the human person,

Considering the obligation of States under the Charter, in particular Article 55, to promote universal respect for, and observance of, human rights and fundamental freedoms,

Having regard to Article 5 of the Universal Declaration of Human Rights and Article 7 of the International Covenant on Civil and Political Rights, both of which provide that no one shall be subjected to torture or to cruel, inhuman or degrading treatment or punishment,

Having regard also to the Declaration on the Protection of All Persons from Being Subjected to Torture and Other Cruel, Inhuman or Degrading Treatment or Punishment, adopted by the General Assembly on 9 December 1975,

Desiring to make more effective the struggle against torture and other cruel, inhuman or degrading treatment or punishment throughout the world,

Have agreed as follows:

PART I

Article 1.—1. For the purposes of this Convention, the term "torture" means any act by which severe pain or suffering, whether physical or mental, is intentionally inflicted on a person for such purposes as obtaining from him or a third person information or a confession, punishing him for an act he or a third person has committed or is suspected of having committed, or intimidating or coercing him or a third person, or for any reason based on discrimination of any kind, when such pain or suffering is inflicted by or at the instigation of or with the consent or acquiescence of a public official or other person acting in an official capacity. It does not include pain or suffering arising only from, inherent in or incidental to lawful sanctions.

2. This article is without prejudice to any international instrument or national legislation which does or may contain provisions of wider application.

Article 2.—1. Each State Party shall take effective legislative, administrative, judicial or other measures to prevent acts of torture in any territory under its jurisdiction.

2. No exceptional circumstances whatsoever, whether a state of war or a threat of war, internal political instability or any other public emergency, may be invoked as a justification of torture.

3. An order from a superior officer or a public authority may not be invoked as a justification of torture.

Article 3.—1. No State Party shall expel, return or extradite a person to another State where there are substantial grounds for believing that he would be in danger of being subjected to torture.

For the purpose of determining whether there are such grounds, the competent authorities shall take into account all relevant considerations including, where applicable, the existence in the State concerned of a consistent pattern of gross, flagrant or mass violations of human rights.

Article 4.—1. Each State Party shall ensure that all acts of torture are offences under its criminal law. The same shall apply to an attempt to commit torture and to an act by any person which constitutes complicity or participation in torture. 2. Each State Party shall make these offences punishable by appropriate penalties which take into account their grave nature.

Article 5.—1. Each State Party shall take such measures as may be necessary to establish its jurisdiction over the offences referred to in Article 4 in the following cases:

(a) When the offences are committed in any territory under its jurisdiction or on board a ship or aircraft registered in that State;

(b) When the alleged offender is a national of that State;

(c) When the victim is a national of that State if that State considers it appropriate.

2. Each State Party shall likewise take such measures as may be necessary to establish its jurisdiction over such offences in cases where the alleged offender is present in any territory under its jurisdiction and it does not extradite him pursuant to Article 8 to any of the States mentioned in Paragraph 1 of this Article.

3. This Convention does not exclude any criminal jurisdiction exercised in accordance with internal law.

Article 6.—1. Upon being satisfied, after an examination of information available to it, that the circumstances so warrant, any State Party in whose territory a person alleged to have committed any offence referred to in Article 4 is present shall take him into custody or take other legal measures to ensure his presence. The custody and other legal measures shall be as provided in the law of that State but may be continued only for such time as is necessary to enable any criminal or extradition proceedings to be instituted.

2. Such State shall immediately make a preliminary inquiry into the facts.

3. Any person in custody pursuant to paragraph 1 of this Article shall be assisted in communicating immediately with the nearest appropriate representative of the State of which he is a national, or, if he is a stateless person, with the representatives of the State where he usually resides.

4. When a State, pursuant to this article, has taken a person into custody, it shall immediately notify the States referred to in Article 5, Paragraph 1, of the fact that such person is in custody and of the circumstances which warrant his detention. The State which makes the preliminary inquiry contemplated in Paragraph 2 of this Article shall promptly report its findings to the said States and shall indicate whether it intends to exercise jurisdiction.

Article 7.—1. The State Party in the territory under whose jurisdiction a person alleged to have committed any offene referred to in Article 4 is found shall in the cases contemplated in Article 5, if it does extradite him, submit the case to its competent authorities for the purpose of prosecution.

2. These authorities shall take their decision in the same manner as in the case of any ordinary offence of a serious nature under the law of that State. In the cases referred to in Article 5, Paragraph 2, the standards of evidence required for prosecution and conviction shall in no way be less stringent than those which apply in the cases referred to in Article 5, Paragraph 1.

3. Any person regarding whom proceedings are brought in connection with any of the offences referred to in Article 4 shall be guaranteed fair treatment at all stages of the proceedings.

Article 8.—1. The offences referred to in Article 4 shall be deemed to be included as extraditable offences in any extradition treaty existing between States Parties. States Parties undertake to include such offences as extraditable offences in every extradition treaty to be concluded between them.

2. If a State Party which makes extradition conditional on the existence of a treaty receives a request for extradition from another State Party with which it has no extradition treaty, it may consider this Convention as the legal basis for extradition in respect of such offences. Extradition shall be subject to the other conditions provided by the law of the requested State.

3. States Parties which do not make extradition conditional on the existence of a treaty shall recognize such offences as extraditable offences between themselves subject to the conditions provided by the law of the requested State.

4. Such offences shall be treated, for the purpose of extradition between States Parties, as if they had been committed not only in the place in which they occurred but also in the territories of the States required to establish their jurisdiction in accordance with Article 5, Paragraph 1.

Article 9.—1. States Parties shall afford one another the greatest measure of assistance in connection with criminal proceedings brought in respect of any of the offences referred to in Article 4, including the supply of all evidence at their disposal necessary for the proceedings.

2. States Parties shall carry out their obligations under Paragraph 1 of this Article in conformity with any treaties on mutual judicial assistance that may exist between them.

Article 10.—1. Each State Party shall ensure that education and information regarding the prohibition against torture are fully included in the training of law enforcement personnel, civil or military, medical personnel, public officials and other persons who may be involved in the custody, interrogation or treatment of any individual subjected to any form of arrest, detention or imprisonment.

2. Each State Party shall include this prohibition in the rules or instructions issued in regard to the duties and functions of any such person.

Article 11.—Each State Party shall keep under systematic review interrogation rules, instructions, methods and practices as well as arrangements for the custody and treatment of persons subjected to any form of arrest, detention or imprisonment in any territory under its jurisdiction, with a view to preventing any cases of torture.

Article 12.—Each State Party shall ensure that its competent authorities proceed to a prompt and impartial investigation, whenever there is reasonable ground to believe that an act of torture has been committed in any territory under its jurisdiction.

Article 13.—Each State Party shall ensure that any individual who alleges he has been subjected to torture in any territory under its jurisdiction has the right to complain to, and to have his case promptly and impartially examined by, its competent authorities. Steps shall be taken to ensure that the complainant and witnesses are protected against all ill-treatment or intimidation as a consequence of his complaint or any evidence given.

Article 14.—1. Each State Party shall ensure in its legal system that the victim of an act of torture obtains redress and has an enforceable right to fair and adequate compensation, including the means for as full rehabilitation as possible. In the event of the death of the victim as a result of an act of torture, his dependants shall be entitled to compensation.

2. Nothing in this article shall affect any right of the victim or other persons to compensation which may exist under national law.

Article 15.—Each State party shall ensure that any statement which is established to have been made as a result of torture shall not be invoked as evidence in any proceedings, except against a person accused of torture as evidence that the statement was made.

Article 16.—1. Each State Party shall undertake to prevent in any territory under its jurisdiction other acts of cruel, inhuman or degrading treatment or punishment which do not amount to torture as defined in Article 1, when such acts are committed by or at the instigation of or with the consent of acquiescence of a public official or other person acting in an official capacity. In particular, the obligations contained in Articles 10, 11, 12, and 13 shall apply with the substitution for references to torture of references to other forms of cruel, inhuman or degrading treatment or punishment. 2. The provisions of this Convention are without prejudice to the provisions of any other international instrument or national law which prohibits cruel, inhuman or degrading treatment or punishment or which relates to extradition or expulsion.

PART III

Article 31.—1. A State Party may denounce this Convention by written notification to the Secretary-General of the United Nations. Denunciation becomes effective one year after the date of receipt of the notification by the Secretary-General.

2. Such a denunciation shall not have the effect of releasing the State Party from its obligations under this Convention in regard to any act or omission which occurs prior to the date at which the denunciation becomes effective, nor shall denunciation prejudice in any way the continued consideration of any matter which is already under consideration by the Committee prior to the date at which the denunciation becomes effective.

3. Following the date at which the denunciation of a State Party becomes effective, the Committee shall not commence consideration of any new matter regarding that State.

Appendix F
Geneva Convention Relative to The Treatment of Enemy Prisoners of War (Select Articles)

Adopted at Geneva and opened for signature 12 August 1949
United States Senate Resolution of Ratification
101 Cong. Rec. S9958-S9973, 84th Cong., July 6, 1955

PART I
GENERAL PROVISIONS

Article 1.—The High Contracting Parties undertake to respect and to ensure respect for the present Convention in all circumstances.

Article 2.—In addition to the provisions which shall be implemented in peace time, the present Convention shall apply to all cases of declared war or of any other armed conflict which may arise between two or more of the High Contracting Parties, even if the state of war is not recognized by one of them.

The Convention shall also apply to all cases of partial or total occupation of the territory of a High Contracting Party, even if the said occupation meets with no armed resistance.

Although one of the Powers in conflict may not be a party to the present Convention, the Powers who are parties thereto shall remain bound by it in their mutual relations. They shall furthermore be bound by the Convention in relation to the said Power, if the latter accepts and applies the provisions thereof.

Article 3.—In the case of armed conflict not of an international character occurring in the territory of one of the High Contracting Parties, each Party to the conflict shall be bound to apply, as a minimum, the following provisions:

(1) Persons taking no active part in the hostilities, including members of armed forces who have laid down their arms and those placed *hors de com-*

bat by sickness, wounds, detention, or any other cause, shall in all circumstances be treated humanely, without any adverse distinction founded on race, colour, religion or faith, sex, birth or wealth, or any other similar criteria. To this end the following acts are and shall remain prohibited at any time and in any place whatsoever with respect to the above-mentioned persons:

(a) violence to life and person, in particular murder of all kinds, mutilation, cruel treatment and torture;
(b) taking of hostages;
(c) outrages upon personal dignity, in particular, humiliating and degrading treatment;
(d) the passing of sentences and the carrying out of executions without previous judgment pronounced by a regularly constituted court affording all the judicial guarantees which are recognized as indispensable by civilized peoples.

(2) The wounded and sick shall be collected and cared for.

An impartial humanitarian body, such as the International Committee of the Red Cross, may offer its services to the Parties to the conflict.

The Parties to the conflict should further endeavour to bring into force, by means of special agreements, all or part of the other provisions of the present Convention.

The application of the preceding provisions shall not affect the legal status of the Parties to the conflict.

Article 4.—A. Prisoners of War, in the sense of the present Convention, are persons belonging to one of the following categories, who have fallen into the power of the enemy:

(1) Members of the armed forces of a Party to the conflict, as well as members of militias or volunteer corps forming part of such armed forces.
(2) Members of other militias and members of other volunteer corps, including those of organized resistance movements, belonging to a Party to the conflict and operating in or outside their own territory, even if this territory is occupied, provided that such militias or volunteer corps, including such organized resistance movements, fulfil the following conditions:
   (a) that of being commanded by a person responsible for his subordinates;
   (b) that of having a fixed distinctive sign recognizable at a distance;
   (c) that of carrying arms openly;
   (d) that of conducting their operations in accordance with the laws and customs of war.
(3) Members of regular armed forces who profess allegiance to a government or an authority not recognized by the Detaining Power.

(4) Persons who accompany the armed forces without actually being members thereof, such as civilian members of military aircraft crews, war correspondents, supply contractors, members of labour units or of services responsible for the welfare of the armed forces, provided that they have received authorization from the armed forces which they accompany, who shall provide them for that purpose with an identity card similar to the annexed model.

(5) Members of crews, including masters, pilots and apprentices, of the merchant marine and the crews of civil aircraft of the Parties to the conflict, who do not benefit by more favorable treatment under any other provisions of international law.

(6) Inhabitants of a non-occupied territory, who on the approach of the enemy spontaneously take up arms to resist the invading forces, without having had time to form themselves into regular armed units, provided they carry arms openly and respect the laws and customs of war.

B. The following shall likewise be treated as prisoners of war under the present Convention:

(1) Persons belonging, or having belonged, to the armed forces of the occupied country, if the occupying Power considers it necessary by reason of such allegiance to intern them, even though it has originally liberated them while hostilities were going on outside the territory it occupies, in particular where such persons have made an unsuccessful attempt to rejoin the armed forces to which they belong and which are engaged in combat, or where they fail to comply with a summons made to them to internment.

(2) The persons belonging to one of the categories enumerated in the present Article, who have been received by neutral or non-belligerent Powers on their territory and whom these Powers are required to intern under international law, without prejudice to any more favorable treatment which these Powers may choose to give and with the exception of Articles 8, 10, 15, 30, Fifth Paragraph, 58-67, 92, 126 and, where diplomatic relations exist between the Parties to the conflict and the neutral or non-belligerent Power concerned, those Articles concerning the Protecting Power. Where such diplomatic relations exist, the Parties to a conflict on whom these persons depend shall be allowed to perform towards them the functions of a Protecting Power as provided in the present Conventions, without prejudice to the functions which these Parties normally exercise in conformity with diplomatic and consular usage and treaties.

C. This Article shall in no way affect the status of medical personnel and chaplains as provided for in Article 33 of the present Convention.

Article 5. —The present Convention shall apply to the person referred to in Article 4 from the time they fall into the power of the enemy and until their final release and repatriation.

Should any doubt arise as to whether persons, having committed a belligerent act and having fallen into the hands of the enemy, belong to any of the categories enumerated in Article 4, such persons shall enjoy the protections of the present Convention until such time as their status has been determined by a competent tribunal.

Article 13.—Prisoners of war must at all times be humanely treated. Any unlawful act or omission by the Detaining Power causing death or seriously endangering the health of a prisoner of war in its custody is prohibited, and will be regarded as a serious breach of the present Convention. In particular, no prisoners of war may be subjected to physical mutilation or to medical or scientific experiments of any kind which are not justified by the medical, dental or hospital treatment of the prisoner concerned and carried out in his interest.

Likewise, prisoners of war must at all times be protected, particularly against acts of violence or intimidation and against insults and public curiosity.

Measures of reprisal against prisoners of war is prohibited.

Article 14.—Prisoners of war are entitled in all circumstances to respect for their persons and their honour.

Women shall be treated with all the regard due to their sex and shall in all cases benefit by treatment as favorable as that granted to men.

Prisoners of war shall retain the full civil capacity which they enjoyed at the time of their capture. The Detaining Power may not restrict the exercise, either within or without its own territory, of the rights such capacity confers except in so far as the captivity requires.

Article 17(4).—No physical or mental torture, nor any other form of coercion, may be inflicted on prisoners of war to secure from them information of any kind whatever. Prisoners of war who refuse to answer may not be threatened, insulted, or exposed to unpleasant or disadvantageous treatment of any kind.

Article 20.—The evacuation of prisoners of war shall always be effected humanely and in conditions similar to those for the forces of the Detaining Power in their changes of station.

The Detaining Power shall supply prisoners of war who are being evacuated with sufficient food and potable water, and with the necessary clothing and medical attention. The Detaining Power shall take all suitable precautions to ensure their safety during evacuation, and shall establish as soon as possible a list of the prisoners of war who are evacuated.

If prisoners of war must, during evacuation, pass through transit camps, their stay in such camps shall be as brief as possible.

Article 21(1).—The Detaining Power may subject prisoners of war to internment. It may impose on them the obligation of not leaving, beyond certain limits, the camp where they are interned, or if the said camp is fenced in, of not going outside its perimeter. Subject to the provisions of the present Convention relative to penal and disciplinary sanctions, prisoners of war may not be held in close confinement except where necessary to safeguard their health and then only during the continuation of the circumstances which make such confinement necessary.

Article 22(1).—Prisoners of war may be interned only in premises located on land and affording every guarantee of hygiene and healthfulness. Except in particular cases which are justified by the interest of the prisoners themselves, they shall not be interned in penitentiaries.

Article 25(1).—Prisoners of war shall be quartered under conditions as favourable as those for the forces of the Detaining Power who are billeted in the same area. The said conditions shall make allowance for the habits and customs of the prisoners and shall in no case be prejudicial to their health.

Article 84.—A prisoner of war shall be tried only by a military court, unless the existing laws of the Detaining Power expressly permit the civil courts to try a member of the armed forces of the Detaining Power in respect of the particular offence alleged to have been committed by the prisoner of war.

In no circumstances whatever shall a prisoner of war be tried by a court of any kind which does not offer the essential guarantees of independence and impartiality as generally recognized, and, in particular, the procedure of which does not afford the accused the rights and means of defence provided for in Article 105.

Article 85.—Prisoners of war prosecuted under the laws of the Detaining Power for acts committed prior to capture shall retain, even if convicted, the benefits of the present Convention.

Article 86.—No prisoner of war may be punished more than once for the same act or on the same charge.

Article 87(1)(2)(3).—Prisoners of war may not be sentenced by the military authorities and courts of the Detaining Power to any penalties except those provided for in respect of members of the armed forces of the said Power who have committed the same acts.

When fixing the penalty, the courts or authorities of the Detaining Power shall take into consideration, to the widest extent possible, the fact that the accused, not being a national for the Detaining Power, is not bound to it by any duty of allegiance, and that he is in its power as a result of circumstances independent of his own will. The said courts or authorities shall be at liberty to reduce the penalty provided for the violation of which the prisoner of war is accused, and shall therefore not be bound to apply the minimum penalty prescribed.

Collective punishment for individual acts, corporal punishment, imprisonment in premises without daylight and, in general, any form of torture or cruelty, are forbidden.

Article 99.—No prisoner of war may be tried or sentenced for an act which is not forbidden by the law of the Detaining Power or by international law, in force at the time the said act was committed.

No moral or physical coercion may be exerted on a prisoner of war in order to induce him to admit himself guilty of the act of which he is accused.

No prisoner of war may be convicted without having had an opportunity to present his defence and the assistance of a qualified advocate or counsel.

Article 104.—In any case in which the Detaining Power has decided to institute judicial proceedings against a prisoner of war, it shall notify the Protecting Power as soon as possible and at least three weeks before the opening of the trial. This period of three weeks shall run as from the day on which such notification reaches the Protecting Power at the address previously indicated by the latter to the Detaining Power. The said notification shall contain the following information:

(1) Surname and first names of the prisoner of war, his rank, his army, regimental, personal or serial number, his date of birth, and his profession or trade, if any;
(2) Place of internment or confinement;
(3) Specification of the charge or charges on which the prisoner of war is to be arraigned, giving the legal provisions applicable;
(4) Designation of the court which will try the case, likewise the date and place fixed for the opening of the trial.

The same communication shall be made by the Detaining Power to the prisoners' representative.

If no evidence is submitted, at the opening of a trial, that the notification referred to above was received by the Protecting Power, by the prisoner of war and by the prisoners' representative concerned, at least three weeks before the opening of the trial, then the latter cannot take place and must be adjourned.

Article 105.—The prisoner of war shall be entitled to assistance by one of his prisoner comrades, to defence by a qualified advocate or counsel of his own choice, to the calling of witnesses and, if he deems necessary, to the services of a competent interpreter. He shall be advised of these rights by the Detaining Power in due time before the trial.

Failing a choice by the prisoner of war, the Protecting Power shall find him an advocate or counsel, and shall have at least one week at its disposal for the purpose. The Detaining Power shall deliver to the said Power, on request, a list of persons qualified to present the defence. Failing a choice of an advocate or counsel by the prisoner of war or the Protecting Power, the Detaining Power shall appoint a competent advocate or counsel to conduct the defence.

The advocate or counsel conducting the defence on behalf of the prisoner of war shall have at his disposal a period of two weeks at least before the opening of the trial, as well as the necessary facilities to prepare the defence of the accused. He may, in particular, freely visit the accused and interview him in private. He may also confer with any witnesses for the defence, including prisoners of war. He shall have the benefit of these facilities until the term of appeal or petition has expired.

Particulars of the charge or charges on which the prisoner or war is to be arraigned as well as the documents which are generally communicated to the accused by virtue of the laws in force in the armed forces of the Detaining Power, shall be communicated to the accused prisoner of war in a language which he understands, and in good time before the opening of the trial. The same communication in the same circumstances shall be made to the advocate or counsel conducting the defence on behalf of the prisoner of war.

The representatives of the Protecting Power shall be entitled to attend the trial of the case, unless, exceptionally, this is held *in camera* in the interest of State security. In such a case the Detaining Power shall advise the Protecting Power accordingly.

Article 106.—Every prisoner of war shall have, in the same manner as the members of the armed forces of the Detaining Power, the right of appeal or petition from any sentence pronounced upon him, with a view to the quashing or revising of the sentence or the reopening of the trial. He shall be fully informed of his right to appeal or petition and of the time limit within which he may do so.

Article 126.—Representatives or delegates of the Protecting Powers shall have permission to go to all places where prisoners of war may be, particularly to places of internment, imprisonment and labour, and shall have access to all premises occupied by prisoners of war; they shall also be allowed to go to the places of departure, passage and arrival of prisoners who are being transferred. They shall be able to interview the prisoners, and in particular the prisoners' representatives, without witnesses, either personally or through an interpreter.

Representatives and delegates of the Protecting Powers shall have full liberty to select the places they wish to visit. The duration and frequency of these visits shall not be restricted. Visits may not be prohibited except for reasons of imperative military necessity, and then only as an exceptional and temporary measure.

The Detaining Power and the Power on which the said prisoners of war depend may agree, if necessary, that compatriots of these prisoners of war be permitted to participate in the visits.

The delegates of the International Committee of the Red Cross shall enjoy the same prerogatives. The appointment of such delegates shall be submitted to the approval of the Power detaining the prisoners of war to be visited.

Article 130.—Grave breaches to which the preceding Article relates shall be those involving any of the following acts, if committed against persons or property protected by the Convention: wilful killing, torture or inhuman treatment, including biological experiments, wilfully causing great suffering or serious injury to body or health, compelling a prisoner of war to serve in the forces of the hostile Power, or wilfully depriving a prisoner of war of the rights of fair and regular trial prescribed in this Convention.

Article 131.—No High Contracting Party shall be allowed to absolve itself or any other High Contracting Party of any liability incurred by itself or by another High Contracting Party in respect of breaches referred to in the preceding Article.

Article 142.—Each of the High Contracting Parties shall be at liberty to denounce the present Convention.

The denunciation shall be notified in writing to the Swiss Federal Council, which shall transmit it to the Governments of all the High Contracting Parties.

The denunciation shall take effect one year after the notification thereof has been made to the Swiss Federal Council. However, a denunciation of which notification has been made at a time when the denouncing Power is involved in a conflict shall not take effect until peace has been concluded, and until after operations connected with release and repatriation of the persons protected by the present Convention have been terminated.

The denunciation shall have effect only in respect of the denouncing Power. It shall in no way impair the obligations which the Parties to the conflict shall remain bound to fulfill by virtue of the principles of the law of nations, as they result from the usages established among civilized peoples, from the laws of humanity and the dictates of the public conscience.

Appendix G
Geneva Convention Relative to The Protection of Civilian Persons in Time of War (Select Articles)

Adopted and opened for signature 12 August 1949
United States Senate Resolution of Ratification
101 Cong. Rec. S9958-S9973 , 84th Cong., July 6, 1955

PART I
GENERAL PROVISIONS

Articles 1, 2, and *3* are common in all four Geneva Conventions.

Article 4.—Persons protected by the Convention are those who, at a given moment and in any manner whatever, find themselves, in case of a conflict or occupation, in the hands of a Party to the conflict or Occupying Power of which they are not nationals.

Nationals of a State which is not bound by the Convention are not protected by it. Nationals of a neutral State who find themselves in the territory of a belligerent State, and nationals of a co-belligerent State, shall not be regarded as protected persons while the State of which they are nationals has normal diplomatic representation in the State in whose hands they are.The provisions of Part II are, however, wider in application, as defined in Article 13.

Persons protected by the Geneva Convention for the Amelioration of the Condition of the Wounded and Sick in Armed Forces in the Field of August 12, 1949, or by the Geneva Convention for the Amelioration of the Condition of Wounded, Sick and Shipwrecked Members of Armed Forces as Sea of August 12, 1949, or by the Geneva Convention relative to the Treatment of Prisoners of War of August 12, 1949, shall not be considered as protected persons within the meaning of the present Convention.

Article 27.—Protected persons are entitled, in all circumstances, to respect for their persons, their honour, their family rights, their religious convictions and practices, and their manners and customs. They shall at all times be humanely treated, and shall be protected especially against all acts of violence or threats thereof and against insults and public curiousity.

Women shall be especially protected against any attack on their honour, in particular against rape, enforced prostitution, or any form of indecent assault.

Without prejudice to the provisions relating to their state of health, age and sex, all protected persons shall be treated with the same consideration by the Party to the conflict in whose power they are, without any adverse distinction based, in particular, on race, religion or political opinion.

However, the Parties to the conflict may take such measures of control and security in regard to protected persons as may be necessary as a result of the war.

Article 31.—No physical or moral coercion shall be exercised against protected persons, in particular to obtain information from them or from third parties.

Article 32.—The High Contracting Parties specifically agree that each of them is prohibited from taking any measure of such a character as to cause the physical suffering or extermination of protected persons in their hands. This prohibition applies not only to murder, torture, corporal punishment, mutilation and medical or scientific experiments not necessitated by the medical treatment of a protected person, but also to any other measures of brutality whether applied by civilian or military agents.

Article 33.—No protected person may be punished for an offence he or she has not personally committed. Collective penalties and likewise all measures of intimidation or of terrorism are prohibited.

Pillage is prohibited.

Reprisals against protected persons and their property are prohibited.

Article 34.—The taking of hostages is prohibited.

Article 49.—Individual or mass forcible transfers, as well as deportations of protected persons from occupied territory to the territory of the Occupying Power or to that of any other country, occupied or not, are prohibited, regardless of their motive.

Nevertheless, the Occupying Power may undertake total or partial evacuation of a given area if the security of the population or imperative military reasons so demand. Such evacuations may not involve the displacement of protected persons outside the bounds of the occupied territory except when for material reasons it is impossible to avoid such displacement. Persons thus evacuated shall be transferred back to their homes as soon as hostilities in the area in question have ceased.

The Occupying Power undertaking such transfers or evacuations shall ensure, to the greatest practicable extent, that proper accommodation is provided to receive the protected persons, that the removals are effected in satisfactory conditions of hygiene, health, safety and nutrition, and that members of the same family are not separated.

The Protecting Power shall be informed of any transfers and evacuations as soon as they have taken place.

The Occupying Power shall not detain protected persons in an area particularly exposed to the dangers of war unless the security of the population or imperative military reasons so demand.

The Occupying Power shall not deport or transfer parts of its own civilian population into the territory it occupies.

Article 71.—No sentence shall be pronounced by the competent courts of the Occupying Power except after a regular trial.

Accused persons who are prosecuted by the Occupying Power shall be promptly informed, in writing, in a language which they understand, of the particulars of the charges preferred against them, and shall be brought to trial as rapidly as possible. The Protecting Power shall be informed of all proceedings instituted by the Occupying Power against protected persons in respect of charges involving the death penalty or imprisonment for two years or more; it shall be enabled, at any time, to obtain information regarding the state of such proceedings. Furthermore, the Protecting Power shall be entitled, on request, to be furnished with all particulars of these and of any other proceedings instituted by the Occupying Power against protected persons.

The notification to the Protecting Power, as provided for in the second Paragraph above, shall be sent immediately, and shall in any case reach the Protecting Power three weeks before the date of the first hearing. Unless, at the opening of the trial, evidence is submitted that the provisions of this Article are fully complied with, the trial shall not proceed. The notification shall include the following particulars: (a) description of the accused; (b) place of residence or detention; (c) specification of the charge (with mention of the penal provisions under which it is brought); (d) designation of the court which will hear the case; (e) place and date of the first hearing.

Article 72.—Accused persons shall have the right to present evidence necessary to their defence and may, in particular, call witnesses. They shall have the right to be assisted by a qualified advocate or counsel of their own choice, who shall be able to visit them freely and shall enjoy the necessary facilities for preparing the defence.

Failing a choice by the accused, the Protecting Power may provide him with an advocate or counsel. When an accused person has to meet a serious charge and the Protecting Power is not functioning, the Occupying Power, subject to the consent of the accused, shall provide an advocate or counsel.

Accused persons shall, unless they freely waive such assistance, be aided by an interpreter, both during preliminary investigation and during the hearing in court. They shall have the right at any time to object to the interpreter and to ask for his replacement.

Article 73.—A convicted person shall have the right of appeal provided for by the laws applied by the court. He shall be fully informed of his right to appeal or petition and of the time limit within which he may do so.

The penal procedure provided in the present Section shall apply, as far as it is applicable, to appeals. Where the laws applied by the Court make no provision for appeals, the convicted person shall have the right to petition against the finding and sentence to the competent authority of the Occupying Power.

Article 75.—In no case shall persons condemned to death be deprived of the right of petition for pardon or reprieve.

No death sentence shall be carried out before the expiration of a period of at least six months from the date of receipt by the Protecting Power of the notification of the final judgment confirming such death sentence, or of an order denying pardon or reprieve.

The six months period of suspension of the death sentence herein prescribed may be reduced in individual cases in circumstances of grave emergency involving an organized threat to the security of the Occupying Power or its forces, provided always that the Protecting Power is notified of such reduction and is given reasonable time and opportunity to make representations to the competent occupying authorities in respect of such death sentences.

Article 93.—Internees shall enjoy complete latitude in the exercise of their religious duties, including attendance at the services of their faith, on condition that they comply with the disciplinary routine prescribed by the detaining authorities.

Ministers of religion who are interned shall be allowed to minister freely to the members of their community. For this purpose, the Detaining Power shall ensure their equitable allocation amongst the various places of internment in which there are internees speaking the same language and belonging to the same religion. Should such ministers be too few in number, the Detaining Power shall provide them with the necessary facilities, including means of transport, for moving from one place to another, and they shall be authorized to visit any internees who are in hospital. Ministers of religion shall be at liberty to correspond on matters concerning their ministry with the religious authorities in the country of detention and, as far as possible, with the international religious organizations of their faith. Such correspondence shall not be considered as forming a part of the quota mentioned in Article 107. It shall, however, be subject to the provisions of Article 112.

When internees do not have at their disposal the assistance of ministers of their faith, or should these latter be too few in number, the local religious authorities of the same faith may appoint, in agreement with the Detaining Power, a minister of the internees' faith or, if such a course is feasible from a denominational point of view, a minister of similar religion or a qualified layman. The latter shall enjoy the facilities granted to the ministry he has assumed. Persons so appointed shall comply with all regulations laid down by the Detaining Power in the interests of discipline and security.

Appendix H
The Federal Anti-Torture Statute
(Title 18, Part I, Chapter 113C, U.S.C. §§2340-2340A)

§2340. Definitions

As used in this chapter—

(1) "torture" means an act committed by a person acting under the color of law specifically intended to inflict severe physical or mental pain or suffering (other than pain or suffering incidental to lawful sanctions) upon another person within his custody or physical control;

(2) "severe mental pain or suffering" means the prolonged mental harm caused by or resulting from—

   A. the intentional infliction or threatened infliction of severe physical pain or suffering;

   B. the administration or application, or threatened administration or application, of mind-altering substances or other procedures calculated to disrupt profoundly the senses or the personality;

   C. the threat of imminent death; or

   D. the threat that another person will imminently be subject to death, severe physical pain or suffering, or the administration or application of mind-altering substances or other procedures calculated to disrupt profoundly the senses or personality; and

(3) "United States" means the several States of the United States, the District of Columbia, and the commonwealths, territories, and possessions of the United States.

§2340A. Torture

(a) Offense.—Whoever outside the United States commits or attempts to commit torture shall be fined under this Title or imprisoned not more than 20 years, or both, and if death results to any person from conduct prohibited by this Subsection, shall be punished by death or imprisoned for any term of years of for life.

(b) Jurisdiction.—There is jurisdiction over the activity prohibited in Subsection (a) if—
   (1) the alleged offender is a national of the United States; or
   (2) the alleged offender is present in the United States, irrespective of the nationality of the victim or alleged offender.

(c) Conspiracy.—A person who conspires to commit an offense under this Section shall be subject to the same penalties (other than the penalty of death) as the penalties prescribed for the offense, the commission of which was the object of the conspiracy.

Appendix I
The Federal War Crimes Act of 1996
(Title 18, Part I, Chapter 118, U.S.C. §2441)

§2441. War Crimes

(a) Offense.—Whoever, whether inside or outside the United States, commits a war crime, in any of the circumstances described in Subsection (b), shall be fined under this title or imprisoned for life or any term of years, or both, and if death results to the victim, shall also be subject to the penalty of death.

(b) Circumstances.—The circumstances referred to in Subsection (a) are that the person committing such war crime or the victim of such war crime is a member of the Armed Forces of the United States or a national of the United States (as defined in Section 101 of the Immigration and Nationality Act).

(c) Definition.—As used in this section the term "war crime" means any conduct—
  (1) defined as a grave breach in any of the international conventions signed at Geneva 12 August 1949, or any protocol to such convention to which the United States is a party;
  (2) prohibited by Article 23, 25, 27, or 28 of the Annex to the Hague Convention IV, Respecting the Laws and Customs of War on Land, signed 18 October 1907;
  (3) which constitutes a violation of common Article 3 of the international conventions signed at Geneva, 12 August 1949, or any protocol to such convention to which the United States is a party and which deals with non-international armed conflict; or
  (4) of a person who, in relation to an armed conflict and contrary to the provisions of the Protocol on Prohibitions or Restrictions of the Use of Mines, Booby-Traps and Other Devices as amended at Geneva on 3 May 1996 (Protocol II as amended on 3 May 1996), when the United States is a party to such Protocol, willfully kills or causes serious injury to civilians.

Appendix J
War Powers Resolution of 1973
Pub. L. No. 93-148, 87 Stat. 555
93rd Congress, H.J. Res. 542
(Title 50 U.S.C. §§1541-1548)

JOINT RESOLUTION

CONCERNING THE WAR POWERS OF CONGRESS AND THE PRESIDENT

Resolved by the Senate and the House of Representatives of the United States of America in Congress assembled,

SHORT TITLE

Section 1.—This joint resolution may be cited as the "War Powers Resolution."

PURPOSE AND POLICY

Section 2.—(a) It is the purpose of this joint resolution to fulfill the intent of the framers of the Constitution of the United States and insure that the collective judgement of both the Congress and the President will apply to the introduction of United States Armed Forces into hostilities, or into situations where imminent involvement in hostilities is clearly indicated by the circumstances, and to the continued use of such forces in hostilities or in such situations.

(b) Under Article 1, Section 8, of the Constitution, it is specifically provided that the Congress shall have the power to make all laws necessary and proper for carrying into execution, not only its own powers but also all other powers vested by the Constitution in the Government of the United States, or in any department or officer thereof.

(c) The constitutional powers of the President as Commander-in-Chief to introduce United States Armed Forces into hostilities, or into situations where imminent involvement in hostilities is clearly indicated by the circumstances, are exercised only pursuant to

(1) a declaration of war,

(2) specific statutory authorization, or

(3) a national emergency created by attack upon the United States, its territories or possessions, or its armed forces.

CONSULTATION

Section 3.—The President in every possible instance shall consult with Congress before introducing United States Armed Forces into hostilities or into situations where imminent involvement in hostilities is clearly indicated by the circumstances, and after every such introduction shall consult regularly with the Congress until United States Armed Forces are no longer engaged in hostilities or have been removed from such situations.

REPORTING

Section 4.—(a) In the absence of a declaration of war, in any case in which United States Armed Forces are introduced—

(1) into hostilities or into situations where imminent involvement in hostilities is clearly indicated by the circumstances;
(2) into the territory, airspace or waters of a foreign nation, while equipped for combat, except for deployments which relate solely to supply, replacement, repair, or training of such forces; or
(3) in numbers which substantially enlarge United States Armed Forces equipped for combat already located in a foreign nation; the President shall submit within 48 hours to the Speaker of the House of Representatives and to the President pro tempore of the Senate a report, in writing, setting forth—
    (A) the circumstances necessitating the introduction of United States Armed Forces;
    (B) the constitutional and legislative authority under which such introduction took place; and
    (C) the estimated scope and duration of the hostilities or involvement.

(b) The President shall provide such other information as the Congress may request in the fulfillment of its constitutional responsibilities with respect to committing the Nation to war and to the use of United States Armed Forces abroad.

(c) Whenever United States Armed Forces are introduced into hostilities or into any situation described in Subsection (a) of this Section, the President shall, so long as such armed forces continue to be engaged in such hostilities or situation, report to the Congress periodically on the status of such hostilities or situation as well as on the scope and the duration of such hostilities or situation, but in no event shall he report to the Congress less often than once every six months.

CONGRESSIONAL ACTION

Section 5.—(a) Each report submitted pursuant to Section 4(a)(1) shall be transmitted to the Speaker of the House of Representatives and to the President pro tempore of the Senate on the same calendar day. Each report so transmitted shall be referred to the Committee on Foreign Affairs of the House of Representatives and to the Committee on Foreign Relations of the Senate for appropriate action. If, when the report is transmitted, the Congress has adjourned *sine die* or has adjourned for any period in excess of three calendar days, the Speaker of the House of Representatives and the President pro tempore of the Senate, if they deem it advisable (or if petitioned by at least 30 percent of the membership of their respective Houses) shall jointly request the President to convene Congress in order that it may consider the report and take appropriate action pursuant to this Section.

(b) Within sixty calendar days after a report is submitted or is required to be submitted pursuant to Section 4(a)(1), whichever is earlier, the President shall terminate any use of United States Armed Forces with respect to which such report was submitted (or required to be submitted), unless the Congress

(1) has declared war or has enacted a specific authorization for such use of United States Armed Forces,

(2) has extended by law such sixty-day period, or

(3) is physically unable to meet as a result of an armed attack upon the United States. Such sixty-day period shall be extended for not more than an additional thirty days if the President determines and certifies to the Congress in writing that unavoidable military necessity respecting the safety of United States Armed Forces requires the continued use of such armed forces in the course of bringing about a prompt removal of such forces.

(c) Notwithstanding Subsection (b), at any time that United States Armed Forces are engaged in hostilities outside the territory of the United States, its possessions and territories without a declaration of war or specific statutory authorization, such forces shall be removed by the President if the Congress so directs by concurrent resolution.

INTERPRETATION OF JOINT RESOLUTION

Section 8.—(a) Authority to introduce United States Armed Forces into hostilities or into situations wherein involvement in hostilities is clearly indicated by the circumstances shall not be inferred—

(1) from any provision of law (whether or not in effect before the date of the enactment of this Joint Resolution), including any provision contained in any appropriation Act, unless such provision specifically authorizes the introduction of United States Armed Forces into hostilities or into such situations and stating that it is intended to constitute specific statutory authorization within the meaning of this Joint Resolution; or

(2) from any treaty heretofore or hereafter ratified unless such treaty is implemented by legislation specifically authorizing the introduction of United States Armed Forces into hostilities or into such situations and stating that

it is intended to constitute specific statutory authorization within the meaning of this Joint Resolution.

(b) Nothing in this Joint Resolution shall be construed to require any futher specific statutory authorization to permit members of United States Armed Forces to participate jointly with members of the armed forces of one or more foreign countries in the headquarters operations of high-level military commands which were established prior to the date of enactment of this joint resolution and pursuant to the United Nations Charter or any treaty ratified by the United States prior to such date.

(c) For purposes of this joint resolution, the term "introduction of United States Armed Forces" includes the assignment of members of such armed forces to command, coordinate, participate in the movement of, or accompany the regular or irregular military forces of any foreign country or government when such military forces are engaged, or there exists an imminent threat that such forces will become engaged, in hostilities.

(d) Nothing in this joint resolution—

(1) is intended to alter the constitutional authority of the Congress or of the President, or the provision of existing treaties; or

(2) shall be construed as granting any authority to the President with respect to the introduction of United States Armed Forces into hostilities or into situations whererin involvement in hostilities is clearly indicated by the circumstances which authority he would not have had in the absence of this Joint Resolution.

SEPARABILITY CLAUSE

Section 9.—If any provision of this Joint Resolution or the application thereof to any person or circumstance is held invalid, the remainder of the Joint Resolution and the application of such provision to any other person or circumstance shall not be affected thereby.

EFFECTIVE DATE

Section 10.—This joint resolution shall take effect on the date of its enactment.

NOTES

Introduction: Under the Color of Law

1. Carrie Johnson and Anne E. Kornblut, "Holder's Decision To Probe CIA Hints At a New Dynamic," *Washington Post*, Aug. 28, 2009.

2. Peter Baker, David Johnson and Mark Mazzetti, "Abuse Issue Puts the C.I.A. and Justice Dept. at Odds," *New York Times*, Aug. 28, 2009.

3. (1) Memorandum for John Rizzo, Acting General Counsel of the Central Intelligence Agency, from Assistant Attorney General Jay S. Bybee, August 1, 2002, Re: Interrogation of al-Qaeda Operative. (2) Memorandum for John A. Rizzo, Senior Deputy General Counsel, Central Intelligence Agency, from Stephen G. Bradbury, Principal Deputy Assistant Attorney General, May 10, 2005, Re: Application of 18 U.S.C. §§2340-2340A to Certain Techniques That May Be Used in the Interrogation of High Value al-Qaeda Detainee. (3) Memorandum for John A. Rizzo, Senior Deputy General Counsel, Central Intelligence Agency, from Steven A. Bradbury, Principal Deputy Assistant Attorney General, May 10, 2005, Re: Application of 18 U.S.C. §§2340-2340A to the Combined Use of Certain Techniques in the Interrogation of High Value al-Qaeda Detainees. (4) Memorandum for John A. Rizzo, Senior Deputy General Counsel, Central Intelligence Agency, form Steven G. Bradbury, Principal Deputy Assistant Attorney General, May 30, 2005, Re: Application of United States Obligations Under Article 16 of the Convention Against Torture to Certain Techniques that May Be Used in the Interrogation of High Value al-Qaeda Detainees.

4. Karen De Young, "General's Review Creates Rupture As Military Backs Call for More Troops in Afghanistan, Civilian Advisers Balk," *Washington Post*, Sept. 22, 2009. For the view that U.S. troops are losing Afghanistan because they are waging a conventional war against an unconventional opponent see Hy S. Rothstein, *Afghanistan and the Troubled Future of Unconventional Warfare*, Naval Institute Press, 2006. For insight on the evolution of contemporary terrorist movements see Marc

Sageman, *Leaderless Jihad: Terror Networks in the Twenty-First Century*, University of Pennsylvania Press, 2008.

5. ACLU News Release, Oct. 29, 2009, available at http://www.aclu.org/national-security/president-signs-law-giving-dod-authority-exempt-photos-torture-foia.

6. Jameel Jaffer and Alexander A. Abdo, Open Letter to Secretary of Defense Robert M. Gates, October 20, 2009, p. 2.

7. Glenn Greenwald, "A Court Decision that Reflects What Type of Country the U.S. Is: Even When Gov't Officials Purposely Subject an Innocent Person to Brutal Torture, They Enjoy Full Immunity," Nov. 3, 2009, available at http://www.salon.com/news/opinion/glenn-greenwald/2009/11/03/arar/print.html.

8. Section 2340(1) of the anti-torture statute criminalizes with fines, imprisonment, and even death, if death should result to the victim, "any act by a person acting under the color of law specifically intended to inflict severe physical or mental pain or suffering (other than pain or suffering incidental to lawful sanctions) upon another person within his custody or physical control."

9. Memorandum from Assistant Attorney General Jay S. Bybee, Department of Justice, to White House Counsel Alberto R. Gonzales, August 1, 2002, Re: Standards of Conduct for Interrogation under 18 U.S.C. §§2340-2340A, in *The Torture Papers: The Road to Abu Ghraib*, (hereinafter *TTP*), eds. Karen J. Greenberg & Joshua L. Dratel, Memo 14, p. 204 (New York: Cambridge University Press, 2005).

10. *Supra* Introd., n. 9, at 204.

11. Four Separate Geneva Conventions came into existence for the protection of war victims on August 12, 1949: The Geneva Convention for the Amelioration of the Condition of the Wounded and Sick in Armed Forces in the Field; The Geneva Convention for the Amelioration of the Condition of the Wounded, Sick and Shipwrecked Members of Armed Forces at Sea; The Geneva Convention Relative to the Treatment of Prisoners of War (hereinafter GPW); and the Geneva Convention Relative to the Protection of Civilian Persons in Time of War (hereinafter GCP). On July 6, 1955, the United States Senate passed a resolution ratifying the Geneva Conventions (101 Cong. Rec. S9958-S9973, 84th Cong. 1st Session).

12. The question of whether GPW, Article 4(A)(3) qualifies a Taliban fighter as a POW is a question for a competent tribunal to determine on a case-by-case basis. We may safely infer, however, that *bona fide* al-Qaeda members appear liable for crimes of war, since al-Qaeda members are terrorists who, by choosing strategies of random deadly violence directed against defenseless non-belligerents, fail to conduct their operations *in accordance with the laws and customs of war* by GPW, Article 4(A)(2)(d). As we shall discover, a bitter consequence of President Bush's jettisoning of customary international law norms (from which are derived the laws of war) is that it becomes political hypocrisy for him or his successors to later invoke them as needed in order to attain criminal convictions of terrorists.

13. Memorandum from John Yoo, Deputy Assistant Attorney General, U.S. Department of Justice, Office of Legal Counsel, to General Counsel William J.

Haynes II, Department of Defense, January 9, 2002, Re: Application of Treaties and Laws to al-Qaeda and Taliban Detainees, in *TTP*, Memo 4, p. 54.

14. Author's translation of the Latin text of Hugo Grotius, *De Jure Belli ac Pacis Libri Tres*, ed. P. C. Molhuysen, p. 502 (Lyons, Holland: A. W. Sijthoff, 1919): Non autem statim respublica aut civitas esse desinit, si quid admittat iniustum, etiam communiter, nec coetus piratarum aut latronum civitas est, etiamsi forte aequalitatem quandam inter se servent sine qua nullus coetus posset consistere.

15. Memorandum from Donald Rumsfeld, Secretary of Defense, to Chairman of the Joint Chiefs of Staff, January 19, 2002, Re: Status of Taliban and al-Qaeda, in *TTP*, Memo 5, p. 80.

16. *Supra* Introd., n. 9, at 172.

17. Specifically GPW, Articles 5, ¶2; 13; 17, ¶s 4 and 5; 25, ¶1; and GCP, Article 4, ¶1. The prohibition against coercive interrogation techniques and torture of captives is explicitly contained in GPW, Article 17, ¶4 ("no physical or mental torture, nor any other form of coercion, may be inflicted on prisoners of war to secure from them information of any kind whatever. Prisoners of war who refuse to answer may not be threatened, insulted, or exposed to unpleasant or disadvantageous treatment of any kind") which must be read in the context of both GPW, Article 5, ¶2 ("should any doubt arise as to whether persons, having committed a belligerent act and having fallen into the hands of the enemy, belong to any of the categories [defining a POW] enumerated in [GPW] Article 4, such persons shall enjoy the protection of the present Convention until such time as their status has been determined by a competent tribunal") and GCP, Article 4 ("persons protected by the Convention are those who, at a given moment and in any manner whatsoever, find themselves, in case of a conflict or occupation, in the hands of a Party to the conflict or Occupying Power of which they are not nationals"). According to the Schlesinger Report of August 2004, CENTCOM issued an order at the beginning of hostilities in Operation Enduring Freedom (OEF) in Afghanistan on October 17, 2001, that called for the recognition of Geneva's humanitarian protections, and made it clear that "if [U.S.] armed forces personnel were in doubt as to a detained individual's status, [GPW] rights would be accorded to the detainee until a [GPW] Article 5 tribunal made a definitive status determination" (*TTP*, p. 947). On January 19, 2002, Secretary of Defense, Donald Rumsfeld revoked CENTCOM's order and replaced it with a new directive to the Joint Chiefs of Staff by which he decreed that "Al-Qaeda and Taliban individuals under the control of the Department of Defense are not entitled to prisoner of war status for purposes of the Geneva Conventions of 1949" (*TTP*, Memo 5, p. 80). On February 7, 2002, President George W. Bush reiterated Rumsfeld's January 19 directive by means of an Executive Order in which he claims it his constitutional right as President to suspend Geneva in the conflict with al-Qaeda and the Taliban in Afghanistan and "elsewhere throughout the world" (*TTP*, Memo 11, p. 134, Subsections 2(a)(b)). Although President Bush unilaterally ordered that "none of the provisions of Geneva apply to our conflict with al-Qaeda in Afghan-

istan or elsewhere throughout the world," Subsection 2(a), and that he has the "authority under the Constitution to suspend Geneva as between the United States and Afghanistan," he nevertheless maintained the right to demand that "states, organizations, and individuals who gain control of U.S. personnel [be] responsible for treating such personnel humanely and consistent with applicable law" (Section 4).

18. The United Nations Convention Against Torture (CAT) was ratified in the U.S. Senate in 1994. CAT defines torture in Article 1 as "any act by which severe pain or suffering, whether physical or mental, is intentionally inflicted on a person for such purposes as obtaining from him or a third person information or a confession." Article 16 of the CAT mandates that "each State Party shall undertake to prevent in any territory under its jurisdiction other acts of cruel, inhuman or degrading treatment or punishment which do not amount to torture as defined in Article 1." Other blanket prohibitions against torture and other invasive interrogation techniques governing the behavior of U.S. forces *outside* the territory of the United States exist in 18 U.S.C. §2340A, Subsection (a): "whosoever outside the United States commits or attempts to commit torture shall be fined under this title or imprisoned not more than 20 years, or both, and if death results to any person from conduct prohibited by this Subsection, shall be punished by death or imprisoned for any term of years or for life." See also 18 U.S.C. §2441, Subsection (a) which penalizes the commission of a war crime with fines, imprisonment, and even death, if death results to the victim; while Subsection (c)(1) defines a war crime as "a grave breach in any of the international conventions signed at Geneva 12 August 1949, or any protocol to such convention to which the United States is a party."

19. Articles 5 through 11 of the United Nations Universal Declaration of Human Rights (1948) make explicit that persons detained over alleged offenses against the law of nations as possible war criminals, and those held as POWs, are not to be held incommunicado without trial and deprived the presumption of innocence independent of a hearing by a competent tribunal: "Article 5: No one shall be subjected to torture or to cruel, inhuman or degrading treatment or punishment. Article 6: Everyone has the right to recognition everywhere as a person before the law. Article 7: All are equal before the law and are entitled without any discrimination to equal protection of the law. Article 8: Everyone has the right to an effective remedy by the competent national tribunals for acts violating the fundamental rights granted him by the constitution or by law. Article 9: No one shall be subjected to arbitrary arrest, detention or exile. Article 10: Everyone is entitled to full equality to a fair and public hearing by an independent and impartial tribunal, in the determination of his rights and obligations and of any criminal charge against him. Article 11: Everyone charged with a penal offence has the right to be presumed innocent until proved guilty according to law in a public trial at which he has had all the guarantees necessary for his defense" (*The Human Rights Reader*, eds. Walter Laqueur and Barry Rubin, p. 198, Philadelphia: Temple University Press, 1979).

20. Both the United States (as of July 1955) and Afghanistan (as of September 1956) are High Contracting Parties to the Geneva Conventions. No American President, not even Congress or the Judiciary, has legal authorization under Geneva or the Constitution of the United States to unilaterally determine that Geneva shall not apply to the conflict with the Taliban and al-Qaeda in Afghanistan, or to any other conflict. Such a determination transcends the rule of law, violating not only the explicit text of Geneva but strict constitutional limitations on the President's treaty-making powers. Changing international agreements requires the advice and consent of the Senate, plus two-thirds vote therein in order for any new treaty to become law. Once a treaty becomes law it cannot then be suddenly abandoned by a President who might view its application or implementation as overly meddlesome in his conduct of the nation's foreign affairs. Even the Divine Nature, says Grotius, is restricted in His majesty by natural laws that even He cannot alter (*De Jure Belli ac Pacis Libri Tres,* book 1, ch. 1, §10.5).

21. Author's translation of Balthazar Ayala, p. 123 of the original 1582 edition, rpt. ed. John Westlake (Washington D.C.: Carnegie Institution of Washington, 1912): Dictator vero optima lege creaturus, summum imperium belli, pacis, poenarum ac praemiorum sine provocatione habebat: ut liber impedimentis omnibus melius ad summam rerum consulere posset.

22. *Supra* Introd., n. 19.

23. "Any individual subject to this order shall be . . . (e) detained in accordance with such other conditions as the Secretary of Defense may prescribe," Subsection 3(e) of the President's Executive Military Order of November 13, 2001, in *TTP,* Memo 2, pp. 27-28. Full text located in *Appendix A.*

24. *Const.,* Art. 1, §8, ¶s 9, 10, 11. The congressional right to determine "rules concerning captures on land and water" extends to the determination of rules governing the treatment of human captives in time of war; ¶11 specifically spells out Congress's power of *declaring of war* and the *granting of letters of marque and reprisal.* The congressional right to "constitute tribunals inferior to the supreme court" applies mainly to the power of establishing circuit courts of appeal, but expresses no limitation on the type of tribunal to be established, except to say that such must be "inferior to the supreme court." According to Hamilton, Federalist 83, ¶5, "a power to constitute courts, is a power to prescribe the mode of trial." If this be true, then the creation of rules governing the trial of suspected terrorists is legislative, and not executive, domain.

25. Plutarch, *Parallel Lives of the Greeks and Romans: Life of Pompey,* ch. 24, §5, tr. Bernadotte Perrin, *Plutarch's Lives* (Vol. 5 of 11), p.175 (London: William Heinemann, 1917).

26. Plutarch's choice of delicate words followed by a list of no less than sixteen temple locations where violations of sanctity occurred is a euphemistic way of saying that young women were raped in large numbers. The victimization of temple virgins who remain chaste for religious reasons is especially hideous. *Supra* Introd.,

n. 25, at 174: τῶν δὲ ἀσύλων καὶ ἀβάτων πρότερον ἱερῶν ἐξέκοψαν ἐπιόντες τὸ Κλάριον, τὸ Διδυμαῖον, τὸ Σαμοθρᾴκιον ("[the pirates] assailed places of refuge and sanctuaries hitherto pure and inviolate, ravaging the temples of Claros, Didyma, Samothrace" *etc.*)

27. Appian of Alexandria, *Roman Histories*, 12.14.94, tr. Horace White, *Appian's Roman History* (vol. 2 of 4), p. 416 (Cambridge: Harvard University Press, 1962).

28. This plenary judicial power is evident from Plutarch, *supra* Introd., n. 25, at 184, where Pompey is reported to have treated humanely those of the pirates who surrendered willingly to him (πειρατηρίων ἐνίοις δεηθεῖσιν ἐπιεικῶς ἐχρήσατο), and, after seizing their ships and persons, did them no further harm (καὶ παραλαβὼν τὰ πλοῖα καὶ τὰ σώματα κακὸν οὐδὲν ἐποίησεν). Having pardoned, with powers of final arbitration, all lesser offenders, Pompey was able to garner valuable intelligence information from the participants that allowed him to capture, try, and imprison the very worst of the offenders. Plutarch suggests, *supra* Introd., n. 25, at 186, that it was clemency and not the use of cruelty that was most responsible for ending the piratic raids within three months, as Pompey eventually relocated the lesser offenders released from his custody to a rehabilitation program whereby they were reintroduced to civilized life and made to dwell either in cities or on farms as tillers of the soil in the lands of Cilicia.

29. Appian, 12.14.94, *supra* Introd., n. 27, at 416.

30. Plutarch, *supra* Introd., n. 25, at 178.

31. Appian, 11.8.51, *supra,* Introd., n. 27, at 200.

32. According to the constitution that defined the ancient Roman republic from the years 509 to 31 BC formal executive power as Commander-in-Chief of the armed forces was shared between *two* co-consuls, as opposed to one unitary sovereign (*princeps*). (Rome came under imperial governance and a new supreme power or principate was vested in Augustus Caesar a few decades after the deaths of Pompey and Julius Caesar in the last days of the republic.) In time of national emergency one consul would peaceably yield his executive powers to direct war to the single authority of his co-consul. Balthazar Ayala cites, for instance, the case of Agrippa Furius who voluntarily resigned his executive powers to Titus Quintius in an expedition against the Aequians and Volscians. Ayala notes that among the Greek generals at the Battle of Marathon, a similar vein of cooperation arose when Aristides handed over sole command to his better trained colleague Miltiades, encouraging others to do the same (*supra* Introd., n. 21, p. 123-24, 1582 edition). Alexander Hamilton remarks that, by long practice, "it became an established custom with the consuls to divide the administration between themselves by lot; one of them remaining at Rome to govern the city and its environs; the other taking the command in the more distant provinces. This expedient must no doubt have had great influence in preventing those collisions and rivalships, which might otherwise have embroiled the peace of the republic" (*The Federalist*, No. 70, ¶9)

33. Plutarch, *supra* Introd., n. 25, at 182: "whence Piso stood in real danger of having his consulship taken away, Gabinius already having the requisite law written out" (ὅθεν ὁ Πείσων ἐκινδύνευσε τὴν ὑπατείαν ἀφαιρεθῆναι, Γαβινίου νόμον ἔχοντος ἤδη συγγεγραμμένον).

34. Plutarch, *supra* Introd., n. 25, at 182.

35. Memorandum from John Yoo, Deputy Assistant Attorney General, Office of Legal Counsel, Department of Justice, to Timothy Flanigan, Deputy Counsel to the President, September 25, 2001, Re: The President's Constitutional Authority to Conduct Military Operations Against Terrorists and Nations Supporting Them, in *TTP*, Memo 1, p. 3.

36. For instance, Section 212 of the USA Patriot Act 2001, (available at http://www.epic.org/privacy/terrorism/hr3162.html) concerning "emergency disclosure of electronic communications to protect life and limb" authorizes private businesses who provide services to customers "to divulge a record or other information pertaining to a subscriber to or customer of such service . . . to a government entity, if the provider *reasonably believes that an emergency involving immediate danger of death or serious physical injury to any person justifies disclosure of the information.*" This provision effectively deputizes ordinary citizens as organs of surveillance, while bypassing the authority of a judge to issue a warrant for such searches. Section 213 of the act grants government entities authority to delay notice of the execution of a search warrant, "if the court finds reasonable cause to believe that providing immediate notification of the execution of the warrant may have an adverse result." This clause essentially allows federal agents repeated entry into a private residence for purposes of surveillance without having to inform the resident(s) being searched of the fact that they are being searched. For further discussion see Dahila Lithwick and Julia Turner, "A Guide to the Patriot Act," *Slate*, September 8, 2003.

37. Jay Stanley, "The Surveillance-Industrial Complex: How the American Government Is Conscripting Businesses and Individuals in the Construction of a Surveillance Society,"p. 3 (American Civil Liberties Union, August 2004).

38. President George W. Bush, Executive Military Order of November 13, 2001, Subsection 2(a)(2), in *TTP*, Memo 2, p. 26.

39. *Const.*, Art. 1, §8, ¶s 9, 10, 11, and 14.

40. The Reservation to Geneva allows U.S. officials to administer the death penalty to captives duly convicted of war crimes before a competent tribunal regardless of whether such offences were punishable by death under the law of the occupied territory in force before the occupation began.

41. It was unthinkable for the OLC to lift GPW, Article 5 requirements of humane treatment for those awaiting a trial by competent tribunal to sort the innocent from the guilty. Secretary of State Colin Powell and State Department Legal Advisor Wm. H. Taft IV both gave stern warning that flouting Geneva requirements would be both tactically counterproductive and contrary to two centries of United States military tradition (*TTP*, at 122, 129). Both officials eventually found alterna-

tive employment outside the administration, Powell in 2003 and Taft in 2005. International law was already on the side of America before September 11, as no *bona fide* member of al-Qaeda engaging in training for future terrorist attacks could possibly qualify as an individual adhering to the customs and laws of war. It must also be remembered that GPW, Articles 22 and 97 protect prisoners of war from incarceration in penitentiaries and other prison facilities because customary international law does not regard it a crime to take up arms in defense of one's self or one's country. However, since terrorists focus their violence upon defenseless non-belligerents, it is traditionally thought that their behavior does not respect the customs and laws of war. Although, as we shall see, the Bush II OLC dispenses entirely with customary international law on the grounds that it represents an unconstitutional encumbrance on the executive in the conduct of war, that same law could have easily been used to convict international terrorists as war criminals, since bin Laden-style terrorism violates all seven of the traditional requirements for justice in war. And this fact alone would have also ensured criminal conviction of terrorists before an international war crimes tribunal (which is where bin Laden should be tried, if he is ever captured). The consensus among jurists and statesmen throughout the ages has been that wars are just when they are: 1. declared and conducted by authorized sovereigns, i.e., the requirement of *auctoritas principis*; 2. founded upon some just cause (*causa justa*); and 3. motivated by the right intent (*intentio recta*). These three *ad bellum* requirements are stated in Saint Thomas Aquinas, *Summa Theologiae* II. II. q. 40, art. 1, in E. F. Stanisla & Paul Maré, eds., vol. 3, p. 378, col. 2 (Paris: 1889). Saint Bonaventura, *Speculum Animae*, ch. 1, in A. C. Peltier, ed., vol. 7, p. 534, col. 1 (Paris: Ludovicus Vivè, Biblopola Editor, 1864). Al-Qaeda terrorists arguably violate these *ad bellum* requirements because they do not, as non-state entities, possess sovereign authority to declare war, nor do they have just cause in taking defenseless life, nor do they have right intent in carrying out their suicide missions. Al-Qaeda terrorists also violate the traditional requirements for justice *in* the conduct of war (*jus in bello*) by systematically failing: 4. to pursue a goal of lasting peace (*pacis intentio*); 5. to undertake war in self-defense (*defensio sui*); 6. to seek to recover only that which was taken (*recuperatio rerum*); and 7. to focus punishment (*punitio*) upon belligerents, while avoiding defenseless non-belligerents. These *in bello* requirements structure the concept of *proportionality of punishment* in the waging of war. For requirement 4 see Saint Augustine, *De Civitate Dei*, book 19, ch. 12, §§1-2, ed. J. P. Migne, *Patrologiae Latinae* 41.637-638 (Paris: 1900). Saint Bonaventura, *De Beatitudinis Evangelicis*, ch. 6 (*de pace*), A. C. Peltier, ed., vol. 8, p. 324, col. 2 (Paris: Ludovicus Vivè, Biblopola Editor, 1864). Alberico Gentilis, *De Jure Belli Libri Tres*, book 1, ch. 5, p. 45 (1612 edition), ed. James Brown Scott, vol. 1 (Oxford: The Clarendon Press, 1933). Hugo Grotius argues for requirement 5 twice in *De Jure Belli ac Pacis*, first at book 1, ch. 2, §1, ¶4, in ed., tr. William Whewell, vol. 1, pp. 31-32 (Cambridge: Cambridge University Press, 1853), and then, in combination with requirements 6 and 7, at book 2, ch. 1, §2, ¶2 (Whewell, vol. 1, p. 205) where he claims that "most writers lay down three just causes of war: self-defense, recovery of property, and punishment of wrongs." These causes define limits in the conduct and waging of war, and are therefore distinct from *ad bellum* requirements. A nation, in other words, may have perfectly just grounds for going *to* war against an adversary, but then proceed to commit acts of wanton brutality against innocent persons, thereby compromising justice *in* war. Balthazar Ayala argues for requirement 1 in Id., book 1, ch. 2, §7, and for requirements 5 and 6 in book 1, ch. 2, §11. Gentilis argues for requirement 1 in Id., book 1, ch. 2, pp. 22-34, and requirement 4 in Book 1, ch. 5, p. 45, and requirement 5 in book 1, ch. 13, pp. 92-96. It must be remembered that these traditional *ad bellum* and *in bello* requirements exist within the body of customary international law, and that OLC interpreters repeatedly advised President Bush on several occasions *not* to feel constrained in his decision-making process by importing concepts from customary international law that might limit his horizon of options in combating terrorism, e.g., the Yoo-Haynes II January 9, 2002, Memorandum, *TTP*, at 70, 75; the Bybee-Gonzales January 22, 2002 Memorandum, *TTP*, at 111, 113, 115.

42. *Ex parte Quirin* 317 U.S. 1, at 21 (1942).

43. Louis Fisher, *Presidential War Power*, second edition, revised, p. 206 (Lawrence: University Press of Kansas, 2004).

44. *Supra* Introd., n. 42, at 22-23.

45. *Supra* Introd., n. 42, at 25.

46. A person need not have committed a criminal act within the territory of the United States in order to have Fourteenth Amendment rights to due process and equal protection under the law at trial. In fact Article 3 of the Constitution, which outlines the various dimensions of Supreme Court jurisdiction, specifically includes cases involving actions, persons, and detentions falling *outside* the territory of the United States.

47. In a Draft Decision (for the President) Re: the Application of the Geneva Convention on Prisoners of War to the Conflict with Al-Qaeda and the Taliban, January 25, 2002, then-Counsel to the President Alberto R. Gonzales advises President Bush that "a determination that GPW does not apply to al-Qaeda and the Taliban eliminates any argument regarding the need for case-by-case determinations of POW status" (*TTP*, Memo 7, at 119). But days later, then-Secretary of State, Colin Powell argued that the President need not suspend Geneva requirements with respect to the Taliban and al-Qaeda in order to reap the advantages of avoiding tedious case-by-case determinations of POW status, if he just simply issue a blanket executive legal determination that none of the detainees are entitled to POW status. Powell says of the Gonzales-Bush II Memo of January 25, 2002 that it "identifies several positive consequences if the President determines that GPW does not apply. The memorandum should note that these consequences would result equally if the President determines that the GPW does apply but that the detainees are not entitled to POW status" (*TTP*, Memo 8, p. 122). Powell appears to recognize that Geneva

common Article 2 automatically applies the principles and requirements of the Conventions to *all* cases of partial or total occupation of the territory of a High Contracting Party (such as Afghanistan) by United States forces, but his reasoning remains irretrievably flawed because the President cannot both decide that GPW does apply and, at the same time, make a blanket determination that all detainees are *not* entitled to POW status, since, if GPW is applied, then GPW, Article 5, ¶2 applies, which precludes any government official of a High Contracting Party from making blanket determinations of POW status for persons captured in war. Doubt about the POW status of a detainee only arises (under Geneva) if the detainee is suspected of having violated the laws of war. In such case, an Article 5 hearing could try, convict, and sentence any proven member of al-Qaeda. We should recall that many of our soldiers were subjected to extended periods of inhuman confinement, isolation, and intense physical and psychological torture by ruthless North Korean captors during the Korean War, and that these officials justified their lawbreaking by arguing that United States forces were operating as *illegal* combatants, and so, were not deserving of POW status. The blanket categorization of your enemy as non-POW does not confer rights of coercive interrogation or inhuman treatment of any kind to the detaining power. We should recall that the Nazi government early in its war on the Eastern Front also issued a blanket determination that the Geneva Conventions (of July 27, 1929, Relative to the Treatment of Prisoners of War) were not in any way to be applied to captured Soviet personnel, in spite of Helmuth James von Moltke's repeated warnings, as *Oberkommando der Wehrmacht*, that humanitarian restrictions on POW treatment were contained in customary international law at least as early as the eighteenth century. See Scott Horton, "Through a Mirror, Darkly: Applying the Geneva Conventions to a New Kind of Warfare," in *The Torture Debate in America*, (hereinafter *TDA*), ed. Karen J. Greenberg, p. 136, 140 (Cambridge: Cambridge University Press, 2006).

48. According to Joseph Margulies, lead attorney in *Rasul v. Bush* (2004), "establishing the relationships [between U.S. military intelligence and Afghans] that will ensure a steady flow of reliable intelligence is a question of time, not money. In an impoverished country beset by factionalism, the Pentagon's ill-advised bounty program [offering $5,000 per Taliban, $20,000 per al-Qaeda member in leaflets disbursed over Afghanistan in the weeks following 9/11] produced predictable results: a steady flow of miserable prisoners trussed up and tossed into the back of pickup trucks, delivered by villagers with their hands out-stretched." *Guantánamo and the Abuse of Presidential Power*, p.69 (New York: Simon & Schuster, 2006).

49. Margulies, *supra* Introd., n. 48, at 6, 38, 86, 88; Adam Zagorin and Michael Duffy, "Inside the Interrogation of Detainee 063," *Time*, July 20, 2005, 26.

50. Mark Denbeaux, "Report on Guantánamo Detainees: A Profile of 517 Detainees through Analysis of Department of Defense Data," at 2, 3. Seton Hall University School of Law, Feb. 6, 2006. Available at http://law.shu.edu/news/guantanamo_report_final_2_08_06.pdf.

51. Memorandum for Commander, Joint Task Force 170, Guantánamo Bay, Cuba, from Lt. Col. Diane E. Beaver, Staff Judge Advocate, October 11, 2002, Re: Legal Brief on Proposed Counter-Resistance Strategies, in *TTP*, Memo 20, p. 229.

52. *Supra*, Introd., n. 51, at 229.

53. Memorandum from Alberto R. Gonzales, Counsel to the President, to President George W. Bush, Decision Re: Application of the Geneva Convention on Prisoners of War to the Conflict with al-Qaeda and the Taliban, January 25, 2002, in *TTP*, Memo 7, p. 118. Judge Gonzales asserts that any argument which would warn of the danger of future possible erosion in U.S. military culture due to a blanket Presidential determination to suspend Geneva "fails to recognize that our military remain bound to apply the principles of GPW because that is what you [President George W. Bush] have directed them to do"(*TTP*, Memo 7, p. 121). Gonzales appears wholly oblivious to the fact that a policy determination by the President to suspend Geneva sends an *unequivocal* message to our military men and women *not* to apply Geneva's strict humanitarian restrictions prohibiting abuse and mistreatment in the handling, interrogating, and confining of suspected members of the Taliban and al-Qaeda. President Bush made his determination in an Executive Order dated February 7, 2002, Subsection 2(d), in *TTP*, Memo 11, p. 135. In Subsection 5 of the Order President Bush commands somewhat self-contradictorily that suspected Taliban and al-Qaeda detainees will nonetheless be treated humanely and in a manner consistent with Geneva, but only *to the extent appropriate and consistent with military necessity*, thus deliberately leaving the door open for future possible human rights abuses in cases where a quick and timely extraction of information from a suspected terrorist is deemed to be a matter of strategic necessity.

54. Adrian A. S. Zuckerman, "Coercion and the Judicial Ascertainment of Truth," 23 *Isr. L. Rev.* 357, at 361 (1989). Cooperation appears more effective than coercion at retrieving actionable intelligence. See Jeff Zeleny and Charlie Savage, "Official Says Terrorism Suspect is Cooperating," *The New York Times*, Feb. 3, 2010.

55. Author's translation of Aristotle, *Rhetoric*, book 1, ch. 15, 1377a3-6: οὐδὲν γὰϱ ἧττον ἀναγκαζόμενοι τὰ ψευδῆ λέγουσιν ἢ τἀληϑῆ, καὶ διακαϱτεϱοῦντες μὴ λέγειν τἀληϑῆ, καὶ ῥᾳδίως καταψευδόμενοι ὡς παυσόμενοι ϑᾶττον (ed. Immanuel Bekker, vol. 2 of 2, Berlin: 1831).

56. Richard Davies, tr. *Beccaria: On Crimes and Punishments and Other Writings*, ed. Richard Bellamy, p. 41 (Cambridge: Cambridge University Press, 1995). Cesare Beccaria, *Dei delitti e delle pene*, ed. Franco Venturi, §16, p. 41 (Torino: Giulio Einaudi editore, 1970): [L]'impressione del dolore può crescere a segno che, occupandola tutta, non lasci alcuna libertà al torturato che di scegliere la strada piú corta per il momento presente, onde sottrarsi di pena. Allora la risposta del reo è cosí necessaria come le impressioni del fuoco o dell'acqua. Allora l'innocente sensibile si chiamerà reo, quando egli creda con ciò di far cessare il tormento. Ogni differenza tra essi sparisce per quel mezzo medesimo, che si pretende impiegato per ritrovarla.

57. Author's translation of Marcus Aurelius, *Meditations* 6.6: Ἄϱιστος τϱόπος τοῦ ἀμύνεσθαι τὸ μὴ ἐξομοιοῦσθαι, Greek text, ed. C. R. Haines, p. 132 (Cambridge: Harvard University Press, 1916).

58. *Supra* Introd., n. 15, at 80.

59. Report of the International Committee of the Red Cross (ICRC) on the Treatment by the Coalition Forces of Prisoners of War and Other Protected Persons by the Geneva Conventions in Iraq During Arrest, Internment and Interrogation, February 2004, in *TTP*, pp. 392-93.

60. *Supra* introd., n. 59, at 392-93.

61. The term "quaint" was used by White House Counsel Alberto Gonzales to describe Geneva rules governing the quality of life for captured POWs. In his January 25, 2002, memorandum to President Bush, Gonzales argues that "in my judgment, this new paradigm renders obsolete Geneva's strict limitations on questioning of enemy prisoners and renders quaint some of its provisions requiring that a captured enemy be afforded such things as commissary privileges, scrip (i.e., advances of monthly pay), athletic uniforms, and scientific instruments" *(supra* Introd, n. 53, at 119). The idea here is that prisoners form their own independent self-sustaining community during their internment, where they cook their own meals, grow their own food, make their own clothes, while remaining securely quartered within a camp under close surveillance, and that they not be made to suffer gratuitously.

Question One: The Yoo-Flanigan Memo

1. Under Subsection 2(a) of the Authorization for Use of Military Force (AUMF), Pub. L. No. 107-40, 115 Stat. 224 (2001) "the President is authorized to use all necessary and appropriate force against those nations, organizations, or persons he determines planned, authorized, committed, or aided the terrorist attacks that occurred on September 11, 2001, or harbored such organizations or persons, in order to prevent any future acts of international terrorism against the United States by such nations, organizations or persons." The "he determines" phrase gave President Bush the opening he needed to expand the war on terror into Iraq by simply claiming that Saddam Hussein was offering save-haven to al-Qaeda operatives while at the same time both developing and stockpiling Weapons of Mass Destruction (WMD), which could, it was argued, lead to terrorists getting their hands on extremely hazardous weapons, given Saddam's supposed connection to al-Qaeda. It is no coincidence that "according to [then-Secretary of the Treasury Paul] O'Neill, the first topic on the agenda of that initial meeting [of the Bush II National Security Council team] was the invasion and occupation of Iraq." Joe Conason, *It Can Happen Here: Authoritarian Peril in the Age of Bush*, p. 28 (New York: St. Martin's Press, 2007). Of course, it just so happened that the President's Qaeda-Iraq link turned out to be a hoax

based on hearsay evidence gleaned by U.S. intelligence through the use of coercive interrogation techniques carried out by Egyptian authorities upon one Ibn al-Shaykh al-Libi who "provided his most specific and elaborate accounts about ties between Iraq and al-Qaeda only after he was secretly handed over to Egypt by the United States in January of 2002, in a process known as rendition," Douglas Jehl, "Qaeda-Iraq Link U.S. Cited Is Tied to Coercion Claim," *New York Times*, Dec. 9, 2005, A1. Coercive interrogation of al-Libi is patently illegal when done by U.S. *or* Egyptian authorities, because al-Libi unambiguously qualifies as a "protected person" under GPW, Art. 17, ¶4 which says that "no physical or mental torture, nor any other form of coercion, may be inflicted on prisoners of war to secure from them information of any kind whatever. Prisoners of war who refuse to answer may not be threatened, insulted, or exposed to unpleasant or disadvantageous treatment of any kind." Al-Libi should have been, but was not, protected against forcible transfer to Egypt by the United States under GCP, Art. 49, ¶1: "Individual or mass forcible transfers, as well as deportations of protected persons from occupied territory to the territory of the Occupying Power *or to that of any other country*, occupied or not, are prohibited, *regardless of their motive*." (Emphases added.) Al-Libi should have been, but was not, afforded full pretrial POW status whether in Egyptian *or* U.S. custody by GPW, Art. 5, ¶2. Al-Libi should have also been counted as a "protected person" under GCP, Art. 4, ¶1. In a draft opinion memorandum (dated March 3, 2004) for then-White House Counsel Alberto Gonzales, Jack L. Goldsmith III authored the opinion that GCP, Art. 49, ¶1 does *not* prevent the removal of protected persons "from Iraq to another country to facilitate interrogation, for a brief but not indefinite period," if those persons happen to be illegal aliens "pursuant to local immigration law" (*TTP*, p. 368). But the Goldsmith opinion is groundless, for GCP, Art. 49, ¶1 countenances *no exceptions whatsoever* pertaining to the citizenship status of protected persons forcibly transferred from Iraq to another country for interrogation. The only traction Goldsmith has in his argument to wriggle out of GCP, Art. 49 requirements comes from a definition of "deportation" as "forced displacement of . . . persons . . . from the area *in which they are lawfully present*" borrowed from Article 7(2)(d) of the Rome Statute of the International Criminal Court (ICC). But President Bush consistently refused to recognize the ICC as a valid organ of international law, so that Goldsmith's argument legalizing Article 49 violations is grounded in the text of an instrument of law held to be legally non-binding by then-President Bush. See Rome Statute of the International Criminal Court, July 17, 1998, U.N. Doc. A/CONF.183/9, in 37 I.L.M. 999 (1998).

2. *Supra* Introd., n. 35, at 24.

3. Memorandum from Colin L. Powell, U.S. Department of State, to Counsel to the President Alberto R. Gonzales, January 26, 2002, Re: Draft Decision Memorandum for the President on the Applicability of the Geneva Conventions to the Conflict in Afghanistan, in *TTP*, Memo 8, p. 124.

4. For text of GPW see *Appendix F*.

5. Author's translation of the hexameter line εἴ κε πάϑοι τά τ' ἔρεξε, δίκη κ' ἰϑεῖα γένοιτο cited by Aristotle to encapsulate the common conception of justice as retaliation in *Nicomachean Ethics*, book 5, ch. 5, 1132b27.

6. *Supra* Introd., n. 14, at 595. Author's translation of Grotius: [A]equitas iubet parci his qui sine condicionibus se victori permittunt aut supplices fiunt. . . . Adversus haec aequitatis ac iuris naturalis praecepta exceptiones adferri solent minime iustae, nempe si talio exigatur, si terrore opus sit, si pertinacius restitum sit. . . . A captivis et deditis aut dedere se cupientibus periculum non est: ut ergo iuste occidantur oportet crimen antecedat, et quidem tale, quod aequus iudex morte vidicandum censeret.

7. Pub. L. No. 107-40, 115 Stat. 224 (2001).

8. Max Farrand *ed., The Records of the Federal Convention of 1787*. Vol. 2 of 4, 318-19 (New Haven and London: Yale University Press, 1911).

9. Author's translation of Ayala, *supra* Introd., n. 21, at 79: Sicque nimirum consules Romani, penes quos erat summa auctoritas, exercitu accepto, belli quidem gerendi potestatem habuerunt: utque pro suo arbitrio lacesserent, aut invaderent hostem, ac militarem disciplinam sua voluntate regerent; bellum autem indicere, aut finire, nisi ex senatus auctoritate, & iussu populi non potuerunt.

10. None of the scholars cited by Yoo argues that Congress has exclusive power to determine whether or not to engage a foreign enemy in war, since, if Congress held such power, a sitting President would be helpless to order any military response to a sudden attack, and §2(c)(3) of the War Powers Resolution of 1973, a clause well known to each of these scholars, specifically allows the President to introduce United States Armed Forces into hostilities pursuant to a national emergency created by an attack on the United States. Scholars cited by Yoo include Louis Fisher, *Presidential War Power*, 185-206 (1995); John Hart Ely, *War and Responsibility: Constitutional Lessons of Vietnam and Its Aftermath*, 3-5 (1993); Michael Glennon, *Constitutional Diplomacy*, 80-84 (1990); Louis Henkin, *Constitutionalism, Democracy, and Foreign Affairs*, 109 (1990); Harold Hongju Koh, *The National Security Constitution: Sharing Power After the Iran-Contra Affair*, 158-61 (1990); Francis D. Wormuth & Edwin B. Firmage, *To Chain the Dog of War: The War Power of Congress in History and Law* (2nd ed. 1989). See also John Yoo, *Crisis and Command: A History of Executive Power from George Washington to George W. Bush* (New York: Kaplan Pub., 2010).

11. Even if the Bush administration had acted under the color of law by justifying its holding the Guantánamo detainees on GCP Article 5, ¶2 grounds that each such detainee was "a spy or saboteur, or *a person on definite suspicion of activity hostile to the security of the Occupying Power*"—plausible if the detainee is a member of a transnational terrorist network—GCP Article 5, ¶3 would nevertheless demand that each such detainee be treated humanely and, in case of trial, not deprived of the right to a fair and regular trial as prescribed by GCP, Articles 71, 72, 73, 75.

12. CSRT transcripts are available at http://www.defenselink.mil/pubs/foi/detainees/csrt/index.html.

13. Martin Henn, "Preemption and the Limits of Just War: Fundamental Questions of U.S. Policy Formation Over Iran's Emerging Nuclear Weapons Programs," 21 *Public Affairs Quarterly*, no. 4, 363, 367 (2007).

14. According to Grotius, *De Jure Belli ac Pacis*, book 2, ch. 1, §5, anticipatory war in defense of human life is justified only when the danger of attack is present and certain, and not merely opined or conjectured (*supra* q. 1, n. 13, at 365). Alberico Gentili, whose 1612 publication, *De Jure Belli Libri Tres*, served as an original source work and template for Grotius, argues that fear of hostile intent by itself cannot morally justify the use of preemption, since "a just cause of fear is required: suspicion is not enough. Now a just cause of fear is defined as fear of a greater evil—a fear which befalls even a man of the most unflinching dignity," Id. book 1, ch. 14, pp. 98-99, 1612 edition (*supra* q. 1, n. 13, at 366). Francisco de Vitoria acknowledges that anticipatory defense "can only be resorted to at the very moment of danger, or as the jurists say 'in continenti,' and so when the necessity of defense has passed there comes an end to the lawfulness of war" (*Relectiones Theologicae*, text of 1696, ch. 6, §5, *supra* q. 1, n. 13, at 366).

15. Gaillard Hunt, ed. *6 The Writings of James Madison: 1790-1802*, p. 148 (New York: G.P. Putnam's Sons, 1906).

16. Hunt, *supra* q. 1, n. 15, at 312.

17. Louis Fisher, *Presidential War Power*. 2nd edition revised, p. 100 (Lawrence, University Press of Kansas, 2004). John N. Moore also argues for retroactive congressional authorization in "The National Executive and the Use of the Armed Forces Abroad," 21 *Naval War College Rev*. 28, 32 (1969).

18. 2 Stat. 129, 7th Cong., 1st Sess. 4 (1802)—*An Act for the protection of the Commerce and Seamen of the United States, against the Tripolitan Cruisers*. Section 2 of this act allows Jefferson "to instruct the commanders of . . . public vessels . . . to subdue, seize and make prize of all vessels, goods and effects, belonging to the Bey of Tripoli, or to his subjects, and to bring or send the same into port, to be proceeded against . . . according to law." It is clear from the text of this statute that Congress viewed the Barbary Wars as international criminal activity worthy of prosecution in court, but not of a formal declaration of war. The Arab sheikhs originally demanded from the United States a generous tribute in exchange for an abatement of piracy on the high seas, but President Jefferson and Congress rightly refused to pay such tribute.

19. Annals of Cong., 7th Cong., 1st Sess. 431 (1802). *Supra* q. 1, n. 17, at 237 (n. 4).

20. Fisher, *supra* q. 1, n. 17, at 34.

21. Melvin E. Lee, "The Fallacy of Grievance-based Terrorism," *Middle East Quarterly*, vol. 15, no. 1, Winter 2008, 71, 73.

22. Marcus Tullius Cicero (106-43BC), *De Republica*, book 3, ch. 23, §35, text of Clinton Walker Keyes tr. *Cicero: De Re Publica et De Legibus*, p. 212 (Cambridge: Harvard University Press, 1978): Nullum bellum iustum habetur nisi denuntiatum, nisi indictum, nisi repetitis rebus.

23. Hamilton's original Vesting Clause argument is found at *Pacificus* No. 1 in *The Papers of Alexander Hamilton,* vol. 15, ed. Harold C. Syrett, p. 39 (New York and London: Columbia University Press, 1969). Under the pseudonym "Pacificus" Hamilton sought to defend, in a series of seven essays, President Washington's Neutrality Proclamation of 1793, which was issued in order to keep the peace, and to prevent the United States from being drawn into the war between France and Britain over the actions of rogue citizens who, in taking the law into their own hands, might initiate hostilities against either power on the high seas. The constitutional dispute raised by the Proclamation is whether or not the President has constitutional authority to *unilaterally* decide whether the nation shall be at war or peace, given that the power to deliberate and determine upon such questions appears to be vested in Congress by *Const.*, Art. 1, §8, ¶s 9, 10, 11, 12, 13, 14, 15, 16.

24. Hunt, *supra* q. 1, n. 15, at 150-51.

25. Syrett, *supra* q. 1, n. 23, at 42.

26. Syrett, *supra* q. 1, n. 23, at 39.

27. Author's translation of *Polybius: The Histories,* vol. 3, ed., tr., W. R. Paton, p. 303 (Cambridge: Harvard University Press, 1923): καὶ μὴν τὰς ἀρχὰς ὁ δῆμος δίδωσι τοῖς ἀξίοις· ὅπερ ἐστὶ κάλλιστον ἆθλον ἐν πολιτείᾳ καλοκἀγαθίας. ἔχει δὲ τὴν κυρίαν καὶ περὶ τῆς τῶν νόμων δοκιμασίας, καὶ τὸ μέγιστον, ὑπὲρ εἰρήνης οὗτος βουλεύεται καὶ πολέμου. καὶ μὴν περὶ συμμαχίας καὶ διαλύσεως καὶ συνθηκῶν οὗτός ἐστιν ὁ βεβαιῶν ἕκαστα τούτων καὶ κύρια ποιῶν ἢ τοὐναντίον. ὥστε πάλιν ἐκ τούτων εἰκότως ἄν τιν' εἰπεῖν ὅτι μεγίστην ὁ δῆμος ἔχει μερίδα καὶ δημοκρατικόν ἐστι τὸ πολίτευμα.

28. See Bosnia Opinion, 19 Op. O.L.C., Assistant Attorney General Walter Dellinger, Office of Legal Counsel, Memorandum Opinion for the Counsel to the President, November 30, 1995, Re: Proposed Deployment of United States Armed Forces into Bosnia (available at http://www.usdoj.gov.olc/bosnia2.htm) where it is argued that the President, acting without specific statutory authorization, may lawfully introduce United States troops into Bosnia in order to help the North Atlantic Treaty Organization ensure compliance with a recently negotiated peace agreement. Dellinger relies entirely upon the aegis of international legal instruments to legitimize the Clinton deployment of U.S. forces to Bosnia independent of congressional authorization.

29. *TTP*, p. 15.

30. Fisher, *supra* q. 1, n. 17, at 191, argues that President Clinton neither sought nor received congressional authorization for his initial deployment of 20,000 American ground troops to Bosnia in December of 1995, nor did he have such authorization on March 24, 1999, when he ordered hostilities to be initiated against the Federal Republic of Yugoslavia (Serbia and Montenegro).

31. Hunt, *supra* q. 1, n. 15, at 154.

32. Hunt, *supra* q. 1, n. 15, at 153.

33. E.g., John Hart Ely, *War and Responsibility: Constitutional Lessons of Vietnam and Its Aftermath*, p. 24 (Princeton: Princeton University Press, 1993); Fisher, *supra*, q. 1, n. 17, at 69-73. On May 28, 1934, Congress passed a Joint Resolution allowing President Roosevelt to prohibit the sale of arms and munitions to countries then engaged in armed conflict in the Chaco (a region of central South America overlapping Bolivia, Paraguay, and Argentina). According to the Joint Resolution, if the President should find on his own authority that the prohibition of the sale of arms might contribute to peace, then he may issue a proclamation banning such sales "as he may deem necessary." The Curtiss-Wright Export Corporation challenged this resolution on constitutional grounds; but the Court held in *United States v. Curtiss-Wright*, 299 U.S. at 305 that the Joint Resolution did *not* represent an unconstitutional delegation of legislative power to the executive. It is easy then to see why *Curtiss-Wright* is *the* federal case of choice for those in the Bush II OLC who wish to delegate certain legislative powers to the President (for instance, the power to constitute tribunals inferior to the Supreme Court, to define and punish offences against the law of nations, to initiate and authorize military hostilities abroad, to make rules for the government and regulation of the land and naval forces, etc.).

34. In August of 2008, for instance, the Russian army invaded (and two weeks later withdrew) from the Republic of Georgia in the Caucasus. The action may have arisen in response to Bush administration attempts to bring the Ukraine into N.A.T.O. and to equip Poland with anti-ballistic missile technology.

35. Ivo of Chartres laid down the official theological pretext for the Holy Crusades used at the Council of Clermont in his *Decretum Ivonis* of 1093, at Part 10, ch. 87 wherein an eternal reward in the Kingdom of Heaven is promised to any Christian, who, in the act of defending Christians, should die in the killing of infidels. See ed. J. P. Migne, *Patrologiae Latinae 161: Sancti Ivonis Opera Omnia*, at 719, 720 (Paris: 1889). Although there is no talk in Christian theology of bevies of innocent young virgins awaiting the warrior-martyr in heaven, the concept of eternal reward amid religious warfare mimes the practice of the Arab and Berber conquerors of Andalus in the early eighth century. The problem with the presumptive right of heavenly reward in the *Decretum Ivonis*, however, is that it does not spell out exactly what constitutes a *just* defense in warfare; it led also to harsher subsequent reformulations in the *Decretum Gratiani* (Rome: 1152), for instance, (*a*) In certamine, quod contra infideles geritur, quisquis moritur, coeleste regnum meretur ("In battle conducted against infidels, anyone who should perish shall merit the reward of a heavenly kingdom," cause XXIII, question VIII, ch. 49), and (*b*) Crimen punire pro Deo non est crudelitas sed pietas ("To punish crime on behalf of God is not cruelty but piety," cause XXIII, question VIII, part ii, ch. 13, ed. J. P. Migne, *Patrologiae Latinae 187: Decretum Gratiani*, (*a*) at 1234, (*b*) at 1249, 1250 (Paris: 1891). The Crusades made the Church into a revenue-generating entity due to its need to levy the so-called Saladin Tenth, a tax on laity and clergy alike to fund large expeditions into the Middle East to recapture holy sites that had been seized by the Seljuks, who had

replaced the Fatimids of Egypt in the eleventh century as custodians of Jerusalem. This revenue-raising system continued on even after the crusades were over, and sparked ever greater levels of corruption that eventually precipitated the Protestant Reformation.

36. See *Appendix J* for relevant portions of the WPR. Deputy Assistant Yoo argues that actions the President takes pursuant to Subsection 2(c)(3) of the WPR, namely, his deployment of U.S. forces to Afghanistan amid national emergency following the attacks of 9/11, are *not* subject to the reporting requirements of Section 4 nor to the cut-off requirement of Subsection 5(b).

37. "Crisis in the Persian Gulf Region: U.S. Policy Options and Implications," hearing before the Senate Committee on Armed Services, 101st Cong., 2nd Sess. 701 (1990).

38. *Congressional Quarterly Almanac*, 742 (1990).

Question Two: The November 13 Executive Order

1. See *Appendix A* for full text of the November 13 Order.

2. POW status trials by competent tribunal are not guaranteed to persons detained pursuant to this Order.

3. See *Appendix D* for a full list of provisions in the ICCPR flouted by the November 13 Order. The Bush Order cannot even guarantee that detainees will be protected against torture and other cruel, inhuman or degrading treatment generally, since, by Subsection III(e), the Secretary of Defense may, at his personal discretion, adjust the Geneva-style humanitarian conditions listed in III(b)(c)(d) by improvising whatever *other conditions* of detention he wishes to prescribe.

4. The court affirmed in *Rasul* that United States federal courts have jurisdiction to consider legal challenges from foreign nationals captured abroad in connection with hostilities and held at Guantánamo Bay Naval Base, Cuba. The CSRT system was most likely designed by Wolfowitz and company as a public relations ploy to give the appearance of due process at GTMO base. See Margulies's masterfully argued Petitioner's Brief on the Merits, *Rasul v. Bush* (03-334) 542 U.S. 466 (2004), as well as his personal account of the trial process for Shafiq Rasul, *supra* Introd., n. 48. See also Shafiq Rasul, Asif Iqbal, and Rhuhel Ahmed, "Composite Statement: Detention in Afghanistan and Guantánamo," July 26, 2004, available at http://www. ccr-ny.org/v2/reports/report.asp?ObjID=4bUT8M23lk&Content=424.

5. See *Appendix* C for full text of the Order Establishing Combatant Status Review Tribunal, July 7, 2004.

6. *Habeas corpus* (Lat., 'you may have the body'). A writ of habeas corpus allows a person detained without trial access to a judge to decide the legality of his detention. Article 1, §9, ¶2 of the Constitution says "The privilege of the writ of habeas

corpus shall not be suspended, unless when in cases of rebellion or invasion the public safety may require it." Although President Bush issued a "Declaration of National Emergency by Reason of Certain Terrorist Attacks" on September 14, 2001, the threat of further attack does not constitute a case of wholesale invasion or domestic rebellion envisioned by the suspension clause. During the American Revolution an Act of English Parliament suspended habeas corpus against those it defined as *pirates*, namely, commanders and mariners of such privateers and ships of war belonging to the colonies as should have the misfortune of falling into the hands of the crown. These "pirates" were incarcerated in filthy English prisons incommunicado and indefinitely, and were placed beyond the law. Edmund Burke bristled against this Act of Parliament in his eloquent *Letter to John Farr and John Harris, Esqrs., Sheriffs of the City of Bristol; On the Affairs of America, 1777* (¶s 9, 20), by arguing that "all the ancient, honest, juridical principles and institutions of England are so many clogs to check and retard the headlong course of violence and oppression. They were invented for this one good purpose, that what was not just should not be convenient. . . . People without much difficulty admit the entrance of that injustice of which they are not to be the immediate victims. In times of high proceeding it is never the faction of the predominant power that is in danger: for no tyranny chastises its own instruments. It is the obnoxious and the suspected who want the protection of law. . . . The *Habeas Corpus* Act supposes, contrary to the genius of most other laws, that the lawful magistrate may see particular men with a malignant eye, and it provides for that identical case. But when men, in particular descriptions, marked out by the magistrate himself, are delivered over by parliament to this possible malignity, it is not the *Habeas Corpus* that is occasionally suspended, but its spirit that is mistaken, and its principle that is subverted."

7. Military Commissions Act, October 17, 2006, Pub. L. 109 366, 120 Stat. 2601.

8. Denbeaux, *supra* Introd., n. 50, at 2.

9. *Boumediene v. Bush*, 553 U.S. ___, at §IV(C), ¶3 (2008).

10. *Supra* q. 2, n. 9, at §V(B), ¶6.

11. *Supra* q. 2, n. 9, at §V(B), ¶8.

Question Three: The Yoo-Haynes II Memo

1. The term "customary international law" (often called "the law of nations" or simply "international law") signifies a body of *de facto* customs and practices shared in common among the many civilized peoples of the earth regarding the declaration and conduct of war, treaties of peace, postliminy, diplomatic immunity, rights of passage, etc., that are spelled out quite specifically in the texts of the great jurists, historians, statesmen, and constitutions of the past, the content and form of which evolve slowly over time with the growth and development of mankind as a whole.

Customary international law is, therefore, distinct from *positive* international law (or what is often called "treaty law"). The Bush II OLC position is that customary international law has no binding legal effect on the President in his conduct of the Afghanistan conflict because it is not federal (treaty) law.

2. *Statement of United Nations High Commissioner for Human Rights Mary Robinson on Detention of Taliban and al-Qaida Prisoners at U.S. Base in Guantánamo Bay, Cuba, 16 January 2002*. Available at http://www.unhchr.ch/huricane/huricane.nsf/0/C537C6D4657C7928C1256B43003E7D0B?

3. Bulletin E.U. 1/2-2003, Human rights 1/11. European Parliament resolution on the European Union's rights, priorities and recommendations for the 59th session of the U.N. Commission on Human Rights in Geneva (17 March to 25 April 2003). Available at http://europa.eu/bulletin/en/200301/p102001.htm.

4. Special Rapporteur Cumaraswamy issued a press release in response to a ruling by the Court of Appeals for the District of Columbia Circuit in *Al Odah v. United States*, 321 F 3d 1124 (2003) that U.S. courts lack jurisdiction to examine the legality of the detention of the Guantánamo Bay detainees. See *United Nations Press Release*, "U.S. Court Decision on Guantánamo Detainees has Serious Implicaitons for Rule of Law, Says UN Rights Expert," at http://www.unhchr.ch/huricane/huricane.nsf/0/0C5F3E732DBFC069C1256CE8002D76C0?

5. Johan Steyn, "Guantánamo Bay: The Legal Black Hole," Twenty-Seventh F. A. Mann Lecture: 25 November 2003, p. 14: "One of the charges made against Edward Hyde, the First Earl of Clarendon, in his impeachment in 1667 was that he had attempted to preclude habeas corpus by sending persons to 'remote islands, garrisons, and other places, thereby to prevent them from the benefit of the law,' that is by sending persons to places where the writ of habeas corpus would not be available. This loophole was blocked by section 11 of the Habeas Corpus Amendment Act of 1679. For more than three centuries such stratagems to evade habeas corpus have been unlawful in England."

6. Stevenson Jacobs, "Prisoner Says Taliban Forced Him to Cook," Associated Press, Aug. 5, 2004.

7. Hunt *supra* q. 1, n. 15, at 165.

8. Scott McLellan, *What Happened: Inside the Bush White House and Washington's Culture of Deception*, pp. 62-63 (New York: Public Affairs, 2008). According to McLellan's description of the "permanent campaign" mentality in the Bush White House, campaigning for reelection and governing the nation had become wholly indistinguishable.

9. Author's translation of text quoted at Introd., n. 14, at 502. For the genesis of failed-state doctrine at the Bush II OLC, see David D. Caron, "If Afghanistan Has Failed, Then Afghanistan is Dead: 'Failed States' and the Inappropriate Substitution of Legal Conclusions for Political Description," in *TDA*, p. 214.

10. David Gray Adler, *The Constitution and the Termination of Treaties*, p. 96 (New York and London: Garland Publishing, Inc., 1986).

11. Transcript of the President's comments available at http://www.whitehouse.gov/news/releases/2001/09/20010911-16.html.

12. Author's translation of Grotius, *supra* Introd., n. 14, at 613: Demosthenes in epistola pro Lycurgi liberis laudat Philippum Macedonem quod non omnes qui inter hostes fuerant servos fecisset. καὶ γὰϱ οὔτε δίκαια εἶναι πϱὸς ἅπαντας τὰ αὐτὰ οὔτε κάλα ἡγεῖτο, ἀλλὰ τὴν τῆς ἀξίας πϱοσθήκην συλλογιζόμενος τὰ τοιαῦτ᾽ ἐπέκϱινεν. *Neque enim,* inquit, *eadem in omnes aut aequa aut honesta censebat, sed rem exputans cum accessione eius quod quisque meruisset etiam in talibus velut iudicem agebat.*

13. Senate Resolution of Ratification, 101 Cong. Rec. 9958-9973, 84th Congress, 1st Sess. (1955).

14. Michael Ratner and Peter Weiss, "Litigating Against Torture: The German Criminal Prosecution," in *TDA*, pp. 261-66. On November 30, 2004, the Center for Constitutional Rights (CCR), a humanitarian legal organization based in New York, filed a criminal complaint in Germany seeking both investigation and prosecution of 10 high U.S. government officials over alleged involvement in the torture and inhumane treatment of prisoners of war in Iraq. Germany's (2002) Code of Crimes Against International Law (CCIL) criminalizes grave breaches of the Geneva Conventions as well as violations of the customary laws of war. The involvement of high U.S. government officials in these investigations greatly strained relations between the Bush administration and the government of Germany, see "Lawsuit Against Rumsfeld Threatens U.S.-German Relations," http://www.dw-world.de/dw/article/0,1564,142700.html.

15. Vienna Convention on the Law of Treaties, done at Vienna May 23, 1969. Entered into force on January 27, 1980. United Nations, Treaty Series, vol. 1155, p. 331, available at http://untreaty.un.org/ilc/texts/instruments/english/conventions/1_1_1969.pdf.

16. Prisoners at GTMO base were transferred from camp X-Ray to camp Delta in late April of 2002. Delta was designed as a more permanent security facility.

17. See Statement of Secretary of Defense Donald Rumsfeld, January 27, 2002, available at http://www.dod.gov/transcripts/2002/t01282002_t0127cnr.html.

18. Joseph Margulies, *supra* Introd., n. 48, at 66.

19. Lt. Col. Diane E. Beaver, Staff Judge Advocate, Memorandum for Commander, Joint Task Force 170, Re: Legal Brief on Proposed Counter-Resistance Strategies, in *TTP*, Memo 20, p. 229.

20. Secretary Rumsfeld issued his Order in a Memorandum for the General Counsel of the Department of Defense, Re: Detainee Interrogation, in *TTP*, Memo 22, p. 238.

21. Working Group Report on Detainee Interrogations in the Global War on Terrorism: Assessment of Legal, Historical, Policy, and Operational Considerations, April 4, 2003, in *TTP*, Memo 26, at 353.

22. Eleanor C. McDowell, "Contemporary Practice of the United States Relating to International Law," 71 *American Journal of International Law*, 337 (1977).

23. John Yoo presents this argument at *TTP*, Memo 4, p. 51.

24. Syrett, *supra* q. 1, n. 23, at 40.

25. For the Bush II OLC opinion on presumptive Presidential powers to suspend and withdraw unilaterally from ratified U.S. Treaties see (1) Memorandum from John Yoo, Deputy Assistant Attorney General, Office of Legal Counsel, to William Howard Taft, IV, Legal Adviser, Department of State, August 24, 2001, Re: President's Constitutional Authority to Withdraw Treaties from the Senate. (2) Memorandum from John C. Yoo, Deputy Assistant Attorney General, Office of Legal Counsel and Robert J. Delahunty, Special Counsel, Office of Legal Counsel, to John Bellinger, III, Senior Associate Counsel and Legal Adviser to the National Security Council, November 15, 2001, Re: Authority of the President to Suspend Certain Provisions of the ABM Treaty.

26. Syrett, *supra* q. 1, n. 23, at 41.

27. Hunt, *supra* q. 1, n. 15, at 169.

28. Author's translation of Grotius, *supra* Introd., n. 14, at 503: Quare crude nimis dictum est ab eodem Cicerone de republica tertio, ubi iniustus est rex, ubi iniusti optimates, aut ipse populus, non iam vitiosam, sed nullam esse rempublicam: quam sententiam Augustinus corrigens: *Nec ideo tamen*, ait, *vel ipsum non esse populum, vel eius rem dixerim non esse rempublicam, quamdiu manet qualiscunque multitudinis rationibus coetus rerum quas diligit concordi communione sociatus*. Corpus morbidum corpus tamen est: et civitas, quanquam graviter aegrota, civitas est, quamdiu manent leges, manent iudicia, et quae alia necessaria sunt ut ibi ius exteri consequi possint, non minus quam privati inter se. Rectius Dion Chrysostomus, qui legem (eam praesertim quae ius Gentium facit) dicit esse in civitate, ut mentem in corpore humano: ea enim sublata civitatem non esse amplius.

29. *Supra* Introd., n. 13, at 75.

30. Adler, *supra* q. 3, n. 10, at 190.

31. Yoo's criticism of customary international law is based on a position espoused by Curtis A. Bradley and Jack L. Goldsmith, "Customary International Law as Federal Common Law: A Critique of the Modern Position," 110 *Harv. L. Rev.* 815 (February, 1997). For the counter-argument, see Gerald L. Neuman, "Sense and Nonsense About Customary International Law: A Response to Professors Bradley and Goldsmith," 66 *Fordham L. Rev.* 371 (November 1997).

32. The opinion of Justice Gray unambiguously renders all questions of CIL federal questions, since "where there is no treaty and no controlling executive or legislative act or judicial decision, resort must be had to the customs and usages of civilized nations," 175 U.S., at 700.

33. Author's translation of the Latin text of William Whewell, ed., tr., *Hugonis Grotii, De Jure Belli ac Pacis Libri Tres*, Vol. 1, p. 10 (Cambridge: Cambridge University Press, 1853): Jus Naturale est dictatum rectae rationis, indicans actui alicui, ex

ejus convenientia aut disconvenientia cum ipsa natura rationali <ac sociali>, inesse moralem turpitudinem, aut necessitatem moralem, ac consequenter ab auctore naturae Deo talem actum aut vetari, aut praecipi.

34. See, for instance, Aristotle (384-322 BC), *Nicomachean Ethics*, book 5, ch. 7, 1134b18-34, Immanuel Bekker ed., *Aristotelis Opera Omnia*, vol. 2 (Berlin, 1830); T. H. Irwin tr., *Aristotle's Nicomachean Ethics* (Indianapolis: Hackett Publishing Co., 1982); Marcus Tullius Cicero, *On Laws*, 1.10, §28-30; 1.12, §33-34; 1.15, §42-45; 2.4, §9-11, Clinton Walker Keyes, text and trans., *Cicero De Re Publica et De Legibus* (Cambridge: Harvard University Press, 1977); Justinian I (483-565), Byzantine Emperor (r. 527-65), *Digest or Pandects of Justinian*, first part, book 1, title 1, Theodor Mommsen and Paul Kreuger, eds. *Corpus Juris Civilis*, volumen primum, pp. 29-30 (Hildescheim: Weidmannsche Verlasgsbuchhandlung, First pub. Berlin, 1963); Isidore of Seville (*c.* 570-636), Spanish Archbishop and encyclopedist, *Etymologies* 5.2-6 (W.M. Lindsay ed., *Isidori Hispalensis Episcopi: Etymologiarum Sive Originum Libri XX*, 2 vols. (Oxford: The Clarendon Press, 1911); Thomas Aquinas, *Summa Theologica*, II II, q. 57, art. 2, *ibid.*, Stanisla and Maré eds. (Paris: 1887); Hugo Grotius, *De Jure Belli ac Pacis Libri Tres*, book 1, ch. 1, §10.2-4, William Whewell, ed.

35. Author's translation of Aristotle, *Nicomachean Ethics*, book 5, ch. 7, 1134b18-24: τοῦ δὲ πολιτικοῦ δικαίου τὸ μὲν φυσικόν ἐστι τὸ δὲ νομικόν, φυσικὸν μὲν τὸ πανταχοῦ τὴν αὐτὴν ἔχον δύναμιν, καὶ οὐ τῷ δοκεῖν ἢ μή, νομικὸν δὲ ὃ ἐξ ἀρχῆς μὲν οὐδὲν διαφέρει οὕτως ἢ ἄλλως, ὅταν δὲ θῶνται, διαφέρει, οἷον τὸ μνᾶς λυτροῦσθαι, ἢ τὸ αἶγα θύειν ἀλλὰ μὴ δύο πρόβατα, ἔτι ὅσα ἐπὶ τῶν καθ' ἕκαστα νομοθετοῦσιν, οἷον τὸ θύειν Βρασίδᾳ, καὶ τὰ ψηφισματώδη.

36. Cicero, *On Laws*, book 2, ch. 4, §9.

37. Author's translation of Ulpian from the Latin text of Mommsen, *supra* q. 3, n. 34, at 30: Quae res (i.e., servitus) a iure gentium originem sumpsit, utpote cum iure naturali omnes liberi nascerentur nec esset nota manumissio, cum servitus esset incognita: sed posteaquam iure gentium servitus invasit, secutum est beneficium manumissionis. Et cum uno naturali nomine homines appellaremur, iure gentium tria genera esse coeperunt: liberi et his contrarium servi et tertium genus liberti, id est hi qui desierant esse servi.

38. Author's translation of the Latin text of Stanisla & Maré eds., *supra* q. 3, n. 34, at *Summa Theologica* II. II. q. 57, art. 2, obj. 1: et si ita esset quod natura humana semper esset recta, hoc esset semper servandum; sed quia quandoque contingit quod voluntas hominis depravatur, est aliquis causus in quo depositum non est reddendum, ne homo perversam voluntatem habens male eo utatur, puta si furiosus vel hostis reipublicae arma deposita reposcat.

39. 41 U.S. (16 Pet.) 1 (1842). See Neuman on *Tyson*, *supra* q. 3, n. 31, at 374.

40. Steven H. Gifis (quoting from 37 N. W. 2d 543, 547) *Barron's Law Dictionary* (Second Edition), p.81, (New York: Barron's Educational Series, Inc., 1984).

41. In *New York Life Ins. Co. v. Hendren*, 92 U.S. 286, 288 (1875) the court held that, whether written or not, "international law has the force of law in our courts,

because it is adopted and used by the United States. It could have no force but for that, and may be modified as the government sees fit."

42. 41 U.S. (16 Pet.) 1 (1842).

43. Philip C. Jessup, "The Doctrine of *Erie Railroad v. Tompkins* Applied to International Law," 33 *Am. J. Int'l L.*, 740, 743 (1939); compare Neuman, *supra* q. 3, n. 31, at 375 (n. 21).

44. Jessup, *supra* q. 3, n. 43, at 743.

45. The Judiciary Act of 1789, ch. 20, §9(b), 1 Stat. 73, 77 (1789), codified at 28 U.S.C. §1350, provides that "the district courts shall have original jurisdiction of any civil action by an alien for a tort only, committed in violation of the law of nations or a treaty of the United States."

46. President Clinton signed the Rome Statute of the International Criminal Court (see http://untreaty.un.org/cod/icc/statute/99_corr/cstatute.htm), but President Bush II has ignored the instrument entirely, saying that United States officials shall not be subject to its provisions. The Statute remains unratified to this day.

47. Yoo cites in evidence of his claim *Foster v. Neilson*, 27 U.S. (2 Pet.) 253, 314 (1829). See John C. Yoo, "Globalism and the Constitution: Treaties, Non-Self-Executing, and the Original Understanding," 99 *Colum. L. Rev.* 1955 (1999), and "Treaties and Public Lawmaking: A Textual and Structural Defense of Non-Self-Execution," 99 *Colum. L. Rev.* 2218 (1999). For self-executing versus non-self-executing treaties see Lori Fisler Damrosch, "The Role of the United States Senate Concerning 'Self-Executing' and 'Non-Self-Executing' Treaties," 67 *Chi.-Kent. L. Rev.* 515 (1991).

48. *The Paquete Habana*, 175 U.S. 677, at 710.

49. Daveed Gartenstein-Ross, "The Strategic Challenge of Somalia's Al-Shabaab," *Middle East Quarterly*, vol. 16, no. 4, Fall 2009, 29. See Reuters: "Yemen: Qaeda Affiliate Urges Joint Blockade of Red Sea," *New York Times*, Feb. 9, 2010.

50. Syrett, *supra* q. 1, n. 23, at 40.

51. "Inter-American Commission on Human Rights (IACHR): Decision of Request for Precautionary Measures (Detainees at Guantánamo Bay, Cuba)," March 12, 2002, 41 *ILM* 532, at ¶7.

52. For the philosophical ramifications of soldiers following orders in war, see David Estlund, "On Following Orders in an Unjust War," 15 *The Journal of Political Philosophy*, No. 2, 213 (2007); Allen Buchanan, "Institutionalizing the Just War," 34 *Philosophy & Public Affairs*, No. 1, 2; Lionel McPherson, "Innocence and Responsibility in War," 34 *Canadian Journal of Philosophy* 485 (2004); Jeff McMahon, "The Ethics of Killing in War," 114 *Ethics*, 693 (2004); Michael Waltzer, *Just and Unjust Wars*, (New York: Basic Books, 1977).

53. 119 Stat. 2742 (2005), 109th Congress.

54. *TTP*, Memo 26, pp. 340-54.

55. Text of the DTA is available at http://www.pegc.us/detainee_act_2005.html.

56. The anti-torture statute, 18 U.S.C. §2340-2340A (*Appendix H*) should be read in conjunction with the War Crimes Act of 1996 (*Appendix J*).

57. Hugo Grotius, 1583-1645, Dutch jurist and statesman. Samuel von Pufendorf, 1632-94, German jurist and historian. Emerich Vattel, 1714-67, Swiss jurist and diplomat.

Question Four: The February 7 Executive Order

1. Subsection 2(d) of the February 7, 2002, Executive Order of President George W. Bush, in *TTP*, Memo 11, p. 135.
2. *Supra* q. 4, n. 1, at 134, Subsection 2(a).
3. Memorandum from John Ashcroft, Attorney General, to President George W. Bush, February 1, 2002, Re: Justice Department's position on why the Geneva Convention did not apply to al-Qaeda and Taliban detainees, in *TTP*, Memo 9, p. 127.
4. *Supra* q. 4, n. 1, at 134, Section 1.
5. *Supra* q. 4, n. 1, at 134, Subsection 2(b).
6. *Supra* q. 4, n. 1, at 134, Subsection 2(c).
7. *Hostes*, Lat. (*m. pl.*) *foreigners, public enemies*, lawful *combatants* against whom war is publicly declared, as opposed to brigands, pirates, and terrorists, whose actions define categories of criminal behavior.
8. *Supra* Introd., n. 13, at 75.

Question Five: The Bybee-Gonzales Memo

1. *TTP*, Memo 14, p. 173.
2. Levin-Comey Memo, Part II, Section 4, ¶4, in *TDA*, p. 375.
3. Levin-Comey Memo, footnote 8, in *TDA*, p. 362.
4. Mark Bowden, "The Dark Art of Interrogation," *Atlantic Monthly*, October 2003, 56.
5. HCJ 5100/94, *The Public Committee against Torture in Israel v. The State of Israel* 53(4) *PD* 817. English translation of the original Hebrew available at http://elyon1.court.gov.il/files_eng/94/000/051/a09/94051000.a09.pdf.
6. *Supra* q. 5, n. 5, at Statement of Judgment.
7. Bowden, *supra* q. 5, n. 4, at 76.
8. John Schwartz, "Simulated Prison in '71 Showed a Fine Line Between 'Normal' and 'Monster'," *New York Times*, May 6, 2004, A20.
9. Mordechai Kremnitzer and Re'em Segev, "The Legality of Interrogational Torture: A Question of Proper Authorization or a Substantive Moral Issue?," 34 *Isr. L. Rev.* 509, 511 (Fall 2000).
10. Author's translation of Grotius, *supra* Introd., n. 14, at 649: [G]enerosi esse animi stare federibus etiam post aliquid iniuriae acceptum, quo nomine sapiens

Indus Iarchas laudabat regem, qui laesus a vicino federato, οὐ παρέλυσε τοὺς ὅρκους, οὕτω βεβαίως ὀμωμοκέναι φήσας, ὡς μηδὲ ὁπότε ἠδικεῖτο λυπεῖν αὐτὸν: non discessit a iurata fide, aiens tam sancte se iurasse, ut alteri ne post acceptam quidem iniuriam nociturus esset. (Grotius quotes the Greek of Flavius Philostratus, *Life of Apollonius of Tyana*, book 3, ch. 20.)

11. Author's translation of Grotius, *supra* Introd., n. 14, at 593: Accedat illud Augustini: *hostem pugnantem necessitas perimat, non voluntas. Sicut bellanti et resistenti violentia redditur, ita victo vel capto misericordia iam debetur, maxime in quo pacis perturbatio non timetur.* Xenophon de Agesilao: προσηγόρευσε τοῖς στρατιώταις τοὺς ἁλισκομένους μὴ ὡς ἀδίκους τιμωρεῖσθαι, ἀλλ᾽ ὡς ἀνθρώπους ὄντας φυλάσσειν: *monuit milites ut captos non tanquam sontes punirent, sed tanquam homines custodirent.* Apud Diodorum Siculum est: πάντες ἀνατείνοντας μὲν πρὸς τοὺς ἀντιταττομένους, εἴκουσι δὲ τοῖς ὑποπεπτωκόσι. *Omnes (Graeci) opponunt se repugnantibus, parcunt iam subactis.* Eodem iudice Macedones qui sub Alexandro πικότερον ἢ πολεμικώτερον προσεφέροντο τοῖς Θηβαίοις *acerbius egerant cum Thebanis quam belli fas ferebat.* (Grotius quotes passages from Saint Augustine, *Letter to Boniface*, Epistle 189, §6, as well as the Greek Historians Xenophon, *Agesilaus*, ch. 1, §21, and Diodorus Siculus, *Bibliotheca Historica*, book 13, ch. 24, and book 17, ch. 13.)

12. Bybee's definition of "severe pain" is borrowed from statutes defining an emergency medical condition: 8 U.S.C. §1369 (2000); 42 U.S.C. §1395w-22; *id.* §1395x (2000); *id.* §1395dd (2000); *id.* §1396b (2000); *id.* §1396u-2 (2000), see *TTP*, Memo 14, p. 176.

13. The Fay-Jones Report: Investigation of Intelligence Activities at Abu Ghraib, LTG Anthony R. Jones and MG George R. Fay, August 2004, in *TTP*, p. 1056.

14. *Supra* q. 5, n. 13, at 1057.

15. Bybee's exact words are "even if the defendant [i.e. the interrogator] knows that severe pain will result from his actions [on the interrogee], if causing such harm is not his objective, he lacks the requisite specific intent *even though the defendant did not act in good faith*" (*TTP*, Memo 14, p. 175, lines 14-16, emphasis added).

16. David Luban, "Liberalism, Torture, and the Ticking Bomb," in *TDA*, *supra* Introd., n. 47, at 61.

17. See §§27-28 of HCJ 5100/94. Placing a suspect in the Shabach position involves seating him on a small and low chair, whose seat is tilted forward toward the ground. One hand is tied behind the suspect, and placed inside the gap between the chair's seat and back support. The suspect's other hand is tied behind the chair against its back support. The suspect's head is then covered completely with a sack, while extremely loud music is played in the room. Kept for hours in this position prior to interrogation, the suspect becomes disoriented, experiencing severe headaches and back pain. The Frog Crouch involves consecutive and periodical forced crouching on the tips of one's toes for periods of five minutes at a time.

18. *Supra* q. 5, n. 5, at §25.

19. Jane Mayer, "Can the CIA Legally Kill a Prisoner," *The New Yorker*, Nov. 14, 2005, 44.

20. These behaviors are punishable as federal crimes because §2441(c)(3) of the War Crimes Act defines a war crime as "conduct which constitutes a violation of common Article 3," and outrages upon personal dignity, and humiliating or degrading treatment are banned under common Article 3, ¶1, §1(c).

21. Adler, *supra* q. 3, n. 10, at 207.

22. Id., at 190.

23. *Boumediene v. Bush*, 553 U.S. ___ (2008), opinion of Justice Kennedy, Part VI, §A, ¶6.

24. *TTP*, Memo 14, p. 172.

25. Id., p. 172.

26. Jane Mayer, "The Experiment," *The New Yorker*, July 11, 2005, 60, 67.

27. Alfred W. McCoy discusses the effects of torture on U.S. airmen captured in the Korean War, and the U.S. reaction to the use of Soviet mind-control techniques developed during the Cold War in *A Question of Torture: CIA Interrogation, from the Cold War to the War on Terror*, pp. 23-29 (New York: Henry Holt and Company, 2006).

28. Mayer, *supra* q. 5, n. 26, at 63.

29. Id., at 63.

30. *Supra* q. 5, n. 5, at §30, ¶2.

31. Dana Priest, "CIA Holds Terror Suspects in Secret Prisons; Debate is Growing Within Agency About Legality and Morality of Overseas System Set Up After 9/11," *Washington Post*, Nov. 2, 2005, A01.

32. Dana Priest, "Wrongful Imprisonment: Anatomy of a CIA Mistake; German Citizen Released After Months in 'Rendition'," *Washington Post*, Dec. 4, 2005, A01.

33. Priest, *supra* q. 5, n. 32.

34. *Supra* q. 5, n. 5, at §36, ¶1.

35. §948a(1) of the Military Commissions Act (Pub. L. 109-366, 120 Stat. 2601) defines an "unlawful enemy combatant" as "(ii) a person who, before, on, or after the date of the enactment of the MCA of 2006, has been determined to be an unlawful enemy combatant by a Combatant Status Review Tribunal or another competent tribunal established under the authority of the President or the Secretary of Defense [pursuant to President Bush's November 13, 2001, Executive Military Order]."

36. *Supra* q. 5, n. 5, at §36, ¶2.

37. Id., at §19, ¶1.

38. Josh White and R. Jeffrey Smith, "White House Aims to Block Legislation On Detainees," *Washington Post*, July 23, 2005, A01.

39. "Vice President for Torture," *Washington Post*, Editorial, Oct. 26, 2005, A18.

40. As a congressional aide to Rep. Dick Cheney (R-Wyoming) during the Iran-Contra Affair, David Addington helped to draft a legal opinion for the Republican

minority of the House Select Committee investigating the scandal that effectively argued that the law prohibiting aid to the contras represented an unconstitutional infringement of Executive Commander-in-Chief power. In 1989 Addington was made special assistant to Secretary of Defense Dick Cheney. On Addington's role in the shaping of the Bush II OLC policy see Jane Mayer, "The Memo," *New Yorker*, Feb. 27, 2006, 32.

41. *Youngstown Sheet & Tube Co. v. Sawyer*, 343 U.S., at 646, 647, 649 (1952).

42. 8 Op. O.L.C. 101, at 114.

43. *Supra* q. 5, n. 43, at 110.

44. The U.S. prosecutor would send an indictment of an executive branch official to a Grand Jury. If the Grand Jury determines that the accusation contained in the indictment would bring about a criminal conviction of the accused, if proved in a court of law, then the foreman of the Grand Jury endorses the prosecutor's indictment as a true bill, returning it to the prosecutor. Since this process involves a jury handing an endorsed indictment back to the U.S. attorney, the *legal* implication must be that he or she should advance with normal prosecutorial procedures, as opposed to abandoning the bill, and stopping the process.

45. According to *Washington Post* staff writer Dana Priest, "the CIA, working with other intelligence agencies, has captured an estimated 3,000 people, including several key leaders of al-Qaeda, in its campaign to dismantle terrorist networks. It is impossible to know, however, how many mistakes the CIA and its foreign partners have made. . . . To carry out its mission, the [CIA's] Counterterrorist Center relies on its Rendition Group, made up of case officers, paramilitaries, analysts and psychologists. Their job is to figure out how to snatch someone off a city street, or a remote hillside, or a secluded corner of an airport where local authorities wait. Members of the Rendition Group follow a simple but standard procedure: Dressed head to toe in black, including masks, they blindfold and cut the clothes off their new captives, then administer an enema and sleeping drugs. They outfit detainees in a diaper and jumpsuit for what can be a day-long trip. Their destinations: either a detention facility operated by cooperative countries in the Middle East and Central Asia, including Afghanistan, or one of the CIA's own cover prisons— referred to in classified documents as 'black sites,' which at various times have been operated in eight countries, including several in Eastern Europe" (*Supra* q. 5, n. 32).

46. Michael S. Moore, "Torture and the Balance of Evils," 23 *Isr. L. Rev.* 280, 285 (1989).

47. Penal Law, 1977 (L.S.I. Special Volume), §22, in Moore, *supra* n. 46, at 283.

48. Although the Bybee-Gonzales Memo (August 2002) was formally withdrawn at the OLC and replaced with the December 2004 Levin-Comey opinion, Levin-Comey contains an ominous proviso in footnote 8 warning us that no substantive changes to the President's policy of preemptive war are really being introduced: "While we have identified various disagreements with the August 2002 [Bybee-Gonzales] Memorandum," says Levin, "we have reviewed this Office's prior

opinions addressing issues involving treatment of detainees and do not believe that any of their conclusions would be different under the standards set forth in this memorandum" (*TDA*, p. 362). According to *New York Times* staff writer Douglas Jehl, "a cryptic footnote to the [Levin-Comey opinion] about the 'treatment of detainees' referred to what officials [from Justice and the National Security Council] said were other still classified opinions. Officials have said that the footnote meant that coercive techniques approved by the Justice Department under the looser interpretation of the torture statutes were still lawful even under the new, more restrictive standards" (Douglas Jehl, "Report Warned C.I.A. on Tactics in Interrogation," *New York Times*, Nov. 9, 2005, A1).

49. *TTP*, Memo 14, pp. 208-09.

50. Philip Zimbardo, *The Lucifer Effect: Understanding How Good People Turn Evil*, p. 291 (New York: Random House, 2007). See also Matthew Alexander, *How to Break a Terrorist: The U.S. Interrogators Who Used Brains, Not Brutality, to Take Down the Deadliest Man in Iraq*, (New York: Free Press, 2008); Tara McKelvey, *Monstering: Inside America's Policy of Secret Inerrogations and Torture in the War on Terror*, (New York: Carroll & Graf Publishers, 2007); James Risen, *State of War: The Secret History of the CIA and the Bush Administration*, (NewYork: Free Press, 2006).

51. James Risen and Tim Golden, "3 Prisoners Commit Suicide at Guantánamo," *New York Times*, June 11, 2006, A1.

52. Moore, *supra* q. 5, n. 46, at 323. Since the error fits his purpose so well, I infer that Mr. Bybee's misquotation of Moore at *TTP*, p. 211, line 45 is more than typographical and that he deliberately inserted "might" over Moore's original "must" at 23 *Isr. L. Rev.* 280, 323 line 11, 1989.

53. Moore, *supra* q. 5, n. 46, at 285.

54. Id., at 288.

55. Id., at 289.

ABBREVIATIONS

AUMF	Authorization for Use of Military Force (2001)
c.	*circa*; around, approximately
cf.	*confer*; compare
CAT	(United Nations) Convention Against Torture
CCR	Center for Constitutional Rights
CENTCOM	United States Central Command
CIL	customary international law
Const.	United States Constitution
CSRT	Combatant Status Review Tribunal (2004)
DTA	Detainee Treatment Act (2005)
EPW	Enemy Prisoner of War
F. [2d]	Federal Reporter [second series]
F. Supp.	Federal Supplement
GCP	Geneva Convention Relative to Civilian Persons
GPW	Geneva Convention Relative to Prisoners of War
GTMO	Guantánamo Bay Naval Base, Cuba
IACHR	Inter-American Commission on Human Rights
ICCPR	International Covenant on Civil and Political Rights
ICRC	International Committee of the Red Cross
Id.	*idem*; the same
ILM	*International Legal Materials*
JTF	Joint Task Force
Lat.	Latin
LTC; Lt. Col.	Lieutenant Colonel
LTG	Lieutenant General
MCA	Military Commissions Act (2006)
OEF	Operation Enduring Freedom

OIF	Operation Iraqi Freedom
OLC	Office of Legal Counsel
Pet.	Peter's United States Supreme Court Reports
Pub. L.; P. L.	Public Law
TDA	*The Torture Debate in America*
TIPS	Terrorism Information and Prevention System
TTP	*The Torture Papers: The Road to Abu Ghraib*
SERE	Survival Evastion Resistance Escape Program
S. Ct.	Supreme Court Reporter
Stat.	United States Statutes at Large
TVPA	Torture Victims Protection Act (1991)
UCMJ	Uniform Code of Military Justice
U.S.	United States Reports
U.S.C. [A.]	United States Code [Annotated]
WCA	War Crimes Act (1996)
Wheat.	Wheaton's United States Supreme Court Reports
Wall.	Wallace's United States Supreme Court Reports
WPR	War Powers Resolution (1973)

INDEX

MARTIN HENN (Ph.D. Philosophy, M.A. Classics, University of Kansas) has published significant work in the areas of pre-Socratic Greek cosmology, Aristotelian metaphysics and epistemology, early Thomistic theology, ethics, law, and international affairs. He is currently working toward completion of a treatise on the natural origin of human rights, in which he sets out to ground objectivity in ethics on the basis of the inherent natural value of all life; moral duties being grounded in rights whose existence is reducible to a set of primitive naturalistic facts.

www.ingramcontent.com/pod-product-compliance
Ingram Content Group UK Ltd.
Pitfield, Milton Keynes, MK11 3LW, UK
UKHW041633031026
15587UKWH00001B/249

9 780739 143292